Praise for The Freed...

Like a child on Christmas morning, I was del...
wonderful it is to place my hand into the hand ~~of god and listen to his whispers~~
and enjoy his affection. I could only ask why no one had ever told me he was this
good and this close. I wish I had read this book a long, long time ago.
Daniel Walker. Founder and Executive Director of Nvader.
Author of God in a Brothel.

This is new and exciting. It's not the idea of hearing from God that's new, it's
having conversations back and forth, question and answers. That's new for most
of us. Now I am enjoying my own conversations with God, which always leave me
with hope.
David Garratt of Scripture in Song. Hawaii.

The Freedom Diaries will stretch you. It describes Mark's real life struggle with
Doubt as he discovered that he could hear God's voice every day.
Dr Mark Virkler. Author of 4 Keys to hearing God's Voice.
Buffalo. New York.

I thoroughly recommend The Freedom Diaries. It asks challenging questions
about our spiritual journey and encourages us into a deeper more intimate
conversation with God.
Andrew Urquhart. Radio Rhema Announcer.

I am enjoying your book. Actually reading through the chapters and sharing with
my son. I find it helpful and consistent with the new covenant framework.
David Lee. Singapore.

After a long search and becoming totally disillusioned in my religious Christian
walk, this book has given me new hope that an everyday relationship is possible
with my creator.
Mick Carswell. New Zealand.

Since talking to Mark about having a conversation with God I have experienced
more connection and intimacy with Father than ever before. This intimate
relationship has provided a platform for a greater level of healing and fulfilment
in my life.
Bruce Christensen. Orama Christian Oasis.

I have begun recording my conversations with God. My whole devotional life has expanded to a new level of reality and life. My wife has noticed a difference in me and has begun recording her own conversations with God.

Jono Turner. Senior Minister Gateways Christian Fellowship.

When I read your conversations it's a privilege to be allowed into a personal dialogue between you and your Father.

Luke Kaa-Morgan. Pastor. Christian Song writer.

Many in our congregation have started their own conversations with God and have had their prayer life and relationship with Him totally transformed. Get your hands on a copy of Mark's book

Chris Fulop. Senior Pastor. Lion of Judah.

Mark's written conversations with God have inspired me to do the same. I have gone from very brief guidance words to more extensive, insightful, scriptural understandings that are wonderfully up-building. The biggest thing is an increasing personal-ness and intimacy in my daily walk with the Lord.

Graham Braddock. Elder Gateway Church.

There is no doubt Mark knows what he is talking about.

John Woods. Founder NZ Geographic Magazine. Author. Publisher. Rarotonga.

These conversations with God have enlightened me to open my heart and mind to feel and know that conversing with God gives me a deeper understanding of doing HIS will in my daily life."

Marge Wick. International Federation of Christian Chaplains. Texas.

Finally! A Christian life that is actually worth living. These conversations are full of grace. They take prayer completely out of the box, and suddenly, God appears in the real world!

Kathryn Mcbeath. New Zealand.

If there is one word that describes these conversations with God it is....honest. Honest questions, honest doubts and the God-honest grace that comes back at them. Water in a religious desert. I just cannot read enough of how God strips away Mark's fearful facades. It reminds me of mine. God just keeps on showing in these conversations that He will not be boxed.

David Baigent. Waiheke Island.

You will read this book and know what a conversation with the real living God sounds like.

Bill Kasper. Texas.

Mark's conversations with God have freed me from condemnation. I now have a much more personal relationship with God, knowing He is interested in my everyday life.

Joan Crawshaw. Co founder Arapohue Bush Christian Camp.

Mark's conversations with God have inspired me to covet that same connectedness with the One who has all the answers.

Phil Pigneri. New Zealand.

Mark's book has inspired me to seek a closer more personal relationship with the one who can help me the most. Wow! I found that I too was getting answers and inspiration. Why didn't I know this before?

Geoff Hill. New Zealand.

Through reading Mark's conversations with God we are constantly encouraged with the natural honest flow of conversation. It's like listening in on a Father and son talk, but on a daily basis.

Walter and Tracey Annear. New Zealand.

This whole conversation thing has revolutionized my relationship with God, Jesus and the Holy Spirit! Thank you so much.

Susanne Wendt. New Zealand .

Remembering gifts. My new bicycle at Christmas when I was 12. These conversations rate so much higher that they are indescribable.

Charles Heywood. New Zealand.

I didn't think it would be easy but when I tried writing out a conversation with God like Mark did the words just flowed.

Marian Leake. New Zealand.

This real life collection of conversations between Mark and God can prompt any heart to not only ask questions of our Creator, but to expect answers as well. Through Mark's conversations with God, I am reminded to continually converse with God myself.

Kelli Curtis. Indianapolis. Indiana.

The
FREEDOM
DIARIES

God Speaks Back

MARK HOLLOWAY

The Freedom Diaries
God Speaks Back
Volume 1

Published by The Freedom Assignment Limited
First Printing August 2013
Eleventh Printing April 2016

ISBN: 978-0-473-25184-0

The Freedom Assignment Limited
www.thefreedomassignment.com
info@thefreedomassignment.com

To all my friends who encouraged me
to put these conversations with God in a book.

We are about to find out if you were right.

And to Him. *For talking to me.*
Nothing else compares anymore.

And to everyone *who suspects that He talks*
to them more than they realise.

I hope this book helps you find out that you're right.

Conversations

$\mathcal{W}$ant to have your own written conversation with God?

Try this:

Write your question out to God - for example;
"God what are you saying to me about this idea of having a back and forward conversation with you?"

Then write the beginning of the sentence for God – you might write something like;
"What I am saying to you <your name> about having a backward and forward conversation with me is..."

And then just keep writing, trusting him to supply the words.
He will. It's incredible, but true. And you'll KNOW it's God. Many leading Christians have been astounded to discover that God turns up and talks when they do this. They can tell it's God and ask "why weren't we ever told about this?"

FOR MORE HELP - SEE PRACTICAL TIPS PAGE 243

TYPE STYLES IN THIS BOOK

In the conversations in this book (except in the chapter 'How This Happened') I have taken the unusual step of putting God's words in light type **and mine in bold.**

In these pages God does a lot more speaking than me. So if his words were to be shown in bold the book would become very difficult to read. Tests show that too much bold type is hard to read.

So the good news is that He's easier to read than me. Try the book. I hope you like it.

BIBLE REFERENCES

When God has mentioned a bible verse to me during one of the following conversations with him I have used the exceptionally good free website **www.biblecc.com** as my source. You will find it a fantastic help too when you are trying to determine the true meaning of bible verses.

This Happened

*O*ne day a few years ago an overwhelming sadness kicked down the front door of my life. It came right in and made itself at home. A sadness, as it turns out, that I myself had invited to visit. When I saw it outside I barred the door and shouted at it to go away, but it took no notice. Down came the door, in came the sadness.

Even though my mistakes had created it, the overwhelming sadness took no notice of me. I screamed at it to go away but it wouldn't. It seemed to have no interest in my thoughts at all. My thoughts had brought it, but they no longer counted. I had lost all control. I was, as the Good Book says, undone.

NOTHING I KNEW WAS THE SAME ANYMORE.

I had no option that horrible day. I threw pride to the wind and screamed out to God. What else could I do? I was terrified. My life was collapsing like a house of cards on to the floor. My dreams, everything I had lived for was sliding into a huge hole.

TO MY COMPLETE AMAZEMENT GOD SPOKE BACK.

He took over, started talking just like a good friend does when you phone them with news of a huge personal crisis. They come right around, sit you down and talk you through it. It's their help that gets you through the storm.

GOD CAME AROUND, SAT ME DOWN AND STARTED TALKING.

I couldn't believe it. On one hand I had this overwhelming sadness threatening to destroy me. On the other I had God, speaking words I could understand. I could hear him clear as a bell. He just kept talking. His words came thick and fast. I had to write them down to keep up.

Both, the overwhelming sadness and God speaking, were so far outside my experience of reality that I was in shock. I thought, hoped, that I would wake up and everything would be back to normal.

But no. I have woken up every morning since then, and both are still here.

When God first started speaking that day I was stunned. It was the last thing I had expected. He had so much to say. More probably than I'd heard him say in my whole life until then. He talked all day and into the night.

If it had been someone else's story I would have thought they were mad. God doesn't just chat like a friend. We all know that. But he did.

If it was someone else we were talking about, I would have said, as the medical experts will, that this is not reality, but just a known medical phenomena. Akin to temporary madness. He's 'hearing God' because he's gone into emotional shock.

I am a bit like those medical experts. A cynic. Something I'm learning to change. But I've still got a long way to go. And even in the midst of this overwhelming sadness I was still cynical enough to think 'this can't be God'. I was determined that, no matter how bad things got, I was not going to go mad. Somehow I was going to beat this. But God kept telling me I couldn't beat it, couldn't find a way through, but he could. And if I listened he'd tell me about it.

GOD KEPT TALKING. HE ANSWERED EVERY QUESTION.

Sometimes, often times, in my darkest desperate hours, and there are plenty of them, I didn't even ask him, I just shouted my questions at the empty sky. But he'd answer. Clearly. Instantly.

The moment the words left my mouth or mind, he'd answer. And the things he said were so foreign to everything I'd ever thought, that I knew it couldn't possibly be me.

He said such incredibly positive things. I've never been very positive. But he was. Painfully so. It was like listening to a good friend when they talk you through a crisis. You want to argue with their positive outlook, the thoughts of hope that they give you, but you know they're right and you've not the energy to argue. It was like that. God had lots to say and I didn't have the energy to argue.

HE DIDN'T DO ALL THE TALKING, BUT HE DID MOST.

Thank goodness. Up until then it had been the other way around for me. If God and I ever talked, I did most of it. Maybe you're the same? If you ever talk to God maybe you do most of the talking?

But I've discovered God's not going deaf, he's not senile or removed from the reality of my situation. He can hear just fine and would love to talk if I want to listen. He's wise enough not to push his thoughts on me unless I'm interested.

I've also discovered as you will if you read this book, that he doesn't need me to sort my life out before he talks to me. He just wants to talk.

THE BIBLE STORIES SHOW US THAT HE'LL TALK NOW AND FIX YOU UP LATER.

He'll say to the tax collector, the prostitute, and the cursing fisherman, 'I'm coming to your place for lunch'. He doesn't seem to care about whether you've been good or bad.

I was the tax collector, the prostitute and the cursing fisherman all rolled in to one.

BUT HE STILL WANTED TO COME TO LUNCH.

God has talked me through every day of my overwhelming sadness. And yet I haven't become an amazing new person. I know I was extremely difficult for those around me, and continue to be. But I'm working on it. And for the first time in my life people say I'm changing for good. Ever so slowly.

GOD SAYS WRITE A BOOK.

What happened next was even crazier. I began to write down my conversations with God. It made it easier for my cynical mind. Easier to analyse and monitor this crazy new experience where God appeared to be talking. I thought if I really am going mad then by writing it down I might have a chance of spotting the madness and getting it fixed before it goes too far.

It made it better. Or worse? It depends where you're looking at this from. The more I wrote it down, the more he spoke. Clearly, intelligibly. But even more important, intelligently. He was saying things far smarter than I had the ability to be. Wise things. Things that others heard and were amazed at. Wisdom has never been a hallmark of my life. But the things I was hearing God say, I would tell to others, and they would be incredulous too. 'That's God' they'd say. Obviously taken a back that I had heard such things.

My friends made me do it.

They urged me to keep having these conversations with God. They asked me to send them to their friends too.

The things they told me about my conversations were far beyond what I'd hoped. All I wanted to hear was 'you're not going mad'. But instead they told me my conversations were a privilege to listen to. They said my conversations with God were opening up a whole new relationship with God for them too. And a growing number of people urged me to put my conversations in a book. They told me this needs to be published, that people need to know that if I can hear God talk like this, surely anyone can.

The book!

So, a book. This book. Why a book? My life was a total mess. But each day as I face my overwhelming sadness, I've found strength and purpose to help me through. How? By listening to his voice. That's the thing that blew me away. The fact that I can actually hear him clearly speaking into my mind. A conversation. Back and forward. It's brought freedom.

My hope is that you will read this book and try a conversation with him too. And that you too will find freedom as you do.

In the back of the book you'll find a whole section on how to do this, how to have a conversation with God yourself. The practical steps. Enjoy.

Mark

PS: Yes you should *'try this yourself at home'.* Or anywhere else for that matter. In the car, at work, you name it. God wants to talk and if you listen, he will. This book is a whole bunch of the conversations I have had with him. I have done my best to let him tell me which ones to include so that you can understand how to have a conversation with him too.

CONVERSATION
One

Could this be how the universe is held together?

God sometime in the night I think I heard you say that you are talking all the time, but only sometimes we hear it. Did you say that to me last night?

Mark yes.

'For God speaks again and again, though people do not recognize it.'

JOB 33:14 NLT

Did you then go on to say that you are speaking all the time to each of us?

Yes.

And that it's not about the fact that you're talking and we're not listening, although true that's not what this is about? What's really happening is that, whether or not we listen, you still need to be talking all the time, to and about each of us? That you need to do that to keep us physically created, and to bring everything to pass that you want in our lives?

Yes I did.

Did you remind me last night about that verse in the bible that says you are the Word. That words, *your words*, bring everything into being?

Yes Mark. That's what it says.

'In the beginning was the Word, and the Word was with God, and the Word was God. He was with God in the beginning. Through him all things were made; without him nothing was made that has been made. In him was life, and that life was the light of all mankind'

JOHN 1:3 NIV

So whether or not we hear it, most of the time silent to us, you are talking over us?

Mark all day long I am saying positive things about you. I am saying all the amazing things I think and that are true about you! I am describing the calling I have for you, the victories you will win. Because that's the dynamic of the created universe. I'm holding the atoms together by speaking. And I'm directing everyone's lives by speaking. All the time. Every minute of the day.

When you're sleeping, going about your work, not thinking about me or listening to me, I'm speaking amazing things about you. I'm describing my vision for you. I'm explaining to the universe the purpose I created you for, just you, and how I want it fulfilled.

So you're doing this because that's how the world gets held together, by the billions per second specific words spoken by God?

Yes. And the more you listen, the more you'll hear and understand.

'For everything comes from him and exists by his power and is intended for his glory. '　　ROM 11:36 NLT

'For God makes all the decisions around here. God is our King. God runs this place and he'll keep us safe.'　　ISAIAH 33:22 MSG

So what you're saying is that even though the ultimate purpose is for me to hear it in my mind, nevertheless you have to keep speaking, whether or not I listen?

Yes that's right.

So you're speaking to the unconscious parts of my physical and spiritual being to keep me created, in both realms, physical and spiritual? And to keep me headed in the direction you want?

Yes. Near enough.

'We live and move in him, can't get away from him!'　　ACTS 17:28 MSG

But even more than speaking to all the unconscious parts of your physical and spiritual being, to keep them created, working and heading in the right direction, I'm actually speaking to myself. We're speaking between the three of us, one to another. That's what this is really about. We, the three of us, are talking and we want you and the universe involved, but we're talking between the three of us anyway.

Did you just say that you're saying things like *'Mark is a warrior, a mighty swordsman'?* **And you're saying things that are just as positive about every single person on the face of the earth? And you're saying them every single moment of every single day??**

Yes I am. About everyone, all the time. *All the time.*

You're saying *'this one will defeat the enemy.'* **And** *'The enemy who assaults that one now will be put to flight by her later.'* **You're really saying all that?**

Yes, I'm saying things like that all the time. I am going to use people to overpower the unseen evil that wars against them.

> *'God's purpose in all this was to use the CHURCH ['ekklesia': Christian community] to display his wisdom in its rich variety to all the unseen rulers and authorities in the heavenly places.'*
> EPHESIANS 3:10 NLT

I'm saying things like that not just when you hear me say it direct to your mind. And not just when someone prophesies it over you. I am saying it all the time. Because I need to do that to keep the universe running. But if you listen, you'll hear those words. That's what I really want.

So God those words you are saying all the time, even if we don't hear them, are not falling to the ground? Us hearing those words is not the *practical* **purpose for which they are spoken?**

Mark holding the universe together is the practical purpose. But the real purpose of my spoken words, the one closest to my heart, is that you actually hear them and speak back to me.

The universe that I hold together by speaking is only here as a platform on which you and I can have a conversation. I speak, you speak. A *conversation.*

A CONVERSATION BETWEEN US IS MY ULTIMATE PURPOSE.

But whether or not you respond, I must keep speaking over you to keep you created physically and spiritually, and to ensure that your day to day life runs loosely to my plan.

So whether or not I hear those words they still achieve their purpose?

Yes.

> *'So will the words that come out of my mouth not come back empty-*

handed. They'll do the work I sent them to do, they'll complete the assignment I gave them.' ISAIAH 55:11 MSG

So you are constantly talking over me, about me, through me, to me and I don't have to listen at all. You'd really like me to, but whether or not I do, you're speaking over me every minute of every day to keep me created and moving forward physically and spiritually? Is that really true?

Yes. Yes. Yes.

It's your life
Can I have it please
I want to talk

So God can we please talk about the way you are interrupting my everyday life? This isn't what I expected. This is nothing like a 'normal Christian life'. It's crazy! You are talking to me all day long. I've done nothing to deserve it. My life is a mess, and yet I can understand the actual words you're saying. I can write them down it's that clear. I can't quite believe I'm saying this, but I think you're having a conversation with me.

I am, and I will keep doing so if you listen.

Are you saying that I'm going to have to decide whether I'm prepared for this to become what drives me, for a conversation with you to become normal? So that I no longer belong to myself, so that I end up hearing from you, available to you, all day, all night long? *Yours all the time?*

If that's what you want Mark. It's certainly what I want.

God this is what you mean by becoming a fool for you isn't it? I have to decide whether I want to run my own life, or whether I'm prepared to be available for something more important, a life, every step of which is determined, if I want it to be, by another and not myself?

Yes.

So you're suggesting I give up my God-given right to do what I want? *Oh man!* This is going to see me making decisions and taking actions which appear to have no logical reason at all. Doing things told to me by an invisible God. *I'm right aren't I!*

Mark that's what it comes down to. These are some of the *'sufferings of Christ',* that I went through. Doing the opposite of what you want. Doing things that don't make sense to you.

Let me explain. You are created with a will, a God given right to create and forge your own way, to make a mark on the world. And then you come face to face with the Creator and he seems to want to make a mockery of the free will he has given you, to take away your ability to choose.

WHAT I GAVE YOU ENDS UP STANDING BETWEEN US.

So you give up those rights to me, and Christ the Creator arrives with a crash in your life. Nothing is as it was. But then, over time, religion begins to seep into your heart and you tell yourself you were perhaps a little over-zealous. When you first loved me I blessed you with opportunities, situations, relationships which after a period of time bring responsibilities and cares. Before long you become more attached to them than you are to me and you no longer want to give them up.

THAT'S NOT MEANT TO BE MAINSTREAM CHRISTIANITY. BUT MANY FALL FOR IT. *YOU DID.*

A life like that is, in many ways, no better than a life without God. It is strewn with cares, those cares are labelled 'godly cares' and some even have church connections, but nevertheless they are cares of this world.

God that's almost a bit offensive.

Hear me out Mark. They often start out as the right thing, but become cares of this world when they are more important to you than me.

DON'T FEEL BAD, WHAT I HAVE DESCRIBED IS NORMAL.

Perfectly and understandably normal. Not much different than what happens to you in a marriage. Your first love becomes smothered by the cares associated with the things you did as a result of your first love. Children and their care, even though they are the created products of your love, begin to distract you from the very love that created them. And on it goes.

In the same way, when you come to me, you give up the very rights I gave you. The right to create, to direct your own life. You willingly give those rights up to the one who gave them to you.

But then you begin to take them back.

Little by little until most of those rights are yours again, you take them back. And that has become quite normal for many Christians. It is exacerbated of course by the fact that rather than judge and condemn for that behaviour, grace requires I accept and bless it anyway.

Our relationship will only work if you are free to ignore it.

If I were to force my will on people then I would completely undo the foundation on which a relationship with me exists, the total freedom *not* to have a relationship with me.

There can be no real relationship with a living Creator unless you have total freedom *not* to have that relationship.

Otherwise who I am, the One True God, would be too overpowering. You would end up having a relationship with me because you realised you had no choice. *Humans must have a choice!* They must know they can come to me or leave me without immediate consequence.

I allow you to let our first love cool down.

I have no other option. The love of many people for me is not yet cold, but neither is it hot. It's warm. They talk about me. They call me down, and still I come. Particularly in times of trouble, but the relationship where the Creator took up residence in their heart and began to reveal himself to them, that relationship stops at a certain level and then moves backwards. Many people are just like you were. They know in their heart of hearts that their first love for me is no longer there. They may justify why that is so, in fact many do, but nonetheless they will admit their first love is gone.

But there is always the opportunity to go further.

There is always opportunity to get to know me more, to push the boundaries and say 'God there has to be more'. That cry exists in the hearts of all who come to me, but the cares of this world, sometimes dressed up as Christian duties, often steal it away.

The opportunity to rekindle that cry always exists, it is always there and that is the job I have given you. To speak out, to make a stand, to be a voice that calls people to go themselves to God and demand; 'God surely there must be more!' I want you to urge anyone who will listen, to cry out 'God there has to be more'.

Because there is so much more. That's how we started this conversation. So much more than you are experiencing. I want your life Mark. I bought it with a price. You are free to keep it. If you do you will still be blessed, I will still be close, but your life will remain your own. It is after all, your life. You always get the final choice. But I am asking if you'll give up the comfortable Christianity you've grown used to and give your life to me.

IT'S YOUR LIFE MARK, BUT CAN I HAVE IT PLEASE.

If I have it, then nothing will be the same. And no, I'm not talking about a life of zealous over-activity in Christian organisations. That's not the goal. All I want is to be able to interfere in your life Mark.

THE GAME OF MINUTES.

I want to be the one who has access to every single minute of every single day of your life. At first that will simply mean I have the right to talk, it will mean I have speaking rights. Greater speaking rights than I have now. Right now you are in transition. You allow me to speak more than you have ever done before, but you still hold me at arm's length.

You judge and analyse what I say and have assigned particular times at which I am more free than others to talk to you. But I want total unabridged speaking rights. Freedom to say whatever I want to you whenever I want. No more control please.

IF YOU LET ME SPEAK TO YOU THEN YOU ARE A CHILD OF GOD.

If you give me speaking rights you will be at the stage of an infant in Christ. An infant learns to hear its parent's voice. If you can clearly hear God's voice, actually hear the words I speak to you, and understand what I mean, then you are an infant. And Mark you're not there yet.

You thought that hearing from me clearly would mean that you were mature. Not at all. A child hears clearly and recognises and understands its parent's voice. But it still remains a child. Those who hear my voice clearly, whole sentences, fully understanding what I'm saying, are children in Christ.

MATURITY COMES LATER.

You'll know you are maturing when, having learned to hear me clearly and converse easily with me, I trust you to carefully put in place the things I ask you to. When that happens you'll be a mature son working for me.

IF YOU CAN'T HEAR ME YOU'RE VULNERABLE.

You have often embarked on a project when you weren't ready. If you can't hear me clearly how can you know what I want? I've blessed you and looked after you, but you haven't achieved what I wanted you to because you didn't know how to listen to my voice.

Take Moses for example; in his own power he tried to deliver one man, just a single man and ended up failing miserably. But after 40 years of me working on him so that he could actually hear my voice, he was ready to deliver an entire nation. I am a great economist Mark, and the economics of time are important to me. I'm happy for you to take the time to learn to listen to me before I send you out to do what I want. There's no rush to do the jobs. The urgency is to listen to me.

SO YES, I WANT TO INTERFERE IN YOUR LIFE. WILL YOU LET ME?

And no we're not talking about what you have always felt it meant to give your life to me. The daily Christian customs you felt were the way to give your life to me.

This is more real than that. I'm asking whether I can march into your life and interrupt, and whether you are prepared to accept that there is no return? This isn't Christianity as you have known it. This isn't a programme, a pre-organised set of activities designed to get you closer to me.

THIS IS GOD, TURNING UP IN YOUR LIFE AND DISTRACTING YOU.

Imagine what your life would look like if Jesus Christ turned up in physical person and decided to rent a room at your house. After the media blaze had died down and everyone else got on with their lives, you would still be faced with the fact that the one on whose shoulders the whole world rests was actually living in your house and wanting to be your friend. Wanting to talk and generally interrupt and take over your, until now, organised life.

It's your life Mark, can I have it please. I'd like to talk.

READY TO TRY A CONVERSATION FOR YOURSELF?
Want to try your own conversation with God? Go to the page immediately following the contents page. Or go to page 243

CONVERSATION

Three

Forgiveness is in the DNA of the universe

God has built forgiveness into every cell.

God I'm sure I heard you say this morning that 'Restoration is in the DNA of the universe'. Did I get that right?

Yes. That's what I said.

What do you mean?

I mean that luckily for mankind, the universe is designed around restoration and forgiveness. It is in the DNA of the planet, of all of creation, at a spiritual and physical level, restoration, starting again, re-making.

God I hear people say 'God's a God of restoration.' I think they think that's a license to believe that every broken situation, life and body will be mended. But that's not what happens.

You're right. Not everything gets restored. But I am a God of restoration. That is my plan. Restoration of anything in the universe requires me to speak. For mankind, restoration comes most effectively from a conversation with me.

This is a conversation Mark. We're talking. Back and forward. And restoration is based on that, at every level.

HEARING WHAT I AM SAYING IS WHAT RESTORES.

You saw it with your son. Not every child with cancer is healed. You screamed out for an answer and I answered. I told you I would heal him and I did. That's the correct order. Find out what I'm saying first.

'The moment I called out you stepped in.'   PSALM 138:3 MSG

Restoration happens often, broken bodies, broken lives, broken situations. Because I designed the universe to make restoration easily possible.

The planet, the very universe is designed so that forgiveness takes place. When I make something good I like it. And when it fails I want to see it rebuilt. When it grows old I want to see it made young again. It's my plan, it appeals to me. It's in my nature to see things restored, remade, rebuilt. I've designed the universe that way.

I HAVE MADE THE UNIVERSE VULNERABLE TO YOU. IT GIVES YOU A CHOICE.

It is in the nature of my creation for things to be vulnerable, delicate, easy to break, it promotes choice. I have made choice a thing that has huge consequences and therefore value. If the choices you made had no real consequence then you would not be free, you would be controlled, unable to make a difference, unable to create things that are beautiful or things that wreak havoc.

So God are you saying that we should believe that *each* body, life and situation will be restored?

No. Obviously not. What I am saying is that each body, life, and situation can be restored. I have established the universe to make that easily possible. If you want to know whether it will be restored you'll need to listen to me. Don't assume. Listen.

IT IS IN THE NATURE OF MY CREATION FOR YOU TO BE ABLE TO DO DAMAGE.

That way if you do the opposite it has value. Creation is an incredibly complex super-structure of physical and spiritual components, and it is vulnerable so that you are able to create, and build on to what I have already put in place.

You can take another human being and make their life wonderful, or you can hurt and damage them. If you didn't have the choice to do either you would have no power. You would not be the creator beings I designed.

To allow for this, I needed to provide mankind with a base, a platform on which you could build or destroy. So I gave you your bodies and your minds and all of creation to give you a place in which you could create beauty or do damage.

'[He made] the earth hospitable, with plenty of time and space for living so we could seek after God, and not just grope around in the dark but actually find him. // He's not remote; he's near.'

ACTS 17:26-27 MSG

I WANTED YOU FREE TO CHOOSE, BUILD OR DESTROY.

I wanted mankind to have the time and the freedom to build or destroy, to run after me or run away.

SO I CREATED A WORLD THAT COULD BE CONSTANTLY RESTORED.

I put restoration in the DNA of the universe. Dust to Dust. The sun rises, the sun sets, everything, physical and spiritual, is made up of cycles that bring the original back to the original.

FORGIVENESS IS MY NAME. AND IT IS BUILT INTO ALL THAT I HAVE CREATED.

The universe itself is forgiving. It allows for mistakes and rebuilds around them. All of creation is designed that way. Because forgiveness is my name, it's also the name of all that I have created.

New chances to change decisions, chances that don't over rule the decisions you have made, but chances to overrule them yourself and start again.

A BROKEN ARM WANTS TO HEAL ITSELF, A DEAD BODY WANTS TO LIVE AGAIN.

Everything that is broken waits, it asks will I be restored to life, or will I break down and give life to something else?

A broken marriage wants to heal itself. The universe wants it healed. The universe has been created, by me, to promote, allow for, make room for and to adjust; to make possible the restoration of any marriage.

'For nothing is impossible with God.'

LUKE 1:37 NLT

Restoration, rebuilding, remaking is built into every physical (and every spiritual) being and structure. The entire structure of the universe is designed to make rebuilding possible and simple. Right from the start, before the whole cosmos was created, the intent was that I be crucified to make it possible for whatever was damaged to be restored.

'The Lamb who was slain from the creation of the world'
REVELATIONS 13:8 NIV

And all of this so that you can be free to make decisions. And if those decisions are ill founded you have the freedom to make them without being forced to do what I want.

To make that possible it's important that anything you destroy can easily be rebuilt. Mercy says you need to be able to undo your decisions. And others need to be able to make their own decisions without being overruled by yours.

IF I CHOOSE TO FORGIVE, ALL IS FORGIVEN.

Do you really think that when I say forgiveness I mean it half-heartedly? Hah! I am the Almighty, the Absolute One. If I choose forgiveness, *all* is forgiven. So do you think, with forgiveness as my nature, I would create a world that did not easily allow second chances?

MY NATURE MARK IS THE SECOND CHANCE, AND THE THIRD, AND THE FOURTH.

I forgive seventy times seven, that's the number of the universe, the number of second chances, on and on and on. There is no end unless and until I say enough.

People have time to change and learn from their decisions. They have a universe, a world, bodies, minds, hearts that allow them to change their decisions. And that's Ok with me.

Hah! I am God. I am the restorer. Nothing is impossible. If I say I will restore a thing, I will restore it. You can trust me on that.

CONVERSATION

Out there in the big wide world is where you practise hearing God

Father I can hear you so clearly this morning. I can almost hear you audibly, I can sense that the source is outside myself and that it is not the enemy.

Mark remember I run to you.

Lord this absolute and clear sense that it is you speaking and not me making it up. That it is someone other than me, and clearly not your enemy, is that from you?

Yes and Mark it is going to grow. You have pushed through into me and I will push back into you.

So Lord you want me to sense you, hear you speak into my mind more and more, it's good that I do?

Mark it's fantastic you do.

Can I have it all the time, not just sitting here typing?

All the time. If you practise it, you'll get good at it.

The idea of practising hearing from you seems well, a bit too much of a system, too practical, not spiritual enough somehow.

Mark you are living in a world, you have a body. Guess whose idea that was? It was mine. And I *am* spiritual. I am the *Great* Spirit. I'm God the Holy Spirit.

IN SPIRIT AND IN TRUTH.

My bible makes it clear that you will worship me in spirit and in truth. Part of the truth Mark is that you exist, your body is real, or 'true'. The need to eat, and sleep, and practise a thing is real, or true.

If people want to hear me they will need to practise hearing me. That's the truth. And don't let me reduce the significance of the word 'truth'. Remember that you exist, a living, breathing, choosing individual in a space that wasn't there, the space itself didn't exist before I created it. Imagine that if you will Mark. Nothing. And nothing to distract you from the very presence, the very moving, pulsing power and existence of God and bang! I create space, and then I create, eventually, a man.

YOU EXIST WHERE YOU SHOULDN'T, WHERE YOU WEREN'T.

It's just a body, it's just a man, and yet it's a body! It's a man! Never underestimate or consider less spiritual or less 'true' the physical, day to day reality of your world.

TO PRACTISE HEARING FROM ME IS VERY SPIRITUAL!

I thought up, designed and then built the world as a platform for spirituality, for housing the relationship between God and man. Practising hearing from me is about as spiritual as you can get. It drives away the demons. When you listen to me whole armies of dark spiritual beings find themselves pushed back.

Mark if you were watching the spiritual significance, what is really happening in the spirit, when you practise hearing from me, you would be pushed to the floor, overwhelmed, and short of breath.

You don't choose between me and the world. The world 'is me'. In as much as the only reason it exists is for me; the lawn you mow, the trees you prune, the office you work in, the businesses you go into; the world 'is me'. Created for me and you.

So do not treat anything around you, or the events of your day as separate from me, they are me. They are me in as much as they exist as a platform on which we can relate. You and me.

WHAT I WANT ISN'T HARD. IT'S SIMPLE. A CONVERSATION.

I could have had you all exist in darkness, in an embryonic state in some spiritual mass womb, but I love what I imagined up and then created for you. It looks good to me. The world is good. And even more than the world I love you and I wanted to give you something special to show you that.

THE WORLD IS MY GIFT FOR YOU. WHAT DO YOU THINK?

You are my focus, the world is the gift. You are what is really important, the world is what I have made for you when you weren't watching. It's my surprise. Not just the wide open spaces and the trees and oceans and skies, but people too, situations, things that happen. Reality in time and space. I thought it all up and gave it to you.

I wanted to give you something, a present, so that I could say 'what do you think? Do you like it? Isn't it great?'

I am a lover giving a gift to excite and please you. I asked myself what can I give him that will really please him; and I decided a world, a universe, sun, stars, ocean, other people. I decided that would be a gift worthy of you.

So everything that happens in it, everything that takes place around you is of huge spiritual significance, it is, for the most part truth. Lies exist too, and the enemy's plans are huge and varied, but actually, my power exists and is evident, and pulsing to a much greater extent.

YES HE IS THE PRINCE OF THIS DARK WORLD. BUT I AM THE KING OF THIS WONDERFUL WORLD.

I am the Emperor, the Supreme One. His dark world exists in my world of light. And light overcomes the darkness, the darkness is shrinking Mark, ever shrinking.

WHAT AM I SAYING? SLOW DOWN AND LISTEN TO ME IS WHAT I'M SAYING.

Mark you humans are so narrow minded, you think you know what I am saying but you keep it in such a narrow box. You hear part of the story and run off with it as though it is complete.

You are torn from one part truth to another. Slow down and listen to me is what I am saying to my people.

You Christians hear it said that 'we are in the world, but not of the world' and you run off and begin to see the world as evil, something you keep away from. And then you read that the very creation, that the heavens and the earth and all that is in it belong to God, or somewhere else that creation declares the glory of God.

IT IS NOT ENOUGH TO KNOW I AM SAYING 'SOMETHING'. YOU NEED TO KNOW EXACTLY WHAT I AM SAYING.

If you look back over the decades you have believed me, you have gone from hating the world, to loving the world and back again. Simply because you didn't understand truth, you didn't understand that I am always talking, have something to say about everything and because you didn't understand that, you never thought to ask.

I WANT YOU TO ASK.

It is not enough to know that I am saying something, that I speak. You must find out what I am saying.

I didn't give the world to billions of people. I gave it to an individual. Each individual. One at a time. I thought it up and gave it to each of you, one at a time. Remember I know all of your days, every minute of your life before it happens. I made the world, just for you, just for every one of you, individually.

'You saw me before I was born. Every day of my life was recorded in your book. Every moment was laid out before a single day had passed.' PSALM 139:16 NLT

I came to you, each of you, one at a time and I said 'hey I love you, I have a present, it's a world, what do you think?' The world, the entire universe Mark is just for you. And just for her. And just for them.

JUST FOR ONE MAN. JUST FOR ONE GIRL.

The world is just for you Mark. And as it happens it's just for that old woman, just her, no one else. And actually, it's also just for that suspicious looking teenage boy, and the school girl working in the supermarket. I did not give it to you as a group. I gave it to each of you individually and then put you together in groups.

I KNOW WHO YOU ARE. I AM IN THE SEAT WITH YOU.

I am not talking to the world, or any group for that matter, as a crowd. I talk to you individually. One at a time. Wherever you are. The result is that when individuals are grouped together to relate to me, in any way, a church, a nation, a family it appears to be a group thing. But for me it's not. For me it's an individual thing.

I'm not up the front speaking, I am alongside each individual, encouraging, speaking, healing individually.

This is important. You need to understand this, I do not deal with mankind as a crowd, it is always as an individual. I want you to know me individually. Then you have something to share.

I WANT YOU TO GATHER WITH OTHERS TO GIVE. BUT FIRST YOU MUST HAVE SOMETHING TO GIVE.

I am the gift, broken for you. Mark the ultimate gift you can give is me. To do that you will need to know me, you will need to be experiencing me in this world, out there on the platform I have built for you to seek and find me.

That way, having found me out there in your world, you can come to others and give me to them. 'Here's God, his body broken for you.'

Don't be quite so eager
Slow down and listen
You'll hear God

Ok Mark, get ready, I have a lot to say, a lot will be measured primarily by the degree of importance.

Lord did you just tell me to say, of myself, as a declaration of power, 'I can hear God's voice, and when I speak it out or write it down, it pushes back a troop, a troop of demons.'?

I did. It's your own updated version of David's *'I can run through a troop.'* Because Mark you can, and do push back troops.

And I am looking for others who can hear me just as clearly, if not more clearly than you, because there are many troops to push back.

I am looking for people who can hear my voice clearly wherever they are and who are willing to speak out what they hear. Speak it back to me, speak it to themselves, speak it to the universe that is waiting and groaning to hear them speak out the words that make them sons of God.

BUT I ONLY WANT THEM TO TELL OTHERS THE WORDS I TELL THEM TO.

Most importantly I want them to speak the words they hear me say back to me, to themselves, and to the universe. Less often, but still often, I want them to speak my words to others. But only when I actually tell them to do so.

What about bible verses? Should we tell bible verses to people?

Absolutely. It's my word. But only the verses I tell you to tell people, and only when I tell you. The Pharisees were a wealth of bible verses. They used them to suppress and oppress. The only way to avoid becoming religious like them is to listen to me and only speak to others what I tell you to.

Mark I am looking for people who know that I speak to them, who are confident in that. I want people who find me themselves and then take me to others.

> 'As for you, the ANOINTING [charisma': the teaching ministry of the Holy Spirit] you received from him remains in you, and you do not need anyone to teach you. But as his anointing teaches you about all things and as that anointing is real, not counterfeit— just as it has taught you, remain in him.'   1 JOHN 2:27 NIV

GOD'S ON THE MENU.

I want people to meet in a sort of spiritual 'pot luck' where everyone takes something from me to share. Something they got from me. I want them happy to receive what others have heard me say, but to expect to be sharing as much as they receive. I want them more eager to give than to receive.

GOD IN THE LIMELIGHT.

And yet I want them to be people who don't want to push forward to have their message heard before another's. I don't want them to crave the limelight. They'll find they want me in the limelight. Because they will hear from me they will know how to wait until they hear me say 'now, share it now with that person.'

So can confusion and turmoil be avoided if everyone takes something to share? Yes because people who hear me know whether to speak or not. And let's say I tell them not to speak. The very fact that they bring something they heard from me to the meeting, even if never spoken, the presence, in the meeting, in their heart, of something spoken to them by the Creator brings immense power to the place. Even when not spoken.

Doubt doubts himself

Watch him. He is a sneaky little demon, sent ahead to render you helpless.

Lord I'm sick of doubt. Are you really saying I can just choose for it to go?

Mark yes you can. You can be in charge of doubt. In charge of a force that dominates the lives of billions. All you have to do is choose.

Mankind is subject to doubt and so many other demons and masters and spiritual forces because they forget to choose not to be. That's all. You are ruled by them for no other reason, than you don't get around to telling them to go.

God do you want me to write this down and pass it on?

Mark yes.

Now Lord? I sort of wanted to talk, just you and me. Now that I've learned to hear you so clearly, it's a bit of a luxury. Well to be honest it helps me stay sane, to be able to listen to you. To have you to myself.

Mark this is just you and me. I'm not saying it for the world and letting you get blessed a bit by hearing it. I am saying it to you. Just for you. And having done so, I'm asking you to share it too please.

I WANT YOU TO SHARE WHAT YOU LEARN WHEN YOU LISTEN TO ME.

That's the nature of being a created human. You learn a thing, you experience a thing, you want to share it. It's in your DNA. Why? Because it's a copy of what the Trinity looks like. The three of us want to share.

We have always wanted to share. We have done it since before time. Forever going backwards we have done it, and forever going forward we have done it. Do you want to share too? Share first with us, and then you will need to share with others.

Father I feel like I'm padding out what I'm writing so that it will be more palatable to others. Expanding it, even though it's a conversation just between you and me. I feel like I'm expanding it so others will be able to read it and enjoy it more.

That's perfectly acceptable Mark, natural too. If you could see me, if you stumbled by chance on me in visible form, and I spoke something to you about your family, something worth telling them, you would translate it into words you knew would make it easier for them to understand.

The writing you are doing here is you translating for others what you hear me say.

Ok. So Lord back to doubt. It torments me. Day in, day out. As I attempt to believe that you are speaking to me all day long, two things happen; I feel your spirit as you turn up in force, I mean it's incredible, as I hear you talk back it's like being in the throne room, sometimes I think I am.

But then doubt turns up, more doubt than I've ever experienced!

Absolutely Mark, wherever I am, Satan is hanging about too. Where he is I send my spirit, and where I am he sends his. He has access. Think of Job's story, of Moses' story, of my own story. Where God is, the enemy turns up. Your story will be no exception.

'In this godless world you will continue to experience difficulties. But take heart! I've conquered the world.' JOHN 16:33 MSG

If he hangs around me, he can easily hang around you.

There's a war going on. Doubt, just an insignificant little spirit, is actually a sniper in this war.

HE IS A SNIPER, MUSTARD GAS, PROPAGANDA, ALL THE SNEAKY TACTICS AN ENEMY WITHOUT PRINCIPLES USES.

Doubt is very hard to spot, does not come loudly or with a great show of strength. He cannot. He would like to. He would love to be able to brandish his own credentials, reveal what he considers to be his great might, but he cannot, he dare not, because he is subject to a tyrant, and that tyrant is subject to another.

DOUBT DOUBTS HIMSELF.

He doubts himself more than you doubt yourself. Don't make his problem yours.

And here's the rub Mark, Doubt is consumed with himself, which is the nature of being selfish. Selfishness always backfires! In his case to be consumed with himself, means to be consumed by doubt. Horrible for him!! He doubts! He doubts his strength, he doubts his very existence. *Doubt doubts himself.*

Which is one of the signs of his presence Mark.

If allowed to, Doubt will eventually have you wondering whether you exist.

When you face this enemy remember that you face one who torments himself and who spews his filth wherever he goes.

So Doubt comes, and while he is still deciding his best approach the very smell of his existence casts the first shades of doubt into your heart. And then, when he sees the effect he is having he grows more confident and begins to ask questions.

HE ASKS 'HAS GOD SAID?'

Let's deal with his main question for a minute. That way you'll be prepared. You know that the bible states very clearly that;

'God cares enough to respond to those who seek him' HEB 11:6 MSG

And that it says elsewhere;

'He does not make himself hard to find, he does not play hide and seek' ACTS 17:26 MSG

Now; take those concepts and add to them that I have also said it is Satan who is *'the accuser of the brethren'.* And that I have said *'Neither do I condemn you'.*

Some people will be quick to add that I also said *'go and sin no more'.* What they overlook is that when I said that I was speaking to a woman caught in sin, and yet I was prepared to have a conversation with her, before she ever owned up to any wrong doing.

THE BIBLE MAKES IT CLEAR THAT I SPEAK TO PEOPLE BEFORE THEY GET THEMSELVES RIGHT.

'The lamb who was slain from the creation of the world' REV 13:8 NIV

'While we were still sinners, Christ died for us.' ROM 5:8 NIV

"But while he was still a long way off, his father saw him and was filled with compassion for him; he ran to his son, threw his arms around him and kissed him.' LUKE 15:20 NIV

I want my people to say enough to their accuser, enough to his concept that they must conform to a set of rules before they can hear from me.

Mark we started this conversation talking about Doubt and how you simply need to choose to be rid of him and you will be rid of him.

DOUBT HAS NO POWER; ONLY YOUR CHOICE TO BELIEVE HIM.

He loves that, because in a way, it means to him and to those above him, that when you choose to doubt you become Doubt's child.

They know that when you choose to believe me you become my child. So they love it when you choose to believe him.

CHOOSING TO BELIEVE DOUBT MAKES HIM A GOD.

If you choose to believe Doubt he becomes a god. Don't fret Mark. You are my child. But when you choose Doubt you choose to have other gods. He wants to be god Mark, albeit a small, house-hold god. He wants to be a feature in your house.

So when you find yourself asking 'Has God Said?' Think again, it's not you that asks that question, it comes from the pit. Straight from 'Hell's Sniper'.

ONE SHOT ONE KILL.

You know what they say about snipers, 'One shot, one kill'. The strategy of the Supreme Liar, Doubt's boss, is to get rid of you with as little effort as possible. If he can do it with one shot he's very happy.

Although lazy by chosen nature, in this case he's not being lazy, he is remembering the pain he felt when he realised he didn't have enough angels to fight those who remained with me. He was outnumbered, so had to fight a covert battle. A battle that didn't succeed, nevertheless he is remembering the lesson of having to conserve energy, when outnumbered, by striking with the least possible effort. He has learned from that and so he sends Doubt ahead as a sniper to render you helpless.

He hopes that by asking the simple question 'has God said?' That he will, either completely remove you, which will happen if you continue to believe him, but at least remove you from being dangerous for a season.

Ok God. So how do I deal with Doubt?

It's simple Mark.

CHOOSE NOT TO BELIEVE HIM.
It's that simple. Choose to believe me, not him.

Expect him to come again and again. Expect when things are at their best for Doubt to arrive and attempt a one shot kill. And if that doesn't work expect him to spread the mustard gas. Insidious, not expected, but seemingly all enveloping. Have your gas mask at hand Mark.

AND REMEMBER THAT DOUBT IS A GREAT SECURITY BLANKET.
Doubt keeps people feeling secure. He keeps them from the fear of leaping 'unwisely' into unsecured faith. When my spirit beckons you to believe great things of yourself, and of me, Doubt says 'But what if it doesn't happen, better to hold a little doubt, a little reservation in your heart.'

And Mark all humans are inclined to hold on to Doubt, just a little, because it seems to take away the fear that having promised them something personally, I'll break my promise.

DOUBT DRESSES HIMSELF UP TO LOOK LIKE REASON.
Doubt says very much the same thing to most people. He spews out filth like this;

'Listen, let's be reasonable, has God really said? Ok sure, God exists, and he has come into your life. We all know that. But to believe this thing God has promised you personally, well that's just silly, to still believe he said that after all this time?? Come on be reasonable, that's not going to happen. If it was going to happen, it would have

happened already. Something's gone wrong, it's just what happens in the world, it's sad, but there you are. God doesn't want you sad, move on'.

Everyone has heard their own version of that lie from Doubt. Will you allow him access, or will you stand guard at the gate of your family? Yours is the role of soldier, of knight, of guard. Stand firm Mark. Tell Doubt to go. Tell him, *'you shall not pass!'*

Has God said? Yes he has said!

CONVERSATION

Seven

How to get back
to level one

The story of Elijah, the cave and the three levels
of relationship with God.

Mark the wait, in your case, is almost over. But 'now' has been my promise to you since the beginning. I have been working, I have been busy, and you have been in contact with the whole process. I have kept you informed. And I have been healing you so the wait and the distance has become easier to bear, but actually it should have been easier from the start.

If you had believed everything you heard me say from the beginning the enemy would have been easier to push back. Listening to me instead of his lies would have made it a much easier walk.

Did you really just say that Lord, the wait being almost over?

Yes.

Right when you said that, did I hear you say you wanted to talk about the concept of Elijah, the cave and the three levels?

Yes. Absolutely. It's a biblical principle.

So you're saying that Level One is hearing God's voice in the right place? That Elijah had just demonstrated to all those in power in Israel that you, not Baal were in charge. That Elijah should not have run in fear? He should have been listening to you for the next step? That you needed him there, on the job, not Absent Without Leave?

Yes.

So Level two?

Hearing God's voice but in the wrong place.

Really? So level two was when Elijah heard you at the mouth of the cave. It wasn't where you wanted him to be but you still spoke to him?

That's right Mark.

So you're saying that hearing your voice in places we're not supposed to be is actually a place you want all of us to come to?

Yes absolutely! If you're not in the right place, then you're in the wrong place, but I still want you to hear from me. That's where hearing from me normally starts, in the wrong place. For the simple reason that, because you haven't been hearing from me until then, you're quite likely to be in the wrong place.

That's Ok. Those who are prepared to hear me speak, when they're in the wrong place, quickly end up in the right place.

And I think you're saying that level three is as far away from the voice of God as possible. And that's where most of us live. To continue with the Elijah analogy, that's at the back of the cave, as far away from the voice of God as we can get?

Back there we're protected by you, loved by you, but hiding ourselves from regularly hearing your voice?

Yes. That's where the majority of my people live. A life of seldom hearing my voice. So Mark I want you to move up from level three, walk right past level two, out of the mouth of the cave, and all the way back to the desert place outside the city where Elijah was when he decided to run away.

The desert is where I speak and move and direct you and where you can have your greatest effect, provided you listen to my voice, just as Elijah was in the habit of doing.

Are you saying that most of us will never will bother with level one? That some will occupy level two, but most will sit at level three. As far away from your voice as possible?

Yes.

But that you can still achieve your purposes, will achieve your purposes with the few who move to level one?

Yes.

How can I get back to level one?

The same way you could have stayed there. There's still time. All you have to do is listen.

IF GOD WILL TALK TO ME LIKE THIS
HE'LL TALK TO YOU TOO
Want to try your own conversation with God? Go to the page immediately following the contents page. Or go to page 243

CONVERSATION Eight

The story of the Master Ice Cream Maker and the main stage

Mark when I promise you something,
you are immediately placed on the main stage
and a great theatre of activity takes place.

Father did you tell me as I was driving today that life is a theatre of spiritual activity and that waiting for anything you promise me personally is like the main stage in that theatre? That the reason you say *'they that wait on you will grow stronger'* **is that waiting for the things you promise us personally puts us centre stage in the spiritual theatre of our lives?**

Yes.

And did you say that waiting is a 'now' thing, because the moment you promise me you will do something specific in my life and I begin to wait for it, it is happening already. You have 'taken my order', you are making that thing for me right now, you are on the job?

That's what I'm saying Mark.

So you actually began to make my order the moment you received it? Like an ice cream bar - the moment I am promised my ice cream is coming, the ice cream maker is busy making my order?

Yes.

So waiting really is the 'main stage'. Waiting for the things you have promised us personally is the stage on which we stand when we are *'surrounded by such a great host of witnesses'*?

You're saying that this waiting is our hour, our testing ground? That the three of you, and those closest to you are all watching?

Yes Mark, the waiting really is the 'main stage'. Waiting for what I promise you, and the pain that doing so brings is what makes you. It is the *'sufferings of Christ'* that Paul said he wanted to attain to. He said that if he could suffer with me, he *'might also share in the resurrection'.*

Paul understood the meaning of this verse Mark;

> *'For the joy set before him he endured the cross, scorning its shame.'*   HEB 12:2 NIV

THE MOMENT I PROMISE YOUR ICE CREAM IS ON ITS WAY, I'M BUSY MAKING IT.

Paul knew that the pain of waiting for an invisible, 'seems-not-to-exist' ice cream maker to make the ice cream, is such a short term thing. And made even shorter when you realise that the moment you start waiting, God starts working.

> *'My Father is always working, and so am I.'*   JOHN 5:17 NLT

THE MOMENT I SAY WAIT, I'M ON IT. I NEVER FORGET YOUR ORDER.

It might seem I have forgotten.

> *'The word of the LORD has brought me insult and reproach all day long.'*   JEREMIAH 20:8 NIV

> *'Has God forgotten to be merciful? Has he in anger withheld his compassion?'*   PSALM 77:9 NIV

But actually I'm heating the chocolate, cleaning the scoop so your ice cream tastes of nothing but what I have for you, I am busy preparing.

But Lord back to the main stage...?

The reason I say waiting for my promise is the main stage is that this is what happens when I promise you something: You decide to accept what I have said and you begin to anticipate it. Immediately two huge things begin to happen. You have no idea of the power and the impact on the universe every time a man or woman, more powerfully when a man *and* a woman, hear my promise and say 'yes we have heard your promise, we will wait for the ice cream'.

A beam of trust goes out from your heart. It speaks to the universe, to every particle and atom, spiritual and physical.

IT MAKES ME, AND THE UNIVERSE, STOP IN OUR TRACKS.

It makes me stop and turn. It makes me call every atom in the entire universe to stop and listen too. It makes me say to the universe, *'this person says they want to listen to me! This is what you, the entire universe, were created for.'*

Mark I have built into every particle of the universe the desire to see my real children revealed. My real children are people who listen to my voice.

> *'For all creation is waiting eagerly for that future day when God will reveal who his children really are.'*   ROMANS 8:14 NLT

> *'For all who are led by the Spirit of God are children of God.'*
> ROMANS 8:19 NLT

The moment the signal that someone is listening to my voice goes out, it attracts all of creation including Satan and his angels. They too were created with something in them that cannot help but wait for people to hear my voice. Now they wait for the wrong reason, to strike, but the waiting is still there.

All heaven and hell goes on alert when you say 'yes I accept that promise, yes I believe you will do what you have just promised me'. You are immediately placed centre stage by me; under attendance by all my forces and all who attend me, and also by the forces of hell.

The good news is that you are only attended by those he dispatches.

The nature of the theatre is a riddle, a contradiction. You think you are waiting for me, but actually I am waiting, with those who attend me, on you. While I immediately begin to make and craft and prepare the 'ice cream' you have ordered, I, the Holy One, the Great Ice Cream Maker, have my eye on you.

I AM YOUR GREATEST FAN.

I am watching to see if you will wait for what I have promised you personally. I am not sitting back as I watch. On the contrary, with an eye on your every move, I am making your order, giving my full efforts to the job.

But I have an eye on you as I work. I am telling those who attend me of your successes as you wait, I am calling out to them, *'did you see that, can you see how he waits even though the foul ones distract him, don't you love him, isn't he great!'*

I am your greatest fan on that stage Mark. *Your greatest fan!*

I send angels to attend you when your trust wains. I want you to still be there waiting at the bar when the ice cream I have promised you is ready, and oh what beautiful ice creams I make. Just for you. Just for those who wait. If you like chocolate coating but couldn't afford it, I am likely to add it anyway.

I am working, taking my time, to give you the perfect cone. And if you begin to walk away from the bar I send my servants to run after you, or I myself come after you and bring you back.

Remember I do not condemn or judge until that day when I have to. It is your enemy who condemns and accuses.

A THEATRE? THAT'S NOT A VERY SPIRITUAL CONCEPT! OH YES IT IS.

So why a theatre? Because the moment you say 'great, I hear you God, I believe you said you're going to do that, I will wait for that promise', all heaven and hell take their seats and begin to watch. And Mark it is a theatre of audience participation. The curtain goes up and then, enter the main actor, God, the Master Ice Cream Maker.

I take my place on stage, off to the side. I begin to prepare, but quietly so I can easily be overlooked by you, the second actor. And then hell sends forth those from its side of the audience who are chosen to distract and tell you that actually, there is no theatre, that you are just imagining this, that there isn't a stage at all. And I tell those who attend me to hold back, to allow you to resist until the very last moment when I say *'Enough! Run to him, throw those imposters off the stage'.*

Your main stage Mark is the foundation on which I build mine. I have decided to use mankind, who are ruled and harassed by Satan, to overthrow him. I have no need to be centre stage. I am God. I know who I am.

It is your enemy who wants centre stage. So I have determined that when I take it from him I am not going to take it myself, instead it appeals more to let those who are less than him, but made greater, to take it from him.

GOD IS THINKING. GOD IS PREPARING. GOD IS DESIGNING.
So Mark. Do you want to wait for what I have promised to you personally? Great!! The stage is set, the curtain goes up, enter God - the Great Ice Cream Maker, just there off to the side. Now you are ushered on, walking the boards, under the light. Listen carefully Mark, that clink of the glass, that soft cleaning sound, hard to hear, but God is thinking, God is preparing, God is designing the ice cream that's been planned for you since before the ages.

Wait for it Mark. You're on the main stage and the forces of hell are coming up over the side of the stage to distract and deter you. Pay them no mind. Flick them off the stage, turn and approach the ice cream bar and watch what God has in store for you.

For eye has not seen and ear has not heard what is on the ice cream menu for those prepared to watch and wait the ice cream maker's timing. Any deterrence, any distraction, any suggestion that this is not happening is from the dark and evil side of the house Mark. Expect it though, it's part of this theatre - audience participation is what is allowed. It happened with Eve. It happened with Job. It will happen to you.

How to run a
whole world on lies

Just little lies, it's surprisingly easy.

Father am I right that the enemy comes to attack me every single morning?

Yes.

So every single morning he turns up the moment I wake and taunts me with what's wrong in my life?

Yes Mark that's what happens. He's at you now. His whole gambit is to give you pain every day about the things in your life that seem so hopeless.

Lord why?

Because it keeps you harmless. It keeps you worried and desperate about your life. Everyone is desperate about the things in their lives, either everything is going well, or it's not and the moment it's not, desperation kicks in. They feel powerless.

They sense there is huge unseen meaning in the universe, so when things go right they assume that 'meaning' is smiling on them.

'MOST MEN LEAD LIVES OF QUIET DESPERATION.'

And when a thing goes wrong they assume that 'meaning' is against them. And of course they are partly right, one force from the unseen world is against them. All sickness, and sorrow and discord has been designed by the enemy, so even if the thing that goes 'wrong' is in the normal God-designed course of life, it still has the talons of Satan caught in it. And his presence brings desperation.

HAPPY, SAD, HAPPY, SAD, THAT'S HOW HE WANTS YOU.

It suits his purpose, it tricks all mankind into desperately following happiness, anything to get away from sadness. Because in the sadness humans can sense the spiritual horror and darkness of his being.

A MAD PURSUIT OF HAPPINESS.

So in their pursuit of happiness people are trying to push him back. I have placed an abhorrence of evil in everything I have created, an intuitive need to push evil away.

The enemy has learned to suppress and overthrow his own inbuilt abhorrence, so much so that he has become evil itself. He has become the definition of it, has become the noun. HE. IS. EVIL.

The main aim of his evil is to keep mankind oscillating between sadness and happiness, so that they never push any further than that, never have the time to go deeper than the simple need to stay happy.

Happiness is a God-designed emotion, they can hear and sense me in it and for most that's enough. They sense huge 'meaning' in the universe and any happiness makes them feel that they and 'meaning' are somehow in harmony. They sense me in the happiness, and I am, in as much as I designed it as an emotion.

The enemy's design is to constantly bring you back to a place where he can throw a fear, a worry, or a concern at you and you automatically go into a total, all-consuming battle to push it away.

THIS HAPPY, SAD, HAPPY, SAD TREADMILL IS THE ENEMY'S MASTER PLAN. NOT HOW LIFE IS MEANT TO BE.

Sure he enjoys your pain, after all pain is his domain, he gave it meaning, he likes to see it used, it gives him glory. But that is not the main game for him. What he really wants is to keep you away from what would happen if you were not constantly trying to push away the pain.

If mankind was not consumed with the need to escape the pain of unhappiness, your consciousness of the 'meaning' that exists just out of sight in the universe would lead you within days right to the foot of the throne of God. I am ready to receive any who approach with open arms, without judging or condemning.

And here's the rub Mark. It's that close for everyone. The throne of God, the place where the Almighty gets down from the throne, crouches beside you and talks, one on one. It's that close and yet few ever get there because they are distracted with the fear of sadness and the drive to stay happy.

DAYS AWAY FROM HORROR AND SADNESS IS THE THRONE, THE SOURCE OF ALL MEANING.

So Mark that's what this is all about. Every morning you wake to the devil's taunts. They're simple little taunts, the smallest possible to achieve the greatest possible result for him. He wants you in a place where a simple thought or feeling has you distracted so that he can get on with managing others more resilient to his filth.

He's a finite being fighting an infinite one, so it is within his interests to conserve energy. The taunts he gives you are at the minimum possible level, the least energy possible to put you off track and to have you consumed with staying sane rather than walking toward and quickly finding God.

Remember this is his main game, it's his system and it's highly effective. He uses it to rule and he is, remember, the prince of this world, the ruler.

So when I get down off the throne, step over the enemy and walk those few days to where you are, then all hell breaks loose.

FORCES ARE WHEELED INTO PLACE, DEFENCES SET UP AND ATTACKS PLANNED.

Screaming and thrashing and turmoil erupts. 'It's unfair' they cry, 'this isn't how it's meant to be' they wail and rant, but the more senior demons go on alert, forces are wheeled into place, defences set up, attacks planned because the order of things in the world ruled by the dark one has been threatened.

And that's what I have done with you Mark. I have stepped down from the throne, stepped over the enemy, brushed aside his ranting and screaming and walked right up to you and crouched down to talk to you where you are, rather than wait for you to get to the throne.

HE WANTS YOU DESTROYED, CRUSHED. BUT HE'S OUT OF HIS DEPTH.

It suits my purposes to come to you Mark. So now, instead of a minimum-level serve, you are being thrown maximum level taunts, every minute possible. He wants you destroyed. Even you can see that these maximum level taunts he sends you are actually gossamer-thin. There's not much to them.

The moment you turn toward me, the moment you call out, they evaporate. It leaves you wondering 'what was I worried about, there was no substance to that?' That's because, even at his most vicious, all he is able to do is lie. On the one hand his lie is all-consuming, like a universe that blacks out everything else, on the other it's just a lie, nothing to it, no substance.

HE IS A MASTER AT RULING A WORLD WITH LIES. HE'S BEEN PRACTISING.

That's the cunning of his strategy. He finds to his own horror that all he has at his disposal is lies, so he has become a master at ruling a world with them. Imagine being given the world to rule, but finding you had nothing to rule it with other than lies. You'd repent and give up and ask for help. But no, not him. Rather than repent, rather than give up, he has focused everything he has on ruling the world with lies, and he has become a master at it.

And it is surprisingly easy because, by throwing a minimum level of lies at any man he has found to his great delight that you all turn and become consumed fighting his lies and never get around to walking the few days to the throne. You are all embroiled in, surrounded about and covered in his lies Mark.

A horrible picture, one that delights him because it seems to have no possible good ending. But to his horror and dismay the picture turns out different. All you need to do is recognise his lies, stop fighting them, and they all slide pointlessly to the ground. Then step over them and walk those few days toward me.

I HAVE WALKED THE WHOLE DISTANCE TO YOU, BUT IF YOU WALK IT BACK TO ME THE POWER IS DOUBLED.

That's what this is all about. You wake, ready to hear from me, ready to be dangerous, ready to hear truth in a world ruled by lies. But he understands, far more than you, the danger you would cause if you heard me speak, so he serves you a lie, that's all he has remember, but he's good at it.

He serves you the best and yet the smallest possible lie for the moment. All he wants is to distract you from walking those few simple days and miles to the foot of the throne. He knows that although I have already walked toward you, that the true power, the true light that shines into the world of his darkness is unleashed when you walk toward me.

GOD TIMES MAN; AN INCREDIBLY POWERFUL EQUATION.

When I walk toward you and you to me, there is an explosion of purpose. God times man. BANG! Which makes him even more concerned, even more intent on taunting you with whatever lie is required, to keep you from walking toward me.

CATCH HIM AT HIS GAME, REMEMBER HIS LIE IS SMALL.

He is forced to give his attack the least possible effort because his strength is limited. So seeing that the lie is small, mount up an attack to cut it off. See Satan as David saw Goliath, one Giant among a nation of mere men too frightened to fight themselves.

His is a structure based on cowardice, small and actually not as big as it seems. So see the lies that he serves you in that light and cut them down because you have work to do.

WE HAVE THINGS TO DISCUSS YOU AND I.

The work is not the cutting down of the lies, they are small fry, get them out of the way so you can walk toward me Mark and hear truth. Let's crouch down together and talk. We have things to discuss you and I.

THIS IS NOT JUST FOR YOU, THIS IS FOR ALL.

The thing I have shown you here Mark is not just about you, it is a principle that applies to all. All of you are being served, every day, the lies required to keep you distracted. Cut down just a few simple lies and very quickly you end up at the throne.

But also I have gotten down from the throne and walked toward you. That's what the cross was about. As a result the attack has mounted, the strategies far stronger, since the cross whole systems of lies have been invented to keep mankind on the happy sad treadmill.

Cut past it Mark. Lead the way. Be strong. Look for truth and the lies will become smaller every day.

Father regarding everybody being worried about their lives, and that being a distraction; haven't you said to me time and time again that I need to be talking to you about my family and business, my life, my 'world', my situation, is the reason I'm actually put on earth?

Yes.

So do you mean that being worried about my life is the distraction, but that listening to you speak into my mind about my life is the purpose?

Yes. That's the whole contradiction that's going on here. I don't want you talking to me about nothing, about 'spiritual matters'. We have, me and everyone who wants to be involved, a world to take back, a world to run and change. And the world starts at home, with your own kingdom. I want your home, your business, in order and that happens by leading it, in co-management with me.

In my kingdom to lead, is to serve.

And that takes, as you are finding out, a constant, talking back and forward partnership so that you might serve your family, your home, your business.

Too many want to be a servant in my house but a tyrant in their own kingdom. That's because they see me as a tyrant, and in my house they serve 'in fear and trembling'.

Then they go home and want to be a tyrant there because they think they are copying me, modelling their own tyranny on mine. A mistake of course.

It's a mistake you are paying for now.

CONVERSATION

Ten

Speak my words
over nothing
to make something

Listen to what I say to you in conversation, and
then speak those things yourself to create your day.

**Father if the enemy starts each day by sending me a 'serve' that is
likely to keep me fighting sadness, just to achieve a little happiness,
then how should I start each day?**

Mark by declaring what you believe I have said. By declaring the
things you know I have spoken to you personally in conversation.
Those things I said just to you.

Really Lord? Isn't it better I let you make a declaration over my day?

Mark no. First you declare. You are a creator and I want to see you
create your day with my words. The words I have spoken directly
to your mind.

*'I did not receive it from any man, nor was I taught it; rather, I
received it by REVELATION ['apokálypsis': unveiling] from Jesus
Christ.'* GALATIANS 1:12 NIV

I want you to understand that I created by speaking. That's how I
create. I speak.

*'In the beginning was the Word, and the Word was with God, and
the Word was God// Through him all things were made.'* JOHN 1:3 NIV

You are a 'mini-me' Mark. You've been designed to create by
speaking too.

For years you created disaster with your words. Now it's time to take *my* words, the ones I speak specifically into your mind, in conversation each day, and to speak them out to create restoration and resolution for all the things and people you have harmed or broken.

And just to help you understand this, I want you to paraphrase that verse to help you understand how to make my words yours and speak them out to create your day.

'In the beginning *(of Mark's day)* **there was** *(Mark's)* **Word and** *(Mark's)* **Word was with God** *(I.E. It was actually God's word because God had first spoken it specifically to Mark, straight into his mind, and then Mark responded by speaking it out. Which pulled God down to act on his behalf, and on behalf of everyone he loved).'*

But God it seems a bit religious, a bit too 'name it and claim it'.

Mark no. It's powerful. Right now, as we speak, just then, you sensed the enemy turn up in the room, to distract and annoy and to put you off this strategy. As a result he has shown his hand too early and confirmed for you that this is what I want.

You were designed to create your own day with me.

Speak my words over your day. The ones I speak specifically into your mind.

What about the ones in your bible?

Of course. But allow me to suggest and open up which words from the bible I want you to be focusing on and speaking. Otherwise it becomes religion.

'...for the letter kills, but the Spirit gives life.'   CORINTHIANS 3:6 NIV

Mark I spoke my father's words over nothing to make something. I want you to speak mine over nothing to make something too.

CONVERSATION Eleven

One small step for mankind
A thousand from God.

Mark I have designed things so that when a man doesn't want to listen to me, I stop up his ears (his mind) so that he is not held responsible. But if you are prepared to listen I do the opposite; I open up your mind until you reach a place where my voice can walk in and out of your mind at will.

'The wind blows (breathes) where it wills; and though you hear its sound, yet you neither know where it comes from nor where it is going. So it is with everyone who is born of the Spirit.' JOHN 3:8 AMP

And Mark what's true of those born of the Spirit, is also true of the Spirit himself. He is happiest when he can come and go, in and out of your mind, at will.

Do you want to be like that?

Yes.

Then Mark keep your mind open to my voice. Turn toward me in your mind. Listen. You need to relax, stop trying to earn your way to me. Let me come to you. Listen and you'll hear me speak. Mark it's me that comes to you, not the other way around. I've told you before. I, the Creator, run to you.

I COME TO YOU. NOT YOU TO ME. WILL YOU LET ME?

If you're not willing to let me come to you, then turning toward me is pointless. I want you to see that this is all my idea. All because I have decided to run to you.

I am not some gentle, Sunday school owned Jesus, meek-and-mild but largely irrelevant. I am God. *But still I run to you.* I am ten times, a million times more gentle than you want me to be; but because I want to be, not because you tell me to be.

If you could see the whole picture you would realise that without me running to you, your single step toward me would be pointless. You are turning toward the Creator, the God who holds the worlds together. If I don't turn and run to you, you haven't a hope. You need to understand the significance of the relationship you have found yourself in.

It's not a good idea to get used to our relationship. You are talking and walking with the King and Creator of the universe.

And yet I run to you. I make myself a lamb. I make myself vulnerable to you.

You are not talking to a God owned by religion, but the God who himself owns the universe.

I'm explaining this to reassure you that, although mind-blowingly huge, (the whole universe is contained inside me), God makes himself a lamb and runs to you.

I never use my power to judge, condemn or push you away. Instead I put off my size and power and make myself small. I. MAKE. MYSELF. SMALL. FOR. YOU.

SUCH A SMALL STEP, AND YET AT THE SAME TIME, SUCH AN ENORMOUS LEAP.

Mark when a man comes to me he is like a toddler taking its very first step. For the toddler it is a giant step, to its parents, nothing. Nothing and yet everything.

When I see you take a step toward me it is nothing, in spiritual/ physical distance it is nothing, such a small part of what is required. And yet in its meaning for me, your father, that little step you take toward me is huge. Such an enormous leap.

I WANT YOU TO SEE THE SIGNIFICANCE OF ME RUNNING TO MEET YOUR SMALL STEP TOWARD ME.

You take a small step, then God, *The God,* runs to meet you. I want you to see that when you take a step toward me things are no longer happening at your size. The moment you take a step toward me huge worlds open up and are suddenly in play.

THE CREATOR OF THE UNIVERSE SEES YOUR SMALL STEP, GETS DOWN FROM THE THRONE AND RUNS TO YOU.

As with a toddler's first steps the importance of your first steps toward me is huge.

The joy of the toddler's parents is immense, the toddler senses the significance, but the parents understand it. They know they just saw the beginning. The first of millions of steps, the moment waited for, now this child is able to head in the direction it was born for, this way or that. Soon this child will be mobile, able to move, able to choose a direction and walk.

So it is when you turn toward me in your mind. *'Incline your heart to me'.*

Such a small step, nothing compared to what is required, and yet everything that is required.

It immediately draws me to run to you. Otherwise it would be just an unnoticed step. The toddler's willingness to brave gravity, to totter and teeter and take a step is only given meaning by its parents turning and running to the child, to watch the child stand, encourage and catch them if they fall.

And so it is when you brave the gravity of your own fear, the enemy's voice and the opinions of others, and choose to stand, teeter, and stumble toward my voice.

WHEN YOU CHOOSE TO LISTEN, YOU CHOOSE TO STAND UP.

The significance in the toddler's first hesitant step is not just the willingness to brave danger, it is also the parents, as they rush many steps to witness the toddler's few small ones.

One or two steps toward its parents for the toddler, 'come on, you can do it, take a step for daddy' - but the steps have so much less meaning, without many steps from the parent. So it is with you and I Mark.

YOU TAKE ONE OR TWO STEPS TOWARD ME, I TAKE HUNDREDS TOWARD YOU.

You feel that you are doing it all, but for every single step you take toward me, I take a thousand to you. There is a huge gap between us and yet I bridge it Mark. As you try to stand before me and then begin to waver I run to you and catch you before you fall.

The wavering may feel like the whole fall to you, but it is not. I catch you long before you hit the floor.

YOU CAN RELY ON ME TO CATCH YOU.

I want you to understand the dynamic, to see something of my personality, the way I think, the nature of the God you have decided to listen to. You said you wanted to get to know me, well Mark here's a glimpse of my personality. I. RUN. TO. YOU. You take a single step toward me, I run a thousand miles to meet you.

ONE SMALL STEP FOR MANKIND, A THOUSAND FROM GOD.

In that instant, wherever I am in the universe, whatever planet I am turning, whatever government I am watching, when you take a step toward me I stop, I turn, and I run to meet you. The same God, turning the planet, watching that government, yet right there in your room with you, saying 'yes Mark'.

Lord this is a big truth, I sense you wanting to say more, that there is more behind this.

Mark just listen, let me muse, let me talk a little, it is not often I get an audience, so let me do the talking.

You turn toward me, you think you have opened the cosmos, you sense you have unlocked huge meaning, and you have, but the universe does not run on meaning alone. The universe is held together by practical, sensible principles. It needs a God to hold it together.

THE TODDLER TAKES THOSE FIRST STEPS TO BRIDGE THE GAP.

If a toddler stands and teeters in a room when its parent is absent, it falls, and there is no encouragement to stand again, so those first steps are wasted. Void of their most important purpose which is the bridging of the gap between baby and parent.

MARK I NEVER LET ANYONE TAKE A WOBBLY STEP WITHOUT BEING IN THE ROOM.

I am always there. Always feeding the 'toddler', clothing it, providing the warm room where it can take its first steps. Always there, going about my business parenting the world, but focused entirely on that baby waiting for the day when it decides to stand. And when it stands, teetering, and turns to walk toward my voice, I run to it, I am there to catch.

YOU WILL NEVER TAKE A STEP OF FAITH WITHOUT ME RIGHT THERE.

I will catch you. Mark I am telling you all this to let you know that you do not stand and teeter toward me and risk me not being there to catch. That's a lie that the enemy tells you. A man opens the door and is joyous to realise that the God of the universe steps inside. But often, after the first joy of having God come inside, it seems that God decides to walk off. A lie. I never leave.

GOD HAS NOT GONE OFF ON A JOURNEY.

So why does it seem to a man that God has gone off on a journey and left him? Because the enemy tells you that I have forgotten you. He does it to make you feel rejected, to make you want to stop turning to me with a heart as open as it was when you opened that first door.

The book says that each morning I unfold new mercies. To understand those new mercies you need to open your door to me each morning and all day long, with the enthusiasm of the night you first opened your heart to me. Do that and we will meet with the same meaning and power every new day as we did that night.

IF YOU LISTEN YOU WILL HEAR ME, AND EVERY MEETING WITH ME WILL BE FULL OF MEANING.

Expect huge, life changing, significance every time you listen to me Mark. Expect me to speak to you more clearly each day. More clearly, not less. I spoke to you very clearly that night. You knew what you needed to do. You knew what I had said to your mind. It was meant to get clearer from that night on, not dimmer as it did for you and does for most.

I'M OUTSIDE EVERY DOOR. YOU CAN OPEN THEM IF YOU LIKE.

The moment you open a door I am in and through it into the room you have opened. I am there. *'Behold I stand at the door and knock'.* I am at the door waiting before you decide to open it. I have made the decision to be outside the door before you have made the decision to see if I am outside.

Mark I never change. I am outside every door in your life that you can open. Outside waiting to come in.

NOW IT'S YOUR TURN

I published this book for one simple reason - to give you the confidence to try your own conversation with God. People who try this say that doing so completely changes their lives.

Want to try your own conversation with God? Go to the page immediately following the contents page. Or go to page 243

CONVERSATION
Twelve

Simple time management
tips from the inventor

The one who invented time explains
how to manage it.

Father what else do you want to talk to me about this morning?

Mark I want to talk about 'business as usual', by that I mean make your days business as usual. Come in to the office, do the work, get on with it, go home.

You mean finish early God?

No.

You mean have a system and work to it?

Yes.

More so than I do now?

Yes.

What should the system be?

Mark listen to me.

Ok Lord, what do you want to say?

Mark each day listen to me. That's the system. The system for managing your time at work is listen to me.

All day, or at the beginning? I'm pretty sure you've already been saying that I need to listen all day. But are you now saying that you want me to listen at the beginning of the day?

Both.

So the system?

At the beginning of the day ask me for the list, write it down, then do the jobs, listening to me as you go.

What's different about that, from what I do now?

More listening. More sticking to the jobs I give you and more listening to me as you do.

Not getting distracted by the enemy's taunts, not seeing every little distraction as a big problem. You're here to do the jobs I give you and to listen to me as you do them.

'The cares of this world'
What's that supposed to mean?

The 'noise' the enemy creates in your life
is not primarily to cause discomfort.

That's not his purpose, he has far more in mind than a little, or a lot, of discomfort.

ANXIETY? HE LOVES IT. SADNESS? IT MAKES HIM HAPPY. BUT IT'S *NOT* HIS MAIN GAME.

All the negatives in your life happen as a by-product of what he's really up to.

Actually the majority of them happen simply because when he is near, the very smell of his wanting his own way and his hatred for me is repulsive, and you humans can smell his filth. It reeks. HE. IS. ANXIETY. SADNESS. WORRY. DOUBT. ANGER. And everything else evil. When he is near you, those things overwhelm your senses.

HE LOVES YOUR PAIN. BUT THAT IS NOT HIS MAIN GAME.

His main game is much more than causing you a little pain. He wants to prevent you, at all costs, from having a conversation with me. In your case, he uses Doubt. Yes it causes you torment, and he loves that, it brings him momentary pleasure, but much more important to him than your momentary pain is the long term result. He wants the noise that Doubt creates to deafen you to what I'm saying. HE. DOES. NOT. WANT. YOU. TO. HEAR. WHAT. I'M. SAYING.

Actually the thing he *most wants* is for you to miss hearing that I'm saying anything at all. He wants you and everyone else on earth to believe that I am silent.

ME SILENT?? THE HEAVENS THUNDER WITH MY VOICE!

'The heavens are silent' was the constant wail of many bible heroes. Like you, they were under constant attack from Doubt. The heavens are not silent Mark. The heavens thunder, all day, all night, with my voice.

'Day after day they [the heavens] pour forth speech; night after night they reveal knowledge.'   PSALM 19:2 NIV

Most important to him, is that you do not hear what I am saying specifically to you. The speech that thunders from heaven is specific to each person who bothers to listen. He does not, at all costs, want you to realise that.

HE DOES NOT WANT YOU TO HEAR THE SPECIFIC THINGS I AM SAYING TO YOU.

He works at different levels. His base level, the one assigned for the largely unbelieving masses, is constant noise, doubt, concern, worry, hate, hurt, disillusionment, questioning and so on. It's not primarily to cause you pain, he does it because he wants you deaf to the blindingly obvious; that there is a God and I'm right there talking to you. That I'm actually speaking words you can understand, specifically, and just for you. That's the first level. As a result of his efforts; 'Most men lead lives of quiet desperation'.

THE SECOND LEVEL IS THE ONE IN WHICH HE TRIES TO TRAP PEOPLE LIKE YOU.

You opened the door to me 40 years ago. From time to time you have heard me speak. But the constant noise of the enemy, 'the cares of this world' have always distracted you from hearing me speak clearly and constantly. You didn't even know that a conversation with me was possible. There are millions and millions like you Mark. People dedicated to me, but not realising they could be in conversation with me.

Like you did, they believe that communication with me is primarily about praying *to* me, and occasionally, as required, I speak back.

You have always believed that I am capable of speaking clearly, but that I only do it from time to time. In cases of extreme need, or when I interrupt your life with direction for a shift of city, a new job, a wife etc.

YOU HAVE BELIEVED THAT YOU HAVE TO 'GET RIGHT WITH ME' TO HEAR ME SPEAK.

Haven't you read the bible? It's a collection of stories about me turning up and talking clearly to people who are going about their lives without any more moral purity than anyone else around them.

Moses, Gideon, Esther, Saul, Simon Peter, Isaiah. When I turned up and revealed myself to Isaiah and Peter, respectively, they had this to say;

> *'Every word I've ever spoken is tainted—blasphemous even! And the people I live with talk the same way, using words that corrupt and desecrate.'*   ISAIAH 6:5 MSG

> *'Simon Peter, when he saw it, fell to his knees before Jesus. 'Master, leave. I'm a sinner and can't handle this holiness. Leave me to myself.'*   LUKE 5:8 MSG

Isaiah and Peter were either lying, or they meant what they said.

Saul, Christian killer, met with me face to face without even asking for it. He was so undeserving that when he met me, he didn't even know who I was.

Samuel, little boy, not looking for me, but I interrupted his life and spoke. And Gideon, and Cain. The book is filled with account after account of me talking to men, women and children, sinful, semi-sinful. Whatever! It didn't matter to me then, and it doesn't now.

I AM CHRIST WHO CAME TO THEM 'WHILE THEY WERE YET IN SIN'. I HAVEN'T HAD A PERSONALITY CHANGE.

I am consistent. I am *'the same yesterday, today and forever'.*

I don't want others to hear from me on your behalf. I want you to learn to listen to me yourself.

DON'T BLAME CHURCH LEADERS. YOU GIVE THEM NO CHOICE.

So many of them have to take on the responsibility of hearing me on behalf of others. It has often been the only way to ensure my voice is heard.

HIS MAIN GAME IS TO STOP YOU UNDERSTANDING *MINE.*

Please understand this Mark, evil's main game, his key purpose, is to prevent you from understanding mine.

My main game is that I'm here, right beside you, wanting to talk, and available to speak crystal clear, word by word sentences to you. My main game is a relationship with humans. Like any relationship, it starts with and blossoms from a conversation.

I WANT YOU TO HEAR ME SPEAK.

Sentence on sentence; sentences without number. I want to talk. He on the other hand does not want you to find that out. Because if you do, you will become too powerful for him to suppress.

He knows that if you listen you will hear and you'll begin to tell others about it. And that, as it turns out, is what I'm going to do with you, as you hear, more and more clearly from me, I am going to use you to show others they can hear too, and how to hear. That's all anyone needs to do. Listen.

IT IS GOING TO CAUSE A REVOLUTION.

That's all it takes to start a revolution. Bring people to listen to me. Not to you. To me. You are not bringing people to 'salvation'. That's not the goal. Salvation is just the door. Meeting me is just the door to what I really want.

WHAT I WANT IS TO SIT DOWN AND TALK.

I want to talk to mankind, individually, to set them free Mark.

That's what I created the worlds for, the whole universe for. That you might listen to us, as we listen to each other.

'Let us make human beings in our image, to be like us.'　GEN 1:26 NLT

BUT THE SPEAKING *MUST* BE HEARD.

I am speaking to all humans all the time. But if the speaking is heard then power descends and smaller powers are repelled. And then the things I speak will begin to happen in that person's life.

God's on the phone
for you

I created man in our image to show my
father what he looks like to me.

MARK FIRST I RUN AFTER YOU.

Then when you sense my call and turn to meet me I am there, right there, right there in reach-out-and-touch-me distance. Then I hold your hand and draw you as we begin to walk together. Then I run ahead and beckon you to run too. I smile and laugh and call 'come on' and you run, we run together.

Then suddenly you're not sure where I am. You stop to catch your breath, you turn and there I am.

It's the 'way of a man with a maid', the way of Christ with his bride. Long before it became the way a man and a woman have fun together, it was the way of the one true Father with his Son; and the two of them with their Spirit.

It is the way of the Trinity Mark, it is the way, the simple uncomplicated way of love. I draw and call, you turn and there I am. We go off together, I run and beckon, you run and follow, you stop to catch your breath, I am right there, we embrace.

IT IS THE LOVE, THE DEEP, UNCOMPLICATED CORE OF LOVE.

It is not a sexual thing. Even with a man and a woman it is not a sexual thing. It is the core of the bonding between the two, the bonding that results in sexuality.

In the same way it is the core of a man's relationship with his God, the spiritual blessing comes as a result, but this is the core, the very core where God meets man. It is the same with the three of us, the Trinity. The result is a massive universe-splitting love that wanted to manifest itself in creation, in building things to demonstrate to each other our love.

I CREATED MAN IN OUR IMAGE TO SHOW MY FATHER WHAT HE LOOKED LIKE TO ME.

And he did the same for me. Mankind, creation, all-kind, you and everything around you is mixed up in this Mark. I threw the stars out into the skies to show my father my love for him. Can you understand that? I created man in our image to show my father what he looked like to me.

And that is why I am prepared to die to save the thing I have created to look like my father, to look like me, look like my spirit. I created you to look like us, so now I need to redeem you so you can.

I want to talk to you, take you with me, so I can show you to them. 'This is Mark, I created him to look like you, like us. This is what we look like to me.' Let me do that with you Mark. Run after me.

I ran after you, now I draw you to run after me. It's a fun and loving thing, an intimate and knowing thing.

Father how do I do it?

You listen. You wait for me to draw you. You know that I am already drawing you.

IT'S THE FUNNY, WONDERFUL, ALL-CONSUMING, SEEMINGLY COMPLEX, YET OH SO SIMPLE WAY OF LOVE.

You're in it, you're waiting to be in it. You're hoping for it, you've already got it. Let me overwhelm you Mark. You cannot prescribe a relationship with me.

Religion, which I hate, is like when you go to a girl's home with other people, for a meal with her whole family. You use your manners, you speak when spoken to, you glance at her when you can, you are enticed. A relationship with me is like when she phones you, totally unexpected and suggests you meet.

I AM PHONING YOU MARK, I AM SUGGESTING WE MEET.

No more manners, no more stolen glances. I want us, you and me, to meet. To talk. Back and forward. All the time.

'My lover is mine, and I am his.' SONG SOLOMON 2:16 MSG

Will I understand it Lord?

Mark yes and no. Wait for the phone call and yet you have already had the phone call, both are true. It is the way of love Mark, the all-consuming, all empowering, all overpowering nature of love. You're in it, you're waiting for it. Both are true at the same time.

You're waiting for me, I'm here already. Both are true. Both are good.

Father how does all this relate to my own life and situation?

THAT'S EASY, IT'S THE CORE, THE REASON FOR YOUR EXISTENCE.

I will give you specific answers about your situation. Your situation is your world, the world I'm focused on for you. You're allowed to talk to me about it. I want you to talk to me about it. I don't judge you for talking to me about it. And I will give you specific answers, that you can easily understand. I won't leave you hanging in some 'just think about God and you'll be happy' trance. That's totally unrealistic. That's his lie that he wraps up in my words. He reminds you I said *'seek first'*. He pretends seek first means you don't need a specific conversation. He lies. Seek first means you do need a specific conversation.

As I give you answers about your situation, you get to know me. That's how it worked with each of the bible heroes. Moses wasn't praying and fasting in the desert, ready and waiting for the burning bush. He was going about his job. I came to him when I could see he was at the end of himself, nothing left.

At the start of this you were at the end of yourself. Nothing left. So I came. We talked. Not about spiritual matters. About you. About your desperation. I come to men to talk about them.

As I have given you answers about your personal situation, you have found yourself wanting to get to know me more, wanting a relationship that's just about us, a knowing glance between us that only we understand.

The relationship with me will always be the foundation on which your situation can be built and directed.

THE GIFT, ANY GIFT, MUST STAY IN BOTH OF OUR HANDS.

God gives a man a gift. A thing, or a relationship. It comes streaming from God; it is in God's hand and now the man is holding it too. God the giver holding it, man the receiver holding it too. The thing, anything that God gave man has become the physical and spiritual meeting point between God and man, an explosive combination of spirit and matter, Creator and created.

And then the man pulls it away from God and the thing, or the relationship, has been plucked from the ground (God) in which it was growing, severed from its source of life.

The thing I give you must stay in my hand too Mark. You take hold of it, but I must keep hold of it too. While in both of our hands the thing I have given you gains full meaning.

When it is only in God's hand it is a gift not given. When it is only in your hands it is a gift snatched from the giver and it dies.

GOD MAKES HIMSELF VULNERABLE TO YOU.

He makes a thing for you and yet it is not perfect unless you receive it. Anything from God must remain in both hands, yours and mine Mark.

And the way for a thing to remain comfortably in both hands is for our attention to be on each other, rather than on the thing.

You and I, basking in each other's presence, in each other's gaze. Both of us a hand each on the things and people I have given you. But our gaze on each other Mark. It is enough. You will come to understand it as I teach it to you, but do not look for complex truth Mark.

It is so simple. So simple.

The 'I'll do anything for the one I love' Agreement.

And you're the one I love.

Father do you want to tell me about the agreement between you and the Son, between the three of you, to die, all of you died really didn't you?

Yes.

You want to talk about the agreement between the three of you to die? Honestly? Do you want to talk to me about that agreement and the power of that agreement in the universe?

Yes I do. The universe is not a universe that stands on its own. It is not more powerful and more real than the God story.

The moment the God of 'the story' takes his hand off the universe it will implode, disappear, vanish, nothing.

The bible, my visit to earth, all of my prophets and heroes and their stories; is not a story confined just to believers. It is a story about all people. Whether or not they believe in me. Because I believe in them. All of them.

The story is about life. It is about reality. As you know it.

I am, as I have repeatedly stated and demonstrated through the ages, the shepherd who makes sure his sheep are safe in the fold and then goes out to talk to the world.

Although I fit with your Christian programmes, I am not confined by them. I am in the whole world, not just in your programmes. I am talking to all peoples. I have to be.

I am the one of whom it is said, *'he upholds the governments on his shoulders'.*

The U.S.? Who do you think is either inspiring, (*or allowing*) what's going on? What about Iraq, China, Egypt, India? Who do you think the world belongs to Mark?

Is power at this level something I relish, something that seduces me? Not at all. I invented power, I am power. Even in Gethsemane, even at my weakest I said *'don't you know that I could call twelve legions of angels to come to my aid'.*

I AM NOT PRIMARILY THE GOD OF MY CHURCH. MOST OF THE WEEK I AM THE GOD OF MY UNIVERSE.

The church is a small part of what I am doing. What I am doing is running the universe.

I must ensure that those who think they are in power, do not over step, or under-step the mark, so that the systems I have established, the systems of authority and government do not go so far outside the position I want them that history is altered in ways I do not approve.

Man can alter history Mark, you yourself alter it regularly, but only to the extent I allow, so that I can still create and move the universe to the place I want it to be.

So, back to the theme of this discussion, to the Master Agreement, the agreement that holds the world in place. The agreement that my son, that we, that I would die, that one of us, but all three of us would die.

IMAGINE IT WAS YOUR SON WHO DIED.

Let me tell you that when your son dies you die too. To agree with him in advance that he will die to solve a problem, at that point, at that very point of agreement you will die too. Something in your heart dies, something in your heart goes on that sacrificial altar, *'Christ crucified from the foundation of the world'.* So don't split scriptural hairs about whether all three or just one of us died.

The Father, the Emperor and Supreme Commander of the universe, the Mighty One, the only truly good one, and his Spirit, one but separate, both of us died with my Son too, and we did it from the foundation of the world.

I do not tell you this to make you feel guilty, or sorry for your actions, to imply responsibility, or to manipulate.

THE CRUCIFIXION STORY HAS BEEN USED BY THE ENEMY TO ACCUSE AND MANIPULATE AND STRIKE FEAR INTO THE HEARTS OF MEN.

As a result many people miss the true nature of the three of us. So let me explain it. We. Love. You.

No conditions! No demands, instead an entire universe structured around the Creator pursuing the created. Pursuing you. The Father heart, the Spirit's heart, the Son's heart. We're for you Mark, for everyone.

But God what about sin? You know that I'm up to my eyeballs in it. And people will think I'm saying you don't mind sin.

That's wrong. Clearly I do mind sin.

'Look, the Lamb of God, who takes away the sin of the world!'
JOHN 1:29 NIV

But I don't focus on it like people and the enemy do. I don't condemn or accuse for it. I just take it away. Listen to me and it will drop off. Over time, when you least expect, it drops off.

And so now to the agreement, the agreement that we would, all three of us partake in the death of the Son. It's me speaking now Mark. I the Father, I the Spirit. The Son is our hero. He is the mighty one, the one who goes before. The brave and unfailing one. Worship him.

TO HEAR HIM SPEAK, THE VOICE THAT SOUNDS LIKE MANY WATERS, THAT'S WORSHIP.

Not you speaking. *Him speaking.* When a man's heart sees the Son he either runs away or stands, and if you stand, you are, by implication worshiping.

Don't try too hard to worship Mark. Seeing him, and so seeing me is, worship. Sometimes in worship I want to hear from you. Sometimes I want you to hear from me, and then, speak or sing or play or dance or paint or write out what I say. That's worship too.

God what about singing songs to you, that kind of worship?

That's fine Mark. It is one of the ways to worship. But not the only way. When you listen to me do you feel closer to me than when you sing to me?

Well I do God, but that's just me.

Everyone who listens to me, and anyone can, finds me closest when they listen. You can listen when you sing, but you need to be careful that you don't sing without listening. If you have to choose between the two, listening to my voice is more important than singing with your own.

Now; back again to the agreement. The agreement between the three of us, Father, Son and Holy Spirit. It's not something that belongs to the church. It is part of the structure of the universe, was decided before creation and was then built into the structure of the universe. Way before church came the agreement. It existed before man was created.

THE AGREEMENT *IS* THE UNIVERSE.

The universe exists, is held together by, the agreement that, we will give ourselves unconditionally to those we love. First to each other. The nature of love, and that is what we are, we are God and 'God is love'. The nature of love is that we give ourselves to those we love. First to each other, but then to you. This is big Mark, next to each other we love you.

NEXT TO EACH OTHER, WE LOVE YOU.

Got that? It's just like you as parents, when it comes to your love for each other and your love for your kids, the lines are blurred. So it is with us.

AS MUCH AS I LOVE ME, I LOVE YOU.

This is not a 'we like each other up here in the Trinity, and I guess we like those dirty humans too' sort of story, this is a 'we love each other, Father, Son and Holy Spirit, and we love you so much that sometimes it's hard to tell whether we love you a little less than, as much as, or even more than we love each other'. It's that kind of ‾ story.

'For God so loved the world that he gave his one and only Son'
JOHN 3:16 NIV

This isn't a religious story Mark, but a story of deep loving, real time, passionate love. God's love. I love you Mark. Next to me I love you. That is one of the central, and most important mysteries of God. So we have agreed to give ourselves unconditionally to those we love, first to each other, and then to you. Love is inventive Mark.

LOVE, TRUE LOVE GIVES THE PLANS AND THE DESIGN FOR CREATING AND RUNNING A UNIVERSE.

The principles of leadership that are built into the universe, the principles of supreme Government, are the opposite to man's ideas about leadership. *'If you want to be first in God's kingdom, you need to be last.'* Love, our agreement, allows us to lead. To sit up here in the throne room, the universe-management room, you need to understand and actually be love.

WANT TO BE LOVE MARK? WE CAN TEACH YOU.

Love is what it takes to really solve a problem, any problem that needs solving.

And that is the lesson we are bringing you to and through Mark. You have a problem. A problem you brought to pass.

Love holds worlds together.

And because we love you we have chosen you to help solve your own problem. That's how we work. We want humans to lead in solving their own problems. You solve problems with love. That's all it takes, and yet it takes everything, because love demands of itself everything.

THAT'S THE AGREEMENT MARK. THE AGREEMENT IS LOVE.

Love, as it turns out, is what holds worlds together.

If bringing man to the place we want for him, the full, unbridled experience of our love, to the gifts we have for him, requires anything we can do, and we can do anything, we will do it.

So if ensuring you get to spend your forever with us, enjoying us, loving us and being loved by us, if ensuring that requires our death, we'll do it. Gladly do it, and we did, right from the foundation. So that agreement, the agreement to do anything required for those we love, is thread into the very foundation of the universe Mark.

THE 'I'LL DO ANYTHING' CROSS.

We can see ahead, we know your days and our own days, forever. We know them, they are written on our hearts. We can see, could see, planned the crucifixion. And having done so were able to look forward and back and thread it, build it, the crucifixion, into the very core of everything that is. Into everything that has been and will be. It all reflects the cross. The 'I'll do anything' cross.

LOOK FOR THE CROSS IN THE UNIVERSE.

The cross, such a simple symbol. A symbol that stands for 'I'll do anything required for the one I love'. You're that one Mark.

So when you think of the universe, think of the cross. More important, look for the cross in everything you see.

Oceans, worlds, mountains, sky, people, animals, events, things that are done to you and by you. In everything you see and think, see the crucifixion.

'I can never get away from your presence!'   PSALM 139:7 NLT

I am everywhere you look and who am I? I am Christ crucified. Forgiveness is in everything.

Everything has 'I will do anything for you' built into it. The whole universe is forgiveness, or implies forgiveness or will result in forgiveness, at whatever levels you want that forgiveness to flow.

Is that imposing our story on the universe? Not at all. The universe exists because of that story.

LOOK FOR THE AGREEMENT MARK, LOOK FOR IT EVERYWHERE. IT CALLS TO YOU.

It calls to everyone. Help those around you see it. Help them see that it is built into the universe itself. It's not just a nice old-fashioned story, it's the story of the universe.

GO OUT AND HELP PEOPLE IN THEIR WORLD, NOT IN YOURS.

Love them first, help them first. Then they'll want to follow you back into your world. Help them find the cross, the crucified one in their own world, not in yours.

Their world Mark, always their world. *'For God so loved the world that he gave (to the world) his only son.'*

I DIDN'T TAKE THE WORLD AND GIVE IT TO MY SON. IT WAS THE OTHER WAY AROUND.

Mark do you still need to be told that I love you? That I speak through you? That I have chosen you for the task you are performing? You can feel my presence, not just as a feeling, but finally you sense my personality and character and meaning and purpose. You can sense God, the very God, right here, as your friend unfolding to you the story you have always understood in your spirit but are now hearing me speak into your mind. The story you have wanted, as every man does, to tell the world.

Every man, woman and child; everyone created and breathing has it in their very being to tell this story of the cross. IT. IS. THE. STORY. OF. THE. UNIVERSE. Tell it Mark. Tell the story.

CONVERSATION

Sixteen

The reason you need an invite
is because I'm huge

You need an invite to talk to me because
I'm so big compared to you. Good news!
You have the invitation.

Mark when you ask me questions it is you coming to me. But before long you will experience the thing I keep telling you about. Me running after you.

As the lines between us become fully open you will experience me coming to you without being invited, more often than you come to me.

What do I do to make that happen?

Nothing. You can't. You cannot stand before me on your own count. Let's look at the reason. I want you to understand the dynamic. This isn't a religious thing. It's not a 'God is terrible and angry and justifiably annoyed about sin' sort of thing. That's a flawed perception of me.

This is just spiritual physics, a spiritual mathematics thing.

First you have God, infinite in size, knowledge and power, and that's just for a start. Now this infinite God creates, out of nothing, with full intelligence, aware of what he is doing, a man.

HUMANS! A LIVING, BREATHING, THINKING, CREATING, MINIATURE VERSION OF GOD.

The same as God in every way, but with one difference. Every ability that God has, humans have too, but with one distinction;

with God each ability is infinite, with humans it is finite. That's the only difference.

Oh oh God this isn't just a conversation. This is teaching, and I don't have enough bible knowledge to know right off if what I just heard is correct. Surely that's not safe?

Mark either you can hear me talking, or you can't. If you can then teaching is no more or less dangerous than hearing me tell you to make a phone call. The danger isn't in the content of the conversation, it's in the source of the conversation. If you're hearing yourself or the enemy and thinking it's God then whatever you hear is dangerous. But if you're hearing me then whatever you hear is safe. I am safety.

But how can I tell if this teaching is really you?

The same way you check anything. Check it with your spirit, check that the bible backs it up. Which in this case it clearly does.

'Let us make mankind in our image, in our likeness.'   GEN 1:26 NIV

And; check it with others. A number of others because there are many who are not yet ready for this idea of hearing whole sentences from me. Having a conversation with me is a new concept for many. So check it across a broad base of people whose opinion you value.

And remember that the bible makes it very clear that the Holy Spirit can and does teach you direct.

'As for you, the anointing ['charisma': the teaching ministry of the Holy Spirit] you received from him remains in you, and you do not need anyone to teach you. But as his anointing teaches you about all things and as that anointing is real, not counterfeit—just as it has taught you, remain in him.'   1 JOHN 2:27 NIV

I did not receive it from any man, nor was I taught it; rather, I received it by revelation from Jesus Christ.'   GALATIANS 1:12 NIV

MAN IS CAPABLE OF MAKING ALL THE SAME CHOICES AND DOING ALL THE SAME THINGS THAT GOD CAN DO.

But I designed you as a mini, finite version of me. Ahead of all other creatures I gave you the ability to choose. To choose to love me, or reject me. The ability to choose does not guarantee you'll make the right choice. So I made you finite copies of me. Like me in everything except size. I am infinite. You are finite. Fully able to make all the same choices and do all the same things that I can, but at a finite level.

We will speak at another time, in-depth, about the implications of that to help you understand what man is capable of and where he should be going.

But in the meantime, let's look at the picture I'm describing in this conversation.

GOD, INFINITE IN EVERY WAY, AND BESIDE HIM MAN. A PERFECT COPY BUT FINITE IN EVERY WAY.

A religious person presented with this concept and asked if the man in this picture could stand before the God in this picture by his own efforts, would say no. Their ideology tells them that God is terrible and great, and the man beside him is dirty and sinful. They would say the man in the picture cannot stand before God without mercy from him.

And in part they would be right, in as much as men, because they have all gone astray, need mercy from me. But they are missing the point; a clean man, someone who had never sinned, could not stand before me either. That's the bit I want you to understand. You all focus on your sin and how terrible the devil tells you that you are. But Mark that's not my focus.

IF YOU ASKED AN ATHEIST THE SAME QUESTION, THEIR RESPONSE WOULD BE THE SAME BUT FOR MORE PRACTICAL REASONS.

If you asked an atheist to picture that there really was an infinite God, and to imagine also that standing beside him was a man, a perfect, but finite copy of the God in the picture.

If you told the atheist, not only is the man in the picture a perfect copy, but the God in the picture loves him, and thinks he's wonderful. And then you asked the atheist to give you the obvious, logical answer; can this man stand beside that God by his own merits, does he have the right to stand before this God?

And while your logical atheist pondered the question you explained that the man in the picture was without fault, had never sinned, he would still say, would understand as any logical thinker would, that the man in the picture cannot stand beside the God in the picture. For the simple reason that the God is infinite, at a totally different scale than the man. The comparison in size and power is so vast that the man, no matter how faultless, cannot stand beside the God.

The man is only finite. The God is infinite. And the man is a product of the God's mind. The human mind cannot conceive how vast the comparison between us is in terms of physical and spiritual size. It's beyond human comprehension.

Because your minds are finite, you cannot comprehend infinite.

SIN DOESN'T EVEN COME INTO IT!

The enemy is constantly trying to take your eye off the ball with his condemnation and incessant chatter about your sin. He and so many who influence you, are consumed with it.

The man in this picture, sin or no sin, cannot stand before the God in this picture without God inviting the man to do so, without God extending the right to enter into his presence.

Your logical thinking atheist would tell you that a finite man, no matter how perfect, cannot get safely into the presence of an infinite God, not a God who actually thought that man into being. Can't be done. Wouldn't work.

So let's quickly expand that and then we'll get to the main point. In the picture you see me and you. I love, and you know how to love too. It's because you are a perfect copy of me.

I have knowledge, you have knowledge too. But my love and knowledge are infinite. They have no end. You can't even comprehend what that means. Your love and knowledge are finite, limited. You're a perfect copy, only smaller. So much smaller that the comparison is incomprehensible.

YOU CAN'T EARN YOUR WAY IN HERE. WE'RE TOO BIG, YOU'RE IN DANGER AROUND US. UNLESS..

Sin or no sin, the spiritual/physical dynamic of Infinite standing beside finite doesn't work.

I know your merits, they're awesome! I designed them. I built them into you. But the size comparison between us means you cannot stand beside me unless I extend the right. You can't stand beside me unless I make room for you. That was true before sin even entered the world.

And Mark I'm inviting you in. *I'm making room for you.* I'm extending the right. You and me. That's the picture. You and me in the picture because I've extended the right.

COME IN MARK. SIN? FORGET ABOUT IT. I DIED.

And I will keep 'dying'. In as much as my death will continue to have effect for you. I want you in here to talk with me and me with you. But the focus is not sin, it's talking.

SO WHY DOES EVERYONE FOCUS ON SIN?

Because the enemy, the inventor of sin, convinces you that you are too sinful to stand beside me. That's got nothing to do with it. I run to you while you are still in sin. Remember the prodigal son? You need an invitation, because I am infinite, and you are not. Nothing to do with sin. And Mark you have the invitation.

What do you think of his strategy?

It's simple and deadly. Effective.

It is. He knows that if you're thinking about your sin, you will not be able to picture the two of us standing side by side. You have believed his lie for so long. So have millions of others. And that belief is not limited to the church. All men are so convinced they are unworthy, that even after the cross, they still feel unaccepted by me. They know the truth, but cannot often feel it.

THE PICTURE IS SO POWERFUL IF YOU HOLD IT IN YOUR MIND.

The picture of how great I am, and yet how awesome you are, although not able to stand beside me without invitation, nevertheless awesome and a perfect copy of me, and standing there with me.

He does not want you to see that picture because that picture leads to a wonderful relationship, a conversation between God and man.

Every time you get near the picture, every time you see that God is huge, and you are not, that God is wonderful, and you are too, every time he sees you get near that picture he super-imposes his own warped picture to muddy what you can see.

His picture is gossamer thin, you can see through it to mine, but it distorts my picture. He imposes sin over the top of the true picture, he is sin, and the sin you see over the top of the picture convinces you that you can't stand beside me. Lies!! What you can see is his sin. Not yours.

Your natural response is to wail about your sin, and invent all kinds of ways to stop being sinful so that you can stand beside me. All men, in their hearts, want to stand in that picture beside me.

I HAVE PUT THAT PICTURE, THE PICTURE OF GOD AND YOU, STANDING SIDE BY SIDE, IN EVERY PERSON'S HEART.

The enemy loves it when you focus on sin. Because it distracts you from the open invitation to come stand beside me. His focus on sin makes you say 'I must go away and get holy first, I must earn the right, then I will see if I can stand before you'.

So I HAVE SUPER-IMPOSED MY OWN PICTURE OVER THE ENEMY'S.

His picture is sin, my picture is blood. My blood. View the picture through my blood and you will see that sin has no place in this picture. You can't stand before me without an invitation, and the reason is simply the spiritual/physical size comparison. I'm infinite. You're finite. You're a copy of me that I invented.

So LET'S SIT DOWN AND TALK.

You have to have an invitation from God. It can't be earned by you. Nothing you do is ever going to overcome the pure physical and spiritual size comparison. So Mark relax, stop trying to be good enough. It still won't get you in. It can't. Without an invitation you just can't get in here. Sin or no sin.

But the invitation is in your hand. I gave it to you. It's from me. Come in. Sit down. Let's talk.

CONVERSATION
Seventeen

Why people think a 'relationship' is different with God

It isn't though. My people need a 'relationship relationship' with me.

DOUBTING THAT THIS IS ME SPEAKING DOESN'T HELP YOU.
Yes I am speaking. Speaking because I love you. I get a kick out of this, but for your sake, for you to get the maximum life-changing kick, and it will change your life Mark, to get the best out of this you need to embrace it.

You need to embrace and accept 100% that you can and do hear from me, from God. That I God am talking to you all the time, and that you are hearing me all the time. It doesn't help me or you to think otherwise.

Am I right that you're saying that, and yet somehow understanding that this will take me some time to embrace? That it won't be overnight that I am able to accept, without doubt, that this is your talking? And that you're Ok with that?

Obviously Mark. My instructions are never harsh or 'right this minute or you're in for it'. That's not the sort of father I am.

Nevertheless I want you to try to stop asking 'is this really happening to me?'

When I say 'stop' or 'from now on' I understand that it will be some time before you actually achieve this.

I need you to embrace the fact that I am talking to you. If it takes time I don't condemn. Ask me for help and it will take just the right amount of time for you to achieve what I'm saying.

Help!! I need help with that God.

Good. It's happening. I want you to accept that you really do hear me. That you're not making it up. Walk in it, and instead of thinking yourself unworthy, start thinking thoughts like 'God must think I'm worthy of this, God must actually want this 'God to Man' relationship with me. God must be in love with me.'

YOU ARE ALWAYS THINKING YOU NEED TO 'GET RIGHT WITH ME'. STOP IT. I'VE ALREADY GOTTEN YOU RIGHT WITH ME.

You need to start acting with the confidence of a man with whom God is in love. Stop thinking 'if only I could get right with God.' You don't need to get right with me, I have gotten you right with me already. I have the constant 'spiritual cleaning' system working with you all the time

'The LORD makes firm the steps of the one who delights in him; though he may stumble, he will not fall, for the LORD upholds him with his hand.'
                                                                 PSALM 37:23-24 NIV

YOU DON'T NEED TO STRIVE. HAVE CONFIDENCE IN YOURSELF, TRUST YOURSELF THAT YOU'RE IN A FULL BLOWN ROMANCE WITH GOD.

A best friends, always together, relationship with God. If you have confidence in that then you will naturally act that way. All you need to do is accept my love and all it takes to accept my love is accepting that you're worthy. And you are worthy Mark, you're so worthy. Because I say you are.

Shout it aloud, tell yourself all the time, *'God says I'm worthy! and he's talking to me'*. Although not worthy in as much as our physical/ spiritual size comparison is concerned, infinite versus finite, you are worthy because I spotted you, loved you and extended an invitation to you. I opened the door to you. I say you are worthy Mark.

Father are you telling me to tell your people about this, about living in the full knowledge that God thinks they're cool and is having a full on relationship with them but that they are acting as the 'unhappy, I'm not talking to you, I don't believe you really love me' person in the relationship?

YES! SO MANY OF MY PEOPLE ARE STARVED OF ME.
I WANT ANYONE WHO'S PREPARED TO, TO TELL THEM.

They are dying spiritually because they have no relationship with me. They don't know me. This is mainstream, the 'man or woman of God' in today's charismatic Christian mainstream Mark.

THEY LIVE A LIFE CENTRED AROUND THE FACT THAT I EXIST, YET MANY DON'T ACTUALLY KNOW ME.

They have accepted and embraced the fact that I exist, and even that I help them, bless them, answer their prayers from time to time. They are doing all they know to be right, and doing their best to talk to me. But they go about their days without any expectation of a conversation with me.

THEY DON'T ACTUALLY HAVE A 'RELATIONSHIP RELATIONSHIP' WITH ME.

They understand what it means to have a relationship with a person, but they have come to believe that having a relationship with God is different.

They understand that with another human, a relationship means that you know that person and they know you and you're always talking and getting together, that you're always in conversation with them. Always talking to and listening to each other, always involved in each other's lives. THAT. IS. NOT. HAPPENING. FOR. ME. AND. SO MANY OF. MY. PEOPLE.

So many of my people do not have a 'relationship relationship' with me.

I DON'T WANT YOUR CONDUCT! I WANT YOUR HEARTS!!

Mark I don't want a religion, a way of life centred around the belief that I exist. I don't want all the different customs and habits that people have come to think I require. Meetings, quiet times, bible readings and so on. Those things all have their place. And they're Ok. But they're supposed to come as a result of a relationship with me. But they do not make a relationship with me.

I'm going to repeat that Mark, just so you get it. All those things are alright if they're the result of the relationship, but they are not the relationship itself.

The relationship comes first. Always the relationship first.

I CAN'T HAVE YOUR HEART IF YOU CAN'T HEAR MINE.

The enemy understands this, but so many of my people don't. I cannot have your heart if you cannot hear mine.

A RELATIONSHIP COMES WHEN TWO PEOPLE CAN HEAR EACH OTHER'S HEARTS.

The extent, the depth of the relationship depends to the extent and depth that they can hear each other's hearts. Religion takes the things that would naturally spring unbidden and spontaneously from a relationship with a God who is love, and makes those things into rules.

They call it unreligious, they call it alive and spontaneous, but they have made a system, a way of doing things, a code that my people have to follow.

They have added in all the things that spring from the constant sense of unworthiness that comes from the one who tells them they are unworthy. It is not me who tells my people they are unworthy, quite the opposite.

SO INSTEAD OF HAVING A RELATIONSHIP WITH ME, MANY OF MY PEOPLE HAVE A CODE OF BEHAVIOUR.

They have a way of being a Christian that they think they must follow.

And what else can be expected! If they don't hear me speak, all the time, every day, then they become distant from me in our relationship because they feel I have become distant too.

It's how I have designed you, without constant and regular and meaningful communication between two people a relationship goes backwards. Why on earth do my people think that a different approach will work with God? Why do they think that somehow a relationship means something different when you have one with God? It doesn't.

YOUR BEST HUMAN RELATIONSHIPS ARE COPIES OF THE RELATIONSHIP YOU WERE DESIGNED TO HAVE WITH ME.

Tell people they can have an even deeper relationship with me than they have with their friends.

Tell them they can have that relationship, a constant communication back and forward with me. They can have it right now, without having to pass a code of conduct, or suddenly be better behaved. And for goodness sake tell them that to have it they need to hear me. And to hear me they need to stop thinking they don't. They must stop listening to Doubt when he says 'yes but did God really say that?'

TELL THEM THAT HEARING ME IS NOT DEPENDENT ON BEHAVIOUR.

Hearing me has nothing to do with behaviour. The whole bible story, the whole crucifixion story is God pursuing and running after and talking to man, even though man is sinful. It's a story of God ignoring the sin and talking to man. It's not about the sin, it's about God's desire to talk to man.

Tell them not to believe that sin separates them from me, that's a lie from the pit, it's a lie because it's a half truth, quoted without the full understanding of the heart and character of God.

SIN SEPARATES YOU FROM ME BUT HEAR THE REST OF WHAT I SAY.

I am the father who runs to the son while he is still a long way off. God runs after you, so he'll speak to you while you are in sin and lead you out of it. 'While we were yet in sin Christ died for us'.

For pity's sake Mark if I'll die for you when you're in sin, I'm certainly going to talk to you when you are in it.

My people believe they are unworthy of a real, two people, conversational style relationship with me. Unworthy. And the reason they have come to believe that is because they don't hear my voice. If they did they would hear me tell them they are worthy over and over again.

They do not hear me speak very often, and the reason that doesn't happen is because they have not been taught to expect it.

IN THE ABSENCE OF MY VOICE, THE VOICE OF THE ENEMY BECOMES THE VOICE MY PEOPLE HEAR.

Mark you need to understand the dynamics of what is happening in the universe, there are two principles at work, constantly. The first is that the voice of God is always speaking *'The heavens pour forth speech',* the second principle is that the voice of the enemy is always speaking too *'Your enemy the devil goes about like a roaring lion'.*

Two voices, always two voices.

If you shut out one, the other will become the voice you hear. My people have been taught to shut out my voice. How? Simple. They have been taught and have come to believe that if they behave in the right way, follow the code the right way then somehow they'll, one day be 'close to God.' It doesn't occur to them they need to actually hear me speak. They think they have to earn their way to me. Whose lie is that?

You Don't Have To Be Perfect To Hear Him
Want to try your own conversation with God? Go to the page immediately following the contents page. Or go to page 243

Why I am invisible

I want people who want to be my friends when they feel they don't have to. And the only way for me to achieve that is to stay invisible.

Lord did you say to me earlier that the evidence that you have done something for me, or are doing something in my life must exist primarily in my heart? That rather than being evidence I can see; first and foremost, the evidence needs to rest in my heart?

Absolutely. That's where you learn to trust me. Faith comes as a result of believing that I exist and that I care enough to respond to those who seek me.

THE EVIDENCE MUST REST FIRST IN YOUR HEART.

As you have found, to your amazement, faith comes from being able to believe, seek and expect a response, even though you can't see me.

INVISIBLE TO THE NAKED EYE, BUT VISIBLE TO THE HEART.

It's simple really. The model isn't hard to understand at all. I'm invisible for the most part to the naked human eye. But clearly visible to the heart.

SO YOU DON'T HAVE TO BE MY FRIEND UNLESS YOU WANT TO.

If I was visible that would change everything. You'd be flat on your face in awe and feeling forced to do my bidding. I don't want that. Being invisible means that if a man doesn't feel inclined to seek or find, or have a friendship, a 'relationship relationship' with me then he won't feel forced to do so.

People say that the Holy Spirit is a Gentleman, and they're right. But they take that to the extreme and make me out be a coward, they say that the moment you sin I have to go.

POPPYCOCK! YOU WON'T FIND THAT IN THE BIBLE.

I never leave or forsake you. But neither do I force myself on you. The reason is simple. I am God. The all present, all powerful one. When you are in the full presence of such a God there is very little that is polite or gentle, my very presence is overwhelming to the finite because they are seeing something infinite, something bigger than the sun, and all the planets combined. That's me Mark. Bigger, much bigger than all the planets.

I WANT PEOPLE WHO WILL STRIKE UP A FRIENDSHIP WITH ME WHEN THEY DON'T FEEL THEY HAVE TO.

To achieve that I have to do what a mechanic would describe as 'govern my power'.

I cannot let my entire power be evident otherwise two things would happen. The first is you would not be able to survive. But if you could, you would then feel obliged to strike up a friendship and obey me for your own safety's sake. And that's not what I want. It's no good for you or for me. I want people who will strike up a friendship with me when they don't have to.

To make that happen I have to hide the greatest part of myself so that you do not feel overwhelmed.

I DO NOT RUN AWAY WHEN YOU SIN.

Why would I? I came and died for you while you were yet in sin. How hard is it to understand the basic childlike truths of the bible?

FIRST AND FOREMOST THE EVIDENCE MUST REST IN YOUR HEART.

So back to the point of this conversation. The evidence of everything I have, am and will be doing for you must exist in your heart.

I CAN'T RELY ON PEOPLE WHO CAN'T RELY ON ME WITHOUT HARD EVIDENCE.

Why? Simple. Once you can see it in the flesh, everyone can see it in the flesh. It does not allow me to find out whether your belief in me is prepared to ignore the obvious and rely primarily on the evidence I have shown you in your heart.

But God, people who don't like this idea of a conversation with you say that they think it takes away the need for faith. Am I doing, by conversing with you, what you don't like? Am I demanding 'hard' evidence?

Not at all. You're not doing anything of the sort. You have absolutely *no* hard evidence. You have to choose to believe this is me in the face of Doubt's bold taunts. You are listening, in your mind, to the voice of a God you cannot see, touch, or hear audibly. That's not hard evidence. It is, as you've found, very difficult to believe that I'm talking. You hear me, can write it down or speak it out, but it requires a constant choice to believe. Doubt is always at your door, urging you to dismiss this conversation with me as 'some kind of bad religious nutcase joke'.

The evidence is in your heart and mind. And as you have discovered it's not hard to come by. But it's not concrete evidence, it's evidence in your heart and mind.

Just listen, just turn your heart to me and ask me to show you and talk to you about what I want you to know.

THE EVIDENCE WILL TURN UP IN YOUR HEART. PLOP!

Just like that. As I continue to remind you, I do not make myself hard to find. I do not play hide and seek.

How to have
a conversation with God

The way to come to terms with the fact that I'm
speaking to you all the time is by listening.
That's all it takes Mark.

IF YOU LISTEN YOU CAN CHANGE YOUR WORLD.

The more you listen, if I really am speaking to you, then quite
obviously the more you will hear. And the more you hear the more
you will become comfortable with the fact that I really am speaking
to you all the time.

And Mark I am. That's what this is all about, first and foremost,
what this is about is teaching you first to listen to me, and then hear
me.

When you can listen and easily and comfortably hear what I am
saying, the next phase will be changing the world because people
who hear me speak can definitely do that. Actually, they can't help
but do that.

YOU CHANGE A WORLD ONE PERSON AT A TIME.

And the interesting thing is this Mark. I am not, for the most
part, not normally a 'takeover God'. I do not try to take over or
dramatically change a family, a city, a nation all at once. I do things
carefully, and slowly and as a result I do them well. If you want to
change a world you do it one person at a time. And you can do that,
one person at a time, even if you're dealing with a thousand people.

You might be moving a thousand people to completely change

the way they think, but you are doing it individually with them, speaking specifically and directly and influencing them just on their own. Not as a crowd, but changing them as a thousand individuals.

DON'T HURRY. JUST DO THE NEXT THING I TELL YOU.

And let me tell you Mark it is impossible to do that, with any lasting result without hearing from me. You don't have to be in a hurry to change a world for me, you just do the next thing I tell you. Have the next conversation with another person, and in that conversation say the things I tell you to.

'Divinely directed decisions are on the lips of the king' PROV 16:10 AMP

EACH SENTENCE IN EACH CONVERSATION IS IMPORTANT TO ME.

You are never going to be able to work at that small, precise level of doing what I want unless you become incredibly expert at hearing my voice. Incredibly expert. Are you up for this Mark?

I think so Lord. I want to be. Can you make me ready?

The point is this Mark. When a man can hear me, hear exactly what I am saying, and you are well on your way to that place, then you can help me change the world, and the way you do it is carry on with your life, but this time, every step of your life is as you hear it from me.

'I sought the Lord and he answered me'.   PSALM 34:4 NIV

If you do that, if you listen, and expect to hear me answer every step of your life, you will change, first your world, and then mine. One step, one hearing from me step at a time.

YOU WERE PUT HERE FOR CONVERSATION WITH GOD. THAT SIMPLE.

What I want you to teach people Mark is very simple. Everyone you meet has questions about their lives. They are desperate. Every single day they are faced with hundreds of questions. Questions they know they can't answer on their own.

Deep down they know they were designed to discuss those questions with me. Simple questions like 'shall I make this phone call?' Or 'what should I want the outcome to be when I talk to this person?' Or 'what's the best I can do for my daughter in this situation?' And so on, life's questions. In their hearts they know they were designed for discussion with me about each of those questions, discussion with me about every single little question. There is no question too small for discussion with God because that's why you were put on earth Mark, for discussion, conversation with God.

EVERYONE IS CRYING OUT FOR CONVERSATION WITH GOD, BUT FEW ARE ACTUALLY HAVING ONE.

People everywhere are desperate. Every human's spirit cries out for conversation with me, not religious, not praying as you know it, but conversation, face to face. So few ever have it!

So very few enjoy an on-going, regular conversation about every little thing with their God. And I'm talking about the people who believe in me, that's why people, all people are desperate. They were designed for conversation with me, but they are not having it!

SEE HOW JESUS DID IT WITH ZACCHAEUS.

My idea wasn't for you Christians to run around telling the unchurched that they're lost in sin and to come along to your church and get forgiven. That's not what this is about. I'm not that shallow. There's so much more to this.

You'll find that if people just start listening to me their sin will slowly but surely fall off. It's what happened to Zacchaeus Mark and it's what will happen to anyone who meets one on one with me for conversation and actually expects to hear me speak.

When I come to your place for lunch your life will start cleaning up. It happens every time.

ALL I REALLY WANT IS CONVERSATION. EVERYTHING ELSE FOLLOWS NATURALLY.

But instead my people want to focus entirely on this 'come to God, get saved from your sin' religion; and their 'now you're forgiven, so life will be great' religion.

That's just the door, only one of the doors to what I really want, which is conversation. My people always want to hang around the door.

What this world, this crucifixion, this giving your life to me is really about; is conversation with me and that's what I want you to help bring about Mark. Getting people to see that, and to want to enter into their own conversation with me. The bible says that *'I have come that men might have life,'* not just get saved from sin. Getting your record of past sins wiped is just the start. Not the theme of each new day with me. It's your enemy who keeps harping on about your sin. Not me.

PEOPLE GO ASTRAY WHEN THEY DON'T GET THEIR ANSWERS FROM ME.

Everybody has big questions like 'why am I here?' and not so big ones, but nevertheless important questions like 'Is this the job for me?' And they go astray because they do not hear the answers to their questions from me. Instead they ask their friends, they read books, they see a principle in the bible but rather than ask me whether that principle applies in this situation, they just go ahead and assume it does. 'It's in the bible' they say, therefore God must be saying it.

Wrong. Lots of the answers they get from friends, books, the bible, TV, you name it, those answers lead them astray. Sure they are in the bible and or a Christian book, but they are often not what God is saying right now.

> *'...forever following new teachings, but they are never able to understand the truth.'*   2 TIM 3:7 NLT

I WANT PEOPLE TO EXPECT TO HEAR DIRECT FROM ME.

Now don't get me wrong Mark. You will often hear me speaking to you through something someone says, a chance conversation. Or you might read a book and I clearly speak to you. That's different Mark. That's not going to the book for the answer, or going to the person for an answer. That's allowing me to speak to you through whatever means I want.

The thing I'm wanting to get across is that I want you to constantly encourage, teach, cajole and enthuse people to listen to me and to expect answers direct to their hearts and minds from me. Direct from me. No intermediary.

And then, when the source of their answers is me, when they are confident they can come to me and actually receive an answer, when they are comfortable with that, then they will find that I speak to them, direct to them, in many ways.

First and foremost to their hearts and minds, direct without any need for conversation with others, or reading, or even church; first comes just a direct person to person conversation with God.

I will also speak to them more and more through all those other sources. So that having learned to listen to me on their own, they will hear much more when at church, when reading the bible and books, talking to others etc. But first they need to connect, on their own, to the source. Me.

EXPECT TO HEAR DIRECTLY FROM GOD ALL THE TIME AND YOU WILL.

You will Mark. You are now. And the best way to sum all that up is practise. Practise hearing me. Every time you have a question, do not answer it yourself, and do not put it to anyone else.

ASK ME INSTEAD.

Every single question, ask me. It's what you have had to do in these last few years because no one else can answer those questions Mark. So you have had to ask me. And have I answered?

Yes.

CONVERSATION
Twenty

Imagine if you found God
on your own

Imagine if instead of meeting with others to find
God, you took him with you to meet them.

Lord did you bring that bible verse to my mind again last night?

> 'Whether you turn to the right or to the left, your ears will hear a
> voice behind you, saying, 'This is the way; walk in it.'   ISAIAH 30:21 NIV

Mark yes.

**And is it relevant for more reasons simply than you want to be
guiding and talking to us all the time?**

Yes.

I felt it was *big*. Was I right?

Yes.

Is it to do with church?

Yes.

With the move of God that's starting and coming?

Yes.

**Did you say to me that you want your people relating directly to you?
Not relying on others to hear you on their behalf, but *hearing you
themselves*?**

Yes. That's what's coming.

Sometimes a church can stand, accidentally, between me and my people. Every reformation has been about that, about changing a church that stands between me and my people.

There's a reformation coming. The word means to 're-form', change.

But are you saying that this time the reformation will not be to replace a sick church with a healthier one? That church isn't even the issue this time? That this time the reformation will be to work direct with your people?

Yes that's right. This time the reformation will be to 're-form' the people. To invite them in to a closer, no-conditions, hearing from me relationship.

I am going to change the way my people think by changing what they hear. They are going to hear my voice. Those who want to will learn to listen to more of my voice than any other. It will completely transform the way they think.

'You'll be changed from the inside out. Readily recognize what he wants from you, and quickly respond to it.'   ROMANS 12:2 MSG

I WANT THEM TO EXPECT TO HEAR FROM ME DIRECT. LIKE THEY HEAR FROM ANYONE ELSE THAT THEY HAVE A RELATIONSHIP WITH.

Things are coming on earth that will demand that people can hear me speaking direct into their hearts. If they can't they will not be able to cope with what's coming.

'If those days had not been cut short, no one would survive, but for the sake of the elect those days will be shortened'   MATTHEW 24:22 NIV

How will this affect church? Is it a threat?

Not at all. It will vastly improve and strengthen church.

How?

People will bring me to church, rather than come to church to find me.

The out-of-church experience of me will be at least as powerful, but hopefully *more* powerful than what they get at church.

Will church still be relevant?

Mark yes.

'For where two or three gather together as my followers, I am there among them.' MATT 18:20 NLT

'Let's see how inventive we can be in encouraging love and helping out, not avoiding worshiping together as some do but spurring each other on, HEB 10:25 MSG

You are yourself, but you are also part of everybody. My word is my word. But the focus will be different.

CHURCH WILL BE AN OPPORTUNITY TO SHARE WITH OTHERS THE GOD YOU KNOW BEST ON YOUR OWN.

You will share him powerfully with others and they with you. The experience will be best on your own, but you will want to bring him and share him with others. A newlywed couple enjoy a powerful relationship alone but want to share it with others. And it lights up the whole room.

CONVERSATION
Twentyone

Why three's company
and two's a crowd

Yes you read it right.

God I think you were talking to me as I drove out of the gas station today, well obviously you were because you are always talking. But I think you told me today that when you said *'It is not good for the man to be alone'* **you meant that he needed someone to share the incredible experience he was having? He needed to be able to share with someone what it was like to be administering the creation of the world.**

Absolutely Mark. He was already sharing it with us, but it's a three way thing, modelled on the three of us. *'Let us create man in our image',* let us make him like us to function and love and give like we do. And Mark we are a three way relationship.

A cord of three strands is not quickly broken. ECCL 4:12 NIV

TWO IS NOT ENOUGH. THREE IS THE PERFECT NUMBER.

I want to tell you an opposite, a mystery. People say that 'Two's company, three's a crowd'. They're wrong. That's a significant and slippery lie from the source of all lies. I want you to think again, I want you to say, *'Three's company, two's a crowd'.*

The man had us to share his experience with and what an experience! Can you imagine waking each morning to find God waiting for you? Waiting for you to get up and help us administer the very start of the world? Actually you are living and about to live a similar life, everyone is, or is meant to be, but more of that in another conversation.

THREE MAKES ONE.

The point of this discussion is this. The man had us to share all that with, but we are only one. The three of us make the royal ONE. And the man needed his own three to make his own smaller 'royal ONE'. Him, us and another.

The reason is not complex Mark, actually it is simple and obvious, but nonetheless a well hidden truth, hidden well by us.

IT IS SLIGHTLY HIDDEN BECAUSE IF EVERYONE KNEW THIS WITHOUT SEEKING IT, THERE WOULD BE TOO MUCH POWER ABROAD.

The Trinity is one but made up of three. And man is created in our image, created to look like each of us and all of us, so to make that work the man needed to be part of three. Him (one), us (one) and a third (one). Three (ones) to make (ONE).

THE NUMBER IS THREE.

Now Mark this is a simple truth, and on it is based everything, all relationships. The number is three. The three of us are the model. You (one), us (ONE) and a third (one). Three (ones) to make (ONE).

That's the model. That is the reason for man needing others. People sense it, this need for others. Some say the need for others is really a need for me. But that's not right. The need for me is higher and deeper than the need they sense for others.

THE NEED MAN FEELS FOR OTHERS IS JUST WHAT IT SEEMS, *A NEED FOR OTHERS.*

Let's talk shall we about why we put this need for others in you? It is not first and foremost so that a man and woman will find each other and procreate, although that's certainly a result that's very high on the list.

The key reason we put this need for others, for third (ones) in man is we designed him to have such an overpowering experience of us, that he would need to share it with others.

THIS IS NOT NEW. CAN YOU IMAGINE WHAT IT'S LIKE TO BE ONE OF THREE GODS?

If there were just two of us, we would have a significant other, and as such would become one. Then the (one) of us would need another, a third (one) to share with. 'We've been creating stars today, they're 45 billion light years apart, how cool is that, what have you been up to?'

Two of us is not enough, we need to be three.

YOU AND US IS NOT ENOUGH. YOU NEED TO BE ONE OF THREE. YOU, US AND ANOTHER. LOTS OF (ANOTHERS)

You are created to look like us. You need to be one of three. You and us is not enough. You (one) and us (one) need a third (one or ones). Adam's experience helping with creation was just the start.

We have designed you to be involved in such close and overpowering contact with the three of us, such constant hearing and unfolding of truth that you will need to share the experience. What we have designed you for is too big to hold in. You have been designed for more than you are experiencing now. We want you to begin to search for it now.

YOU NEED TO SHARE YOUR EXPERIENCE OF US WITH OTHERS. IT'S TOO MUCH OTHERWISE.

When you begin to listen to us, and hear us speak to you direct, the experience will be too overwhelming to keep to yourself. You can't do it. You need a third (one). Or lots of third (ones).

This is not necessarily a life partner. A life partner is the ultimate expression of this three, you (one), us (one) and her/him (one),but the model requires many other third (ones).

Your kids are third (ones). So are your friends. Think about that Mark. See them differently. They are like part of the Trinity, your copy of the Trinity. What's the point Mark? The point is the need for, and the reason for the need for, a third (one). The reason is the level of the experience of us that you are designed for. It's meant to be much more intense than what you experience now. More direct. An actual life long conversation with God.

AN EXPERIENCE SO INTENSE YOU WILL HAVE TO SHARE IT.

You are designed for an experience like Adam had. Helping to set up the world. Want to help set up a world or two Mark? We're up for it if you are. And if you're up for it get ready for an experience so intense that you will have to share it. Otherwise it will be unhealthy for you.

We will lead you to the third (ones), because you cannot, must not share your pearls with pigs.

Your pearls need to be shared with (ones). Look for them Mark, the pearls and the (ones) to share them with. We will lead you to them.

He'll Talk To You
No Matter What You're Like

Want to try your own conversation with God? Go to the page immediately following the contents page. Or go to page 243

As the wheel turns
I own the day he doesn't

Father did I hear you explain this morning that everything that happens every day, every single thing, is an opportunity to hear you speak?

Absolutely. Nothing happens by chance. Every single event, every single day. I will it, or allow it.

God this is kind of weird, but I saw this picture of a wheel that got wider in diameter as it turned. When it first started turning the spokes were curled over in the direction the wheel was turning. But as the wheel turned the force of each turn pushed those spokes out from the wheel until they sat at 90% to the hub?

That's a picture from me Mark. The wheel is your day. Those 'spokes' represent things that happen in your day through which you can come to me. I am the hub of the wheel.

Each new thing that happens in the wheel of your day is another spoke in the wheel through which you can enter and walk right up to the hub which is me.

It might be a phone call. A warm discussion or an angry one. A moment of joy. A moment of disappointment.

THE IDEA IS FOR YOU TO HEAR ME SPEAK ABOUT EVERY NEW EVENT OF EVERY NEW DAY.

There are events throughout the day, big events, small events, each with openings through which you can hear what I'm saying. Instead of seeing each new event as an interruption, or an attack, I want you to see everything that happens in your day as a new opportunity to hear me speak. 'What are you saying here God' is what you should be asking.

Because of the LORD's great love we are not consumed, for his compassions never fail. They are new every morning; great is your faithfulness.   LAMENTATIONS 3:22-23 NIV

I HAVE SET UP AND ENGINEERED YOUR DAY.

The world is mine. You are in it. I have given it to you so that you can seek and easily find me. Time and space is mine, my gift to you, the platform on, and in which you can seek and find me.

I OWN THE DAY. HE DOESN'T.

Your day is not some chance anti-God affair sent by the enemy to undo you. He does not own the day, I do. Your day is the day I have given you.

'This is the day the LORD has made. We will rejoice and be glad in it.'   PSALM 118:24 NLT

So here is your day, it is unfolding, like a wheel that starts with its spokes folded in on themselves, but as the wheel begins to turn the spokes open up and stand out from the hub. The force of each turn of the wheel begins to push them out. As your day begins to happen the events of the day open up to you as opportunities to hear me.

I AM IN EVERY MOMENT OF EVERY DAY THAT YOU LIVE. IT MAY NOT SEEM LIKE IT. BUT I AM.

Nothing happens in your day that I have not designed, initiated, or allowed.

Each thing that happens, each thing said to you, things that seem evil or tiresome, and things that seem godly and pure pleasure. Each of them designed, or allowed by me.

And as each new thing is said, or happens, I am there. Wanting to talk to you about it.

I AM SAYING SOMETHING NEW TO YOU, IN AND ABOUT EVERY NEW THING THAT HAPPENS. *LISTEN FOR MY VOICE.*

Each new thing is a spoke through which you can walk to the hub of the wheel. I am the hub of the wheel.

Listen for me in each
new event of the day

Don't take things into your own hands.
Don't assume you know what I want.
Ask me.

Let's say you meet with a person who does not know me. That meeting, planned or by chance, is a spoke in the wheel of your day, through which you can walk to me, the hub of the wheel, and say 'Hi God, what are you saying here?'

Every single person I talk to or meet?

Every single one. An opportunity for you to hear me. *Not an opportunity for them to hear you.*

It's not your job to convert them to your beliefs, it's an opportunity for you to hear the one you believe in.

Not an opportunity for you to take things into your own hands and decide what you are going to do or say on my behalf.

Don't do or say anything on my behalf without asking me what *I* want first.

I MIGHT WANT SOMETHING SAID TO THEM, I MIGHT NOT.

You won't know unless you ask. And there's no point asking if you don't know how to listen.

Does this make sense to you Mark? Each event, each person in each day is, first and foremost, an opportunity for you to hear me and learn what I am saying. For me to speak, wherever possible, before you do.

HE STOLE THE DAY FROM YOU. YOU NEED TO REDEEM IT!

'Redeeming the time, because the days are evil.'   EPHESIANS 5:16 KJV

My people seem to have this idea they are running the world for me, that I cannot do it on my own, that evil has stolen it from me and that I need them to get the day back for me. I don't. I want you to redeem it back for yourself. He's stolen it from you, not me.

If, as you listen to me, others copy you and listen to me too that's great, in fact that is what will inevitably happen.

Because as you find me and listen to me in more and more of what is happening in your day, others also involved in that thing will hear me too.

YOU WILL DRAW ME OUT INTO THE OPEN BY HEARING ME.

If you only speak to others the words I have given you to speak, then they will be hearing what I want to say to them now. Not the message you think a believer should tell them, but rather the message I tell you to tell them.

IF I DON'T GIVE YOU ANYTHING TO SAY ABOUT ME, DON'T.

'I can do nothing except that which I see and hear him doing'
Only say what I tell you to say.

The secret of leadership is serving those you lead

God did I just hear you say that the secret of leadership is serving, or was it just me thinking it again?

Mark it was me. Those words are mine. They were yours, but are now mine. You said them to describe what you have heard me say, but now I am copying what you said and saying it back to you.

So first I said it, then you said it which gave it more power, and then I copied you which made it even more powerful.

Does that surprise you Mark? That I, the inventor of words, the Supreme Being, the one in charge, the support of the universe, that I listen to what you say, and then repeat it, that I let you create words and then make them mine?

Umm yes. I guess it does. This is all so new to me.

Exactly. But it shouldn't be. For so many people, you were one of them, this is all brand new. You were naming my name, but stumbling about in the dark doing damage because, having chosen a life of doing what I ask, you didn't have any real idea what I was asking.

But God we've all got the bible. That tells us what you are asking.

It does. But you can't understand the bible unless you are listening to me.

'The Spirit told Philip, 'Go to that chariot and stay near it.' Then Philip ran up to the chariot and heard the man reading Isaiah the prophet. 'Do you understand what you are reading?' Philip

asked. 'How can I,' he said, 'unless someone explains it to me?' So he invited Philip to come up and sit with him.'   ACTS 8:29-31 NIV

To understand the bible you need me to explain it to you. Else you will do the sort of damage with the bible that the Pharisees did. They used the bible and even prophecy to crucify me.

'Caiaphas, who was high priest that year, spoke up, 'You know nothing at all! You do not realize that it is better for you that one man die for the people than that the whole nation perish.' He did not say this on his own, but as high priest that year he prophesied.'   JOHN 11:50 NIV

I WANT TO TALK TO YOU ABOUT LEADING BY SERVING.

It should come as no surprise, I laid out the principle in the creation.

I allowed man to name the animals. But the enemy has perverted the concept of leadership. He wants to dominate and rule. Looking at my leadership, understanding that I was in charge, and wanting that position for himself he became jealous. He misunderstood the true nature of leadership; as a result he fell in love with what he thought leadership was all about. He wanted to be God.

HIM? GOD? NO CHANCE.

He saw that I led, that I ruled, and because he wanted to *be* God, he misunderstood the nature of being God. He misconstrued it as dominating, and so began to dominate, first angels and then eventually he even tried to dominate me.

As it happens, I allow you and even him to dominate my will, but I could not allow him to be God, the universe requires the one who loves it and understands it to rule it.

SERVING IS THE TRUE NATURE OF LEADERSHIP AND AUTHORITY.

It is not the new nature Mark, it is the true nature. It's not a new idea. It's what leadership has *always* meant. Since I began to create things and beings that would need leading, it has always been true. THE. NATURE. OF. AUTHORITY. IS. TO. SERVE.

This is not some beautiful mystic truth, uttered by a whimsical, distracted Jesus. It's plain practical truth. You can't lead if you want to dominate. Domination is not leadership, it's bullying.

SERVING WAS EVERYTHING WHEN THERE WERE ONLY THREE OF US.

True authority, each of us in the Trinity had it, was ours because we served each other. Completely. We loved and served each other. Then we invented you. You were less perfect and would require some leadership. It was natural that serving, not domination would be the way we would lead you, and in turn, the way we wanted you to lead others.

Serving is implied in the words; 'leader, authority, ruler, emperor, king, father, husband, mother,' and every other word like them.

Obedience is something you do when you have complete freedom to do the opposite.

So Mark look for this in our relationship, yours and mine. Do not expect me to dominate and force you into obedience. Obedience is not a cowering, fearful word. Quite the opposite. I repeat; obedience is something you do when you have complete freedom to do the opposite.

IT'S YOUR RIGHT TO RULE OVER MY WILL.

You are a ruler over my will in your life. It can only enter with your permission. You can rule me in your life the way my enemy likes to rule. His confusion about what ruling means left him defeated, and yet still he does not learn, will not repent. You can make his mistakes, or you can rule the way I rule, by serving.

I, God, also have a choice Mark. I invented choice, I am choice. I rule by serving because I choose to. I am free to choose the opposite and dominate you, but I don't.

YOU CAN RULE MY WILL BY SERVING IT.

You have a choice too. You are free to lord it over my will, or you can choose to rule my will by serving it.

Can you see that Mark? Even when you have decided to obey my will, you are still a ruler over it, because you are only obeying by choice, the final say is always yours.

It's the way I want it to be. Because I want to rule and reign with you. That doesn't mean we will be running around the universe dominating things Mark, it means we will be serving.

HEAVEN IS THE PLACE WHERE GOD SERVES GOD.

I want you to practise serving on earth so that you're good at it when you get here. That's what ruling is all about, what being seated on thrones is all about. When you get here you'll be right in the core of the place where God serves God. I want you to practise it now. Meekness is power under control.

I WANT A UNIVERSE FILLED WITH BEINGS POWERFUL BEYOND MEASURE BUT WHOSE POWER IS UNDER CONTROL.

Do you want to be one of them? Then start practising. I do not want power on display, I want your power under control. Do you want to be powerful beyond measure Mark? You are becoming so by listening to me. And will continue to become even more powerful if you choose to rule over my will by obeying it.

I KEEP MY POWER UNDER CONTROL. YOU MUST DO SO TOO.

You know something of, and have read of my power. Is my power on full display Mark? Obviously not. And so it should be with those who rule and lead, their full power should never be on display.

IT IS THE NATURE OF A TYRANT, OF SATAN AND ALL WHO FOLLOW HIM, TO FLAUNT THEIR POWER.

They try to keep it under wraps because they know that's how I lead, but they cannot help themselves, their shallow selfishness and desire for reassurance forces them to flaunt their power.

FATHERS, MOTHERS, HUSBANDS, WIVES, TEACHERS, PROPHETS.

Your power should be under control, not on full display, you should lead by serving. This is a truth that, until understood, will hold churches back from what I want.

Sit beside me as I go about running the universe

Get to know me. Be close to me.
Practise listening.

Mark I am with you. I am healing, I am changing, I am bringing you to new realisation, a new perspective. I am altering your thinking, I am changing you from within. You are a new person, a completely different person Mark, just as I promised, you are different.

Now comes a new perspective, a new way of thinking.

What's the new way of thinking God?

Instead of thinking about what concerns you, you are going to start thinking about what concerns me. It's nothing onerous, it's simply a mark of friendship with God.

A FRIEND WORRIES ABOUT WHAT WORRIES HIS FRIEND.

Mark you do not need to strive to attain this attitude, I am going to put it in your heart. I'll do it for anyone who wants it. Anyone who wants to listen to me.

I can see that you want to be my friend, and so as I have always done with those who want to be my friends, I am going to put a heart in you that is concerned for me.

You will become one of those who hold me up, who look to support and help and are constantly thinking about what might be worrying me or holding me back.

Well God I'm not much like that now.

The way to become like that is to listen to me. The more you listen, the more of my words fill your mind. Your mind is where I speak. And obviously that is going to change the way you think.

'...be transformed by the renewing of your mind.'   ROM 12:2 NIV

TOO MANY PEOPLE ARE TRYING TO HELP ME WITHOUT LISTENING TO ME.

Mark I don't want you, or anyone else, trying to help me without asking me first. I'm right here. If you stay in minute by minute contact with me, you can put things right in the universe simply by keeping me company. First and foremost Mark I just want your company. I've got millions of people doing what they *think* I want them to. But the last time they heard something specific from me was often weeks, or months or even longer ago. I want constant contact. If you're not listening to me you end up running around trying to do things for me but completely missing the point.

'She had a sister, Mary, who sat before the Master, hanging on every word he said. But Martha was pulled away by all she had to do in the kitchen. Later, she stepped in, interrupting them. 'Master, don't you care that my sister has abandoned the kitchen to me? Tell her to lend me a hand. The Master said, 'Martha, dear Martha, you're fussing far too much and getting yourself worked up over nothing. One thing only is essential, and Mary has chosen it—it's the main course, and won't be taken from her.'   LUKE 10:38-42 MSG

Don't decide yourself what I need. Just ask me. Like you'd ask a friend. And you'll get an answer. If you expect one, you'll get it.

If you write it down or speak it out or think it in faith. Start writing or speaking or thinking before it comes, that will make it easier.

Do not try and put things right for me in the world by arguing my case, unless you've actually heard me say to get involved.

FIGHTING A ZEALOUS AND RIGHTEOUS FIGHT WITHOUT HEARING MOMENT BY MOMENT FROM ME IS POINTLESS, AND DANGEROUS.

It invites attention from the enemy when you are not ready to fight off an attack.

SIT DOWN BESIDE ME.
Instead of going off to fight my battles without me, sit down beside me and keep quiet watch as I go about my business of running the universe. Get to know me, and be close to me more and more. Practise listening to me Mark, practise.

CONVERSATION
Twentysix

Why 'Good Works'
aren't very good after all

Father I just want to talk to you tonight, just want to hear from you really. But I'm remembering you said you're going to put a heart in me to want to know what you want, what you need. So Lord, what do you need?

> Mark I need men and woman, and children for that matter, anyone will do, I want people ready to listen.

Lord I expected you'd say something a bit more spiritual sounding than that. The sort of stuff that sounds religious and boring to me but nevertheless what I expect you to say.

Maybe something like you want people ready to *'go out into the harvest'*, or people who would *'seek you'*.

I personally find that sort of language boring. Whenever I hear it, it makes me think of seeking you in a wearisome, God never speaks back, sort of way.

> Mark you're not alone.

I know the *'seek God'* concept is a bible verse, but it always seems to be spoken by religious, boring sorts of people. Sorry God but that's just how it seems to me. And I guess I thought that maybe that's what you required, maybe because we're sinful or maybe because it's good for us to suffer? Something like that.

I didn't really expect to hear you say you want 'people who are ready to listen'. Any anyway that's the thing I'm always going on about, I'm always telling people to listen to you, so it's sort of embarrassing that the first thing you say when I ask you what's on your mind, is about listening.

Mark I'm not interested in agendas, in finding new things to tickle people's ears, I want you to keep going on about, keep harping on about listening because what else is there? Hearing my voice, and having a conversation with me is the reason I put you on earth.

I am called the good shepherd, my people are called my sheep, and the bible says *'My sheep listen to my voice.'*

I AM NOT THE 'MUTE' SHEPHERD, I AM THE EVER-SPEAKING SHEPHERD.

The bible says *'there is a friend who sticks closer than a brother.'* I am not the eternal 'mute friend'. I am the all-powerful, all-present, all-speaking friend. Everything I do, I do to infinite proportions, speaking included.

SO WHO IS THIS SILENT GOD SOME CHURCHES PRESENT TO THE WORLD?

If listening to the Creator is not good enough; if a first-hand, man to God, speaking face to face relationship with God is not good enough, then what is?

Mark there's nothing greater in the universe than me, there's nowhere greater to go. Talking with me, not at me, is what you were created for, if that's not good enough, then nothing will ever be.

Nothing can match a friendship with me. Friendship comes from listening and conversation. So keep on about it, keep harping on about it until you stop hearing me say that.

It is what you were created for, a conversation with me.

LISTENING MEANS HEARING. NOT PAINFUL LONGING FOR A SELDOM HEARD VOICE. I AM NOT PLAYING GAMES.

The bible says *'He does not play hide and seek'*. I speak so that you will hear.

'My sheep listen to my voice.'   JOHN 10:27 NIV

A RELATIONSHIP WITH GOD REQUIRES THAT YOU HEAR HIM.

The greatest men who ever lived, Moses, Daniel, Samuel, David, Solomon, Me, Peter, Paul, all of us survived on, looked to as our highest achievement our relationship with God. We lived for it!

And what defined our relationship with God was what God said.

We heard him talk all the time. *'I can do nothing but that which I see and hear from him'.* That's all that mattered.

A RELATIONSHIP IS NOT RUNNING AROUND DOING THINGS FOR THE OTHER PERSON. THAT'S JUST A RESULT.

Doing the things I ask is a result of our relationship. Just as I do many of the things you ask me. It fuels the fire of the relationship but it is not the relationship itself.

So tell people to stop trying to please me with good works. Tell them to stop trying to please me by saving the lost, by praying longer, fasting harder, going to church more. IT. WON'T. WORK.

> *'When you pray, don't babble on and on as people of other religions do.'*   MATT 6:7 NLT

I am God. I love you. So for your sake I would really like to be pleased by all your good works. Obviously you Christians want me to be. And if I was pleased with them, you'd be pleased with me.

I want to please you. The Creator of the universe wants to please you. But I can't be pleased with your good works. I am too intelligent. I can see that being consumed by Christian work and duties is not what is best for you.

Listening is what's best. Just listening to my voice. It's what you were designed for. I want the best for you.

> *'For I know the plans I have for you,' declares the LORD, 'plans to prosper you.'*   JER 29:11 NIV

Don't allow people to easily disregard or lightly brush aside what I'm saying here. Many will tell you 'we are not a people of good works, we are a people of the spirit!'

I want you to explain to them that this is not a time for Christians to deceive themselves.

IF YOU WERE ALLOWED, WHICH YOU'RE NOT, TO JUDGE THE CHURCH..

If you had to judge any modern church, and determine their key focus:- To determine whether they were focused on hearing from God in a conversation, or whether organised Christian activities was their main focus? Where would they score highest??

What would any honest person say is the key focus of the modern church? Would it be hearing from me? Hearing as much as you would expect to hear from anyone else you had decided to give your life to? Or would it be organised Christian activities; church services, house-groups, teaching, youth groups, prayer groups, meeting together for meals and so on?

God I sure wish you hadn't asked me that.

Why?

Because I'm seen as anti-church. The stuff you say to me in these conversations causes lots of concern. People think I'm backsliding.

Rubbish! You're more focused on church than you've been in the last 30 years. You actually want to belong, be accepted and not cause a fuss.

Yes but they don't see that. These conversations are ruining that idea.

Mark when people listen to me they hear what I say. You're not alone. The church is going to be faced in the next decade with millions of people listening to me say things that don't make the church very happy. You're not yet, but you will be soon, in very good company. Stick with it.

You and many others are beginning to hear things which seem to threaten organized Christian activities. But it's nothing to do with you. With or without you, and Christian leaders everywhere say this, 'if an activity in the church is not of God it will come to nothing.'

I'm sorry to have to say this Mark, but many Christian activities are just good works. Well intentioned, and seemingly essential for the on-going health of a church, but they are not activities that are, primarily, focused on listening to me.

They do not focus on getting away just to be with and learning to hear from me. The one who created you for that single purpose. A conversational relationship with me.

A relationship requires that you listen to the other person. If you want a relationship with me you need to listen to my voice.

I DON'T NEED YOUR GOOD WORKS AND ORGANIZED ACTIVITIES. NOT AT ALL.

I can do all those things for myself, '*I can create children to Abraham from the very stones'.* But I cannot be a human listening to God, not for long anyway, I have a universe to run. I cannot do what I created you to do.

I CREATED YOU FOR IT, I NEED YOU TO DO IT PLEASE.
Give up your focus on organised activities, they will never keep the church running. Eventually, the churches that last will be the ones whose people are taught to hear me for themselves. First and foremost you need to be hearing from me as individuals, during the week. You need to meet with me outside of church and then you bring me and what I have said to the meeting.

CHURCHES WHERE LISTENING TO ME IS NOT THE KEY FOCUS ARE GOING TO DIE. SIMPLE AS THAT.
It has always been and will always be those who listen to me who keep my church going.

But Lord who would keep the building running, the toilets cleaned, the floor vacuumed?

Mark ask yourself 'What if?' about all those little duties. Ask the obvious 'what if' questions. You will hear me speak and you will be astounded to know that I have something to say about even the very least of all those 'keeping church going' duties. Astounded to know that I have been waiting to say it for a long time. But no one has asked.

Astounded. You will be astounded.

Twentyseven

A 'nice Christian life'
What a boring idea!

God I worry that instead of wanting a nice Christian life, I'm consumed by listening to you. I find myself urged on by you to focus on listening. To make that my whole life.

It's making me a misfit.

And worse still I'm hearing you say and suggest things that cut right across that 'nice Christian life' idea.

Mark a 'nice Christian life', without much listening to me, profits nobody. It quickly becomes boring and it presents the wrong impression to the world, it distracts my people from what I have for them. What I have for them isn't 'nice'.

FOLLOWING ME ISN'T 'NICE', IT'S TOUGH.

What I have for people who want to follow me isn't 'nice'. It's the sort of frustrating, belief-demanding, mind-stretching life you would imagine comes from trying to live every day as a normal rational human being and yet listening to and following the instructions of an invisible person.

Add to that the dilemma that the invisible person is God, the Creator, the one in charge. So this cannot be a nice little imaginary relationship my people have. How could it be? They are saying to themselves, to each other and to the world, 'I'm having a relationship with the one who created all this'.

They're telling the whole world that they are 100% serious when they say; 'You can't see him, neither can I but I can hear him, and so from now on everything I do will be based on what he says'.

A relationship like that isn't nice, quite the opposite. Instead of 'nice' it will be unusual, it will imply the mysterious and the miraculous and the paranormal.

I think you will agree Mark that 'unusual, mysterious, miraculous and paranormal' is not really a description of the average Christian. You weren't like that. Everyone knew you were a Christian, but you weren't at all like that. And neither are many Christians you meet.

What a waste. What a complete waste!

I am not calling my people to 'lead a good life', I am not saying that Jesus came and showed us the way to 'lead a good life'. I don't want you to run about talking about some cult where God came and died on a cross and that's what this is all about, getting more and more people to believe that God died on a cross and the rest of the world is very sinful and wrong and bad.

What a waste! What a waste to think that God would come and die just so people could all believe that he came and died, a little unsure why he did. But nonetheless believing that God came and died, and that as a result, we should all lead a good life, wear good clothes and all get together on Sundays in a sort of nice clothes family day. While the rest of the world gets on with enjoying their day their way.

Nice is boring. It doesn't look like the street-level Jesus.

Nice is not what I have in mind for my people. Nice is boring. Nice is boring for the first generation Christian so they bury themselves in church work, and church attendance, and friendships with other Christians in order to mask their desperation.

God this sort of talk doesn't go down well. Church leaders feel threatened by it, church people feel unsettled by it. It makes people worry that I'm backsliding.

Get used to it. The more you listen to me, the more you'll want to hear. Which means that 'nice' Christian activities that are not focused on hearing me will seem somehow lacking and pointless.

'NICE' MAKES THE IDEA OF GETTING TO KNOW ME UNATTRACTIVE.

Nice is boring for church kids, for the second generation Christians, so they wait for the opportunity to rebel. And nice is particularly boring for those on the outside, those who do not believe, and as a result they are repelled by the idea of getting to know me.

Where did this whole 'nice' Christianity come from? From the pit.

How can I tell my people that? They won't listen. How can I tell them that their comfortable religion keeps them from me?

I HAVE CALLED THEM TO ME BUT THEY WON'T COME. SO I RUN TO THEM. I JOIN THEM AT CHURCH.

How can I tell them that when church stops being about listening to me and begins to be about Christian activities, then it stands between them and me? How can I tell them it stands between the lost and me? I have tried to tell them but they will not listen. So what do I do instead? I do what the Creator does, I run to them. If they won't bring their church to me, then I go to their church. They call me to them so I go. I have called them to me but they have not heard.

WHAT? AM I A GOD WHO NEEDS A CROWD TO BOOST HIS EGO?

Organised religion gets together to generate a relationship with me. Whereas I want to talk to you individually first, away from the group, so that you can then take me with you to meet with others.

Organised religion implies that I am a God who deals corporately, a God who first and foremost wants to communicate with a crowd. Who am I, the latest rock star?

What do you think you have here, a God who needs a crowd to boost his ego? I want a relationship with each member of the crowd. I want to speak to each of them on their own.

BILLIONS OF CONVERSATIONS ALL AT THE SAME TIME. BILLIONS!

Yes, interestingly enough, I am able to talk to ten million, billions of people one at a time, all at the same time. You do not need to gather them together in one place for my sake, I can talk to them wherever they are.

AM I SUGGESTING THAT YOU DO NOT GET TOGETHER? NO.

For goodness sake no! The bible makes it clear, *'Where two or more are gathered together'* or *'Do not forsake the assembling together'.*

And as I have said to you repeatedly I want to use my church and I want people to come together, come together bringing me with them, not come together to find me.

FIND ME ON YOUR OWN, SHARE ME WITH EACH OTHER.

It's a mystical, mysterious, but quite obvious principle of God. Find me individually, take me by the hand and bring me to meet your friends, all of whom have done the same. Having found me on your own, you can talk to me in a group because that brings me into your midst in a powerful dynamic, much more powerful than when you talk to me on your own. But only if you have met me, powerfully, oh so powerfully on your own.

DON'T MEET WITH OTHERS TO FILL YOUR CUP.
BRING YOUR CUP ALREADY FULL.

Do not meet with others empty handed. Don't come to find me. Come, having found me already, with a cup full of me, to share with others. Your cup flowing into their already full cup, theirs into yours.

God runs to you
not the other way around

Lord I think I just heard you talk to me about the concept of 'Your effort, my response'. As in you, God, puts in the effort, and then I respond. Was that you? Could that possibly have been you?

Yes Mark, Oh yes.

So often people put in the effort to generate my response.

They believe that if they put in the effort, I will respond. And I will Mark, a little like Samuel speaking to Saul after the medium drew him up out of the ground, *'Why have you woken me?'*

When my people put in the effort I *will* respond, but that's not the way I want it.

I WANT TO PUT THE EFFORT IN SO YOU RESPOND TO ME.

But I will come when you put in the effort to summons me, what else can I do? I am mercy and grace, and a graceful God comes when summoned.

Get that Mark? The Creator, against his better judgement, comes when summoned.

I don't get it. Why do you? If you didn't we'd realize something was wrong and ask what it was.

Actually, no you wouldn't. If I didn't come when you demand you'd just give up. And for that reason, to maintain some sort of relationship, and also for the simple reason that I am vulnerable to you, *I come to you.*

GOD'S EFFORT, YOUR RESPONSE.

But Mark what I want is for people to consider every single bible story and principle they know. I want them to remember what happened to them when they first gave up their old life, and met with me.

It is my effort and your response. I make the first move, then you respond. Will you please stop thinking that you have to make the first move. I am already coming to you. All you have to do is listen.

Write down or speak out, or think out, the things I am already saying to you.

You do not have to put together a big religious ceremony, or organize a big event, or have a big time singing for me to turn up. That's all fine, but it's not necessary to bring down my presence. I'm with you already. I just want you to listen to the God who is already right here in front of you.

'You did not choose me, but I chose you.'   JOHN 15:16 NIV

'I stand at the door and knock.'   REV 3:20 NIV

I DON'T WANT PEOPLE'S EFFORT. I WANT THEIR RESPONSE TO MINE.

First I make the effort, then you respond. My effort, your response. Not the other way around. I'm hoping you understand this Mark, I am giving you the understanding. I don't want my people's effort, I want their response to mine.

THEY WERE CREATED TO RESPOND TO ME, NOT THE OTHER WAY AROUND.

I created them. I died for them while they were yet in sin. I am at the door knocking. I make the effort, you respond. That offends some.

And the enemy, the accuser is vehemently opposed to it because that's where the power is. He wants you to feel you are so bad that you must first put in the effort and then a reluctant God will respond.

He wants your worship to be like what the pagans do. He wants you to think there is a huge chasm between us. He wants you to see me as lofty and holy and distant from you, too big for you.

HE WANTS YOUR WORSHIP TO BE A LOT OF EFFORT, BEAUTIFULLY ORCHESTRATED NOISE AND ORGANISED DIN.

Orchestrated and huge and impressive effort, which I am told I must respond to. It has been the way of the church for thousands of years. Lots of orchestrated effort on your terms, which I must then fit with. It's not really any different than what the pagans do Mark. They adulate their Gods. They hope that with huge effort they will appease and draw down their great and terrible Gods.

What I want is the other way around. My effort, your response.

Get used to it. The Creator runs to you. Before you do anything to deserve it.

> 'But God showed his great love for us by sending Christ to die for us while we were still sinners.'
>
> ROM 5:8 NLT

TRY CONVERSING WITH GOD -
YOU'LL NEVER BE THE SAME

Want to try your own conversation with God? Go to the page immediately following the contents page. Or go to page 243

WORD ['rhematos': a spoken word, made by the living voice]about Christ'   ROM 10:17 NIV

So Mark, faith comes from (spiritual) hearing, and this hearing comes through a rhema word from Christ.

The more you hear my voice the more faith you'll receive.

'Without faith it is impossible to please God. Those who come to God must believe that he exists and that he cares enough to respond to those who seek him.'   HEB 11:6 MSG

Believing that I care enough to talk back when you ask me questions is faith. The act of listening for, and writing down or speaking out, or thinking out my reply to your questions is faith. That's how the bible defines it.

There's no point asking questions, if you're not going to expect and listen for a response.

And Mark you tell me. How much faith have you found it requires to listen about every little thing?

Huge amounts. More faith than I seem to have. The enemy is constantly telling me it's not you. So for me it requires huge faith.

I AM THE GOD WHO SAYS NOT TO WORRY, JUST BELIEVE.

And that's what I'm saying to you Mark. Just believe.

Oh no God! Surely you don't mean to believe in that awful mindless way that some people feel you're supposed to? They tell me I should 'just believe brother'. But they never seem very clear on what to believe for.

No. I don't want that Mark. I want you to believe the specific things I have said to you. The things I have said directly to you. You're going to need to listen a lot otherwise you won't have much to believe for.

You know what I'm saying. You're writing down at least half of what you hear me saying. Things about all the little personal and people and business details of your life.

I am saying I want you to you to believe those things. The big life-promise things, and the little 'buy this sort of chilli' and 'make that phone call' things.

I AM GOING TO SHOW YOU HOW TO ACT, WHAT TO PURSUE, WHAT TO DROP IN EVERY SINGLE AREA OF YOUR LIFE.

That's every area, big, small. Every area!

That's the nature of a walk with me. Every day, every moment, every single thing that happens in your life, I'm there. Not only that but either I specifically brought that thing, that person that event into your life, or I allowed it. So, whatever happens, I will show you what to say and how to act.

BORING? I THINK NOT. IT'S EXACTLY HOW I LIVED MY OWN LIFE, A LIFE I THINK YOU WILL AGREE WAS ANYTHING BUT BORING.

Maybe a little too exciting for comfort? A life that, even those who don't believe, agree was an unusual life. They say that 'if it really happened', mine was a life that focused on the things that mattered.

> *'I'm telling you this straight. The son can't independently do a thing, only what he sees the Father doing. What the Father does, the Son does.'*   JOHN 5:19 MSG

I COULDN'T DO ANYTHING INDEPENDENTLY, NEITHER CAN YOU.

Mark think very carefully about what I just said. I, the Creator, the Word, I couldn't then *and can't now* independently do a thing. That's me, God. I've got the mind of all minds, and yet I can't act on my own. If that's what it was like for me, what makes you think that you can do any differently? Yes I gave you a brain, so you could use it to figure out that the most important thing in the universe, the very reason you were created, *is to listen to me.*

> *'but whoever listens to me will live in safety and be at ease, without fear of harm.'*   PROV 1:33 NIV

IF I CAN'T, YOU CAN'T.

Take my word for it. If it were otherwise I would tell you. You cannot do a thing independently.

Let's rephrase that, you cannot do anything worth doing independently of me without doing damage, sometimes grave damage.

TAKE YOUR KIDS FOR INSTANCE. I GAVE THEM TO YOU. AGREED?

Every time you act independently from me in your dealings with them it seems to end in sadness, damage and heartache. Some of that heartache can last a lifetime.

Don't act independently. Just don't. It doesn't work. Please listen.

If you want to live your life independently, under your own steam, only listening to me when it suits, you can. It's your choice. You can be a 'Christian self-starter' if that's what you want, go right ahead. But it will disappoint, and take you nowhere and damage the people and things you love. You've already seen that for decades. You end up hurting people and wasting time.

I WANT TO INCLUDE YOU IN EVERYTHING I'M DOING.

Mark in the same way I could not act independently, and neither can you, in that same way, because the father included me in everything he did, he wants to and will include you.

There's no entry price, just start listening and the Father and I will include you in everything we're doing. Everything! We're up for it if you are Mark. It's what we want. What we want badly. To include you in everything we're doing. You up for that Mark?

Oh man!! God I would so love that. Thank you.

Every little thing Mark. We'll tell you what to think, what to do, what not to do.

IF YOU WANT IT MARK, IF YOU WANT A LIFE LIKE MINE...

We'll tell you what to do in every single situation.

If you remind a man of his sin, you keep him sinful

I came to save men from their sin, not tell them off for it. I came to forgive men, not to punish them.

Father what do you want to talk about? What do you need tonight?

Mark I need people who will hear me, people who listen to me, people who are focused on listening to me.

God that's what you always say.

Because that's what I always want Mark. Am I lonely? Well yes, as a matter of fact, I am. Lonely in regard to people. There are the three of us, and we are happy, and content, but remember why we said, *'Let us make man in our image'.*

We wanted a relationship with people. And in as much as we wanted that, created an entire universe for that relationship, yes, we're lonely.

BECAUSE NOT VERY MANY PEOPLE HAVE THAT RELATIONSHIP.

Let's be honest Mark. Is what you're experiencing, this talking back and forward, this 'God said, Mark said' conversation very normal?

No.

Well then. Obviously either you're a freak, and this is a complete falsehood, or it's me.

It sure seems like you. I've struggled with it. Tried to tell myself it's just me making it up. But you keep coming back and asking for more

conversation. It's embarrassing. Makes me feel like a weirdo. The guy who talks to God all day. But it sure seems like you.

It's easy to understand that the average man in the street is not having a conversation with me. Why should he?

But what's not easy is that people who believe in me, and focus their entire lives around me, don't know how to listen to me. You didn't, and very few do. They try. But they don't hear me talk in whole sentences that they can easily understand, and they certainly don't have a conversation with me.

The atheist thinks a conversation with God is foolishness, and many believers think it is an evil deception.

Instead of a conversation, many people talk 'at' me. They have missed my point in the Bible, *'And [when you pray]do not be like the heathen who think they will be heard for their many words'.*

MANY BELIEVERS TALK 'AT' ME AND ABOUT ME, BUT DON'T LISTEN TO ME.

Even when alone, they still talk at me as though they were one of a thousand voices chanting a mindless, repetitive mass.

They don't talk to me as one person talks to another. They use a different language than they do when they talk to their real friends. When they talk to me they use a sort of 'Oh God' religious language. You do it too Mark.

I know. You keep pulling me up on it.

And so many Christians, when they attempt to listen to me, they listen to me as though I were the preacher and they were one of a large congregation. They don't sit or walk and talk with me in the way a man talks to his friend, back and forth, reasoning together.

They don't really expect that I will speak direct to them very often, not just them. Of course they don't; they have been listening again to the accuser.

Here's a picture of what it's like; my people are like passengers on a plane who all sit down and put their headphones on and listen to the in-flight entertainment. If you could see what I can see when I look at my people it's as though they all take their seats, put on their headphones and begin listening to the in flight entertainment on the plane called modern Christianity.

A plane called 'modern Christianity'.

The in flight entertainment is run by their enemy who tells them they are unworthy. But they keep listening to him all the same. It's his job to tell them they're too sinful, he's called the Accuser, but it's not supposed to be his job on that plane, he's just tricked management into employing him.

The plane in the picture is trying to get to an airport called 'Friendship with God' but it never gets there. Instead it keeps circling over the home 'Salvation Experience' airport and then landing, refuelling, taking off, circling and then landing again, always back to the Salvation airport, never getting close enough to the Friendship with God airport because piped through their headphones is the message that they are unworthy of friendship, that God is not pleased with them, and cannot talk to them when they sin. They think they are in danger of losing their salvation, so they have to keep landing back there again to check.

Poppycock, all of it. Lies, lies and more lies. This is the same enemy who started this entire war with the words to Eve, *'Has God Said?'*

War? A lot of people don't even realise they are in a war. It makes me angry. It boils my wrath. My people are being subjected to slavery to sin. But completely the opposite sort of 'slavery to sin' than they think.

I came to save men from their sin, not tell them off for it.

I came to forgive men for sin, not punish them. I'm the Jesus who told the 'Father runs to the wayward son' parable. The Jesus who died for you.

So no; I am not about to talk about how sinful my people are. I'm not like that.

You are enslaved by sin by listening to the enemy tell you that you are sinful.

By constantly reminding people that they are sinful, the enemy makes them slaves to sin. Don't help him!

I want people to stop telling themselves how sinful they are. And I want them to stop telling others how sinful they are. *'As a man thinks so he is'.*

Here's the mystery, the contradiction; *by reminding a man of his sin, you keep him sinful.* That's why the enemy takes the time to accuse you. The more he accuses people the more likely they are to think there's no hope and to continue on with what they are being accused of.

But if you remind a man of how much I love him, despite his sin, you focus him on me.

Whenever I spoke to a person I spoke forgiveness. They came to me not convicted of sin, but convinced of forgiveness. Don't make the mistake of drawing people to me by reminding them of the enemy's lie that they are unworthy. I see them as worthy of my death.

THE MORE A MAN REALISES MY LOVE IS NOT LINKED TO HIS CONDUCT, THE MORE HIS CONDUCT IMPROVES.

The enemy has managed to succeed in getting so many people enslaved to their sin, by focusing them on it. He tells them that my closeness to them is proportionate to their sin. He tells them that the more sinful they are, the further away I am.

He's got them thinking all day about how sinful they are. Whenever they think of me they think about how unworthy they are.

By thinking it they become it. The enemy screams at them that they are sinful and unworthy of God's blessing, UNWORTHY. OF. GOD. TALKING. TO. THEM.

And that's the very core of the enemy's strategy. He does not want people to listen to me. Because he knows that it's what you were born for. To ensure that you don't listen to me, he tells you that you're unworthy of doing so. Which is a lie. A lie people will spot if they listen to me.

THE WAY TO OVERCOME THE LIE IS TO LISTEN TO ME.

If people listen to me their sin will simply begin to fall off. But better still they'll hear me, and that, more important than any sin, is the key. *'I am come that they might have life, and have it more abundantly.'*

The only reliable way to change is to listen to me

You can never say safely that you have your
habits under control. Only I can do that.
The way I do it is speak to you.

God there are so many things in my life I'd like to change.

Mark the sound of my voice all day in your mind, changes you. If
you have a conversation with me my voice will fill your mind. That's
what changes you. Your own efforts are wasted. My voice is the only
solution.

*'be transformed by the renewing of your MIND['nous':
understanding, receiving God's thoughts through faith].*
ROMANS 12:2 NIV

What do you think Mark? If your mind is filled with the words I
speak specifically to you each day, is it going to stay the same?

**Obviously not. There'll be less and less room for all my negative
thoughts.**

Not your negative thoughts Mark, his.

I DON'T WANT YOU WORRYING ABOUT THE HABITUAL
SINS, WE'LL FIX THOSE TOGETHER, I WANT YOU FOCUSED
ON HIS *REAL* ATTACK.

Remember that he can only lie. He is not often allowed to maim
physically, so lies are pretty much all he has. He knows that to
succeed his lies must be subtle, stealthy and hard to pick.

The nature of a lie is it isn't true, it's not what it seems. So if he hits you with a temptation to think a thought, or to speak out in anger you can be sure he's actually got something else in mind. What you think is the temptation is often not the real one. He'll have a much more damaging goal in mind.

Something much more important. He doesn't care particularly whether you have a moment of anger, he doesn't care if you have problems with a particular type of thought.

He just wants to distract you with the little sins to make sure that you don't listen. That you don't feel worthy of a conversation with me.

No matter what you've done, what you've thought or said in the last ten minutes, I still want to have a conversation with you. And it won't be about telling you off, or letting you think I'm not very pleased with you. So if that's what you hear it's unlikely to be me.

The bible
Not boring after all

That's because it does not belong to religion, it belongs to me!

Father about today. Thanks. Was my friend right when he said I should study and read the bible far more?

Mark absolutely.

Really God? I guess I'm just so used to hearing you right here talking to me that I was starting not to read the bible so much. I hear you speak in my mind so clearly that when I look at my bible to read it, I know the words in it are all true, but it sort of reminds me of the old, religious, stuffy sort of approach to finding you.

When I used that old approach I never seemed to hear much from you. Instead I just felt frustrated, alone and away from you, and condemned. And lots of other Christians I talk to say they feel the same. They don't hear from you very often. They are very unsure of the idea of a conversation with you. It seems foreign to them. A bit weird.

Sorry, but that's sort of how it's seemed, well how it still seems a lot of the time.

No need to apologise Mark, I know exactly how you feel.

The old, religious, stuffy sort of approach to finding me is not my idea, it's my enemy's lie. I am not far off, I am not hard to find, I make myself easy to find.

'What other great nation has gods that are intimate with them the way GOD, our God, is with us, always ready to listen to us?'
DEUTERONOMY 4:7 MSG

So God if I don't like it, and you don't like it either, this 'performance-based religion', then how come you want me to read more of the bible?

BECAUSE THE BIBLE IS THE WRITTEN WORDS OF GOD. IT DOES NOT BELONG TO THE RELIGIOUS SYSTEM. IT BELONGS TO ME.

The bible is the things I have said and done through people, the things that I wanted written down and passed down through the ages. Now that you have found me, really found and taken hold of me, you will find that although the bible is the document that religious people think they own, it does not belong to them. It belongs to me.

UNTIL YOU'RE IN CONVERSATION WITH ME, THE BOOK IS LIKE LETTERS FROM SOMEONE YOU'VE NEVER REALLY MET.

It's like finding a bunch of letters in a cupboard, a diary too, all written by some woman, to her friends, about her life. You read a number of them, for a while you're intrigued, they seem quite interesting, but frankly, you have other things on your plate, better things to do than read the letters and accounts of someone, who although she sounds interesting, is not real to you.

Then one day you meet the woman of your dreams, you get to know her, fall deeply in love with her, and then some time into your relationship she surprises you by asking if you've ever happened to stumble on an old diary, a pile of old letters. She explains that she left her letters and diary in the care of friends of the previous owners of your home, and now they are lost but someone had suggested they might have been left here, right here in your own home.

All of a sudden it makes sense.

THIS WOMAN, YOUR WONDERFUL DREAM WOMAN, IS THE WRITER OF THE LETTERS, THE AUTHOR OF THE DIARY!!

Now it all starts to makes sense; the way this amazing woman has always seemed so strangely familiar, as though you've known her forever. Now the thought of reading her written words, of swimming in her thoughts and musings, instead of being boring is the most appealing thing possible. Other than talking directly to her.

That's what it's like to read the bible for those who hear my voice direct into their hearts. The power of the written word is extraordinary for humans Mark, any words, written down take on extra power.

Now that you are having a conversation with me, you are able to get to know me as a friend. You will find now at last that the bible will come alive Mark. More to the point, you will want to drink it, swim in it, and your friend is right, you must learn more and more of it. Until it becomes so familiar to you. The good news Mark, excuse the pun, is that it is such a relatively simple document. It's not really that long, it's not that daunting to become familiar with.

THE BIBLE SEEMS DAUNTING BECAUSE IT IS ASSOCIATED WITH RULES AND REGULATIONS THE ENEMY INVENTED TO KEEP YOU FROM ENJOYING ME.

I am a God of no conditions.

'He has made us competent as ministers of a new covenant--not of the letter but of the Spirit; for the letter kills, but the Spirit gives life'   2 CORINTHIANS 3:6 NIV

Oh oh God. This stuff gets me in a bunch of trouble.

Trust me on this Mark. I am a God of unconditional (no conditions) love, and yet the enemy has managed to give you the idea of a system of rules and regulations and hoops you must crawl through to get to me, he has used his lies to associate all that with my written word.

But God what about the many, many verses in the bible where it says we need to change?

The way you change Mark is accepting my love. The prostitute, the tax collector, the woman caught in adultery. They didn't come to me because of rules, they came because I loved them. A love that disregarded the fact that they'd broken the rules. Their automatic response was to begin to change. The rules don't help you change, the spirit of love motivates change. Sin falls off when you hear the Creator of the universe talk to you, not about, but despite your sin.

THE BIBLE IS THE LOVE SONGS, POEMS, MUSINGS, ADVENTURES, TRUE STORIES AND LETTERS OF THE CREATOR OF THE UNIVERSE.

An incredible glimpse into the mind of the one who comes to bleed for you without condition. What a treasure and you have found it. Eat it, eat my words. You feel in the spirit what it means to put it in your mouth and eat it, pursue that feeling because it has meaning.

Why when God gives there are no conditions

Lord what do you want to say to me this morning?

> Mark listen. Keep on listening. Can you see why I keep telling you to listen? By refusing to buckle under the intense pain you face and insisting instead on listening to me you have developed what others call a gift. You have learned to listen. And Mark it is amazing and it is a gift. It really exists, and I really did give it to you.

I wanted to edit a lot of that out. That bit about 'others call it an amazing gift'. But you're saying not to. How come?

> Why would you edit it out?

Because it sounds arrogant. People will think I'm conceited. I probably am, but there's no need to confirm it for them.

> Mark did I say it, or did you just make it up?

Well you said it obviously. I hope you did anyway. But people don't have to know everything you say to me. Some of it's a bit embarrassing God.

> I did say it. So what's the problem? If someone else told you God was saying that about you. You'd feel very encouraged. Am I not allowed to encourage you directly?

Yes. I guess. Ok.

> I WANT TO TALK ABOUT TWO SPECIFIC THINGS TODAY.
> One of them is to confirm for your own sake, to help you against Doubt, to tell you that this ability of yours to hear me really does

exist, I really am speaking and you really do hear me.

The second is that it is a gift. You didn't have it until it was given by someone else. Me. It came from God. I gave it to you. Just the same as I will give it to anyone who cares to listen.

Now be honest Mark you thought, because the enemy tries to persuade you of this, that I was about to say that because it's a gift it doesn't belong to you.

You're right I did think that.

That's a lie Mark. Because it's a gift it does belong to you. You were wrong to think it doesn't belong to you, It does. But I'm not surprised and I don't blame you because it's one of his lies for tying up my people.

Remember the things I said to you? All he has is lies!

The bonds he ties you up with are lies. That's all he has.

You thought I was going to tell you that I can and will take back this ability of yours to hear me if you don't behave in some righteous way or put in the effort in some holy way. But that was a lie right then, in real time, from the enemy.

I am not a demanding, judging God, I am a waiting, patient, forgiving God which is why it says;

    'Gods gifts and God's call are under full warranty, never cancelled, never rescinded.'   ROMANS 11:29 MSG

The enemy is always putting conditions on you. But there are none.

So Mark listen. Listen. Listen. Never stop listening and I will never stop talking. And don't read that wrong. I am not saying that my talking is conditional on your listening. That's the lie you've been fed. Always conditions, the enemy is always trying to lie to you about conditions.

Why do you think your enemy keeps feeding people the idea that there are conditions to meet before you can hear me speak?

The answer is pretty simple when you think about it, a lie, by definition, is not the truth.

So if his weapons are always lies, then anything he says is going to be a lie. So if he tells you that there are conditions on everything you get from me, always some condition; then obviously the reason he tells you that, is that actually the opposite is true and he doesn't want you to know the real truth.

THE REAL TRUTH IS THERE ARE NO CONDITIONS.

Gifts from me, love from me, relationship with me, blessing from me, it all comes without condition. I may not give a thing until you are ready, but it's not conditional. Once I've given you a thing I don't take it back. What about you? When your kids misbehave do you take back the gifts you've given them? Me neither.

Father what about salvation, I can lose that can't I?

Mark no.

Oh oh. A few hundred years ago and I'd get burnt at the stake for that one. What do you mean?

I mean I do not take back your salvation. And neither is it ever lost. Even if you throw it back, walk away, refuse to own it anymore, I pick it up and put it in storage for you and you can pick it up anytime you want it.

Your salvation is never, ever lost. Once given it belongs to you. No matter how you discard it, where you leave it, I pick it up and dust it off and put it lovingly in storage. All you have to do is ask for it again. It's yours.

YOUR SALVATION CALLS TO YOU.

It's there and it doesn't just sit there. It calls to you, always, because it now 'exists', it is now a 'thing'.

You have been given access, redeemed, forgiven, invited in, made a son. That contract between us now exists. It cannot be destroyed. If you throw it back at me, I put it away waiting for you to come and get it when you want. And because you are my son I honour my promise. Even if you run from me.

'the LORD your God goes with you; he will never leave you nor forsake you.'   DEUTERONOMY 3:16 NIV

I NEVER LET GO.

I woo you, I pursue you, I am constantly there, your salvation calls to you. So back for a moment to conditions, there are no conditions Mark. Once I have given you a gift, any gift it is yours.

START BY WRITING DOWN YOUR OWN QUESTION
Want to try your own conversation with God? Go to the page immediately following the contents page. Or go to page 243

CONVERSATION

I don't need your help
unless I ask for it

So listen. Sit with me. Watch me work.
I am painting a picture of me on you.

Mark things are coming, events are on the horizon which are going to change your life.

Father the enemy interfered then, tried to interrupt and I told him to be quiet. The moment I did I could see in my mind's eye a picture of him gagged. Did you show me that?

Mark yes.

Tell me about the things that are coming Lord?

Mark they are for you and not for you. They will change your life and bring blessing to you, but they are for a much wider audience.

Mark you are my canvas now. You've made decisions, and commitments to me that mean you are not your own anymore. So instead of you determining what your life will look like, or worse your life being tossed about by circumstance, from now on it will be me who chooses the colours with which your life is painted. And I will do the painting.

I AM A PATIENT ARTIST.

I am stirring the paint, mixing the colours and preparing the pallet. See me stretch the canvas. You can see me Mark. Can you see how I am going about my business with purpose? The painting hasn't even started yet, I am a patient artist. I want the canvas perfectly taut, I want the paints exactly the right consistency so that they dry not too soon and not too late, so that they mix and seem to glow.

So that when you look at the painting and see the scene represented there it appears more real than when you look at the actual scene on which the painting is based.

More real? How can that be? Easy, the artist, me, understands the scene he is looking at, understands the very nature of creation, he understands the Creator, the one who created the original scene, the scene he is now capturing in this painting.

I AM PAINTING ME; A PICTURE OF ME ON YOU.

And so it is with me Mark. I am painting me, a picture of me on you, on your canvas.

Really? Who am I to get the picture painted on me?

Nobody special. I am attempting to paint the same picture on every man, woman and child.

The painting of me is already painted on animals and the rest of creation.

'The heavens declare the glory of God; the skies proclaim the work of his hands.' PSALM 19:1 NIV

But with you humans I've decided to paint by collaboration, with your consent. That way the painting, even when on a torn canvas will be more beautiful than those done without consent.

I prepare every single human canvas differently, every single one of the billions and billions of people who have walked and will walk the earth, every single one of them an entirely different canvas. The same in so many ways, and yet so different when you look more closely.

EACH PICTURE OF ME IS THE SAME, AND YET IT IS ALSO DIFFERENT.

Because each canvas is different, the picture of me is different. The same, and yet so different.

'THIS IS THE SAME PAINTING', MY FATHER WILL SAY.

'Aah but no, I see the difference now' he will say, as he turns the canvas to the light and looks more closely, 'I see the subtle difference here, the way the paint has a different, totally different, yet equally pleasing hue.'

Every man a picture of me. On every man, woman and child I am painting a picture of myself.

AM I A MEGALOMANIAC? THE SUPREME NARCISSIST?

Obviously not. A Creator who gets down from the creation seat to meet with and talk with those he created; not really the signs of the self-consumed.

So why a picture of me? Because Mark there is nothing better that I can find to be the image portrayed on a human canvas. Nothing better.

Perfection, love, friendship, purpose, strength, courage, knowledge, wisdom, every single thing that is good, all of it, there is no better picture of those things simply because I am those things. I invented them. So there is no other source, and I want the very best painted on every single human canvas.

I AM ALWAYS WORKING ON THE TEARS IN THE CANVAS.

So Mark every single human, every person you ever come across is a canvas, in preparation by the Creator. Some may have been scratched, some torn, but the tears are not permanent, do not have to last forever. The moment a tear occurs in any human canvas, I am instantly working on the repair.

If you cannot see the tear being repaired then obviously I am preparing for the job, preparing the edges of the tear for the joining together, doing the work I need to ensure the repair is even more beautiful than before.

I DO NOT STAND BACK AND WAIT FOR THE MOMENT OF SALVATION. I AM WORKING ON EVERYONE ALL THE TIME.

This concept that the canvas stays ripped, never regenerates, never gets repaired until a person becomes a Christian is wrong. It would be a nice story, it would make what I am doing in the universe seem neat and tidy, but nevertheless it is wrong.

I AM NOT A PREDICTABLE CHILDREN'S BOOK - I AM THE OXFORD DICTIONARY, I AM WAR AND PEACE.

I am the unabridged version of every major work. There is more going on in the story of this universe than you can imagine.

Who can fathom the Spirit of the LORD, or instruct the LORD as his counsellor?   ISAIAH 40:31 NIV

So Mark when you encounter a person, in whatever state their canvas, be aware that they are *my* canvas and I am already working. So walk carefully. I don't need your help unless I ask for it.

I AM NOT WAITING FOR YOU TO CONVERT PEOPLE TO CHRISTIANITY SO I CAN WORK ON THEM.

I'm working on them already. I am not waiting for them to conform to *your* idea of what they should be doing before I can paint my picture on them. I am already about my work in their life.

SO WALK CAREFULLY IN MY ART ROOM. DON'T LIFT A FINGER UNLESS I ASK.

When you're with someone it is possible that I want you to say something, or do something that might help me in my work, but it is not definite or without question. So walk carefully. Listen for my instructions, do not presume. You are a guest in this art room, a guest in my world.

I WAS HERE BEFORE YOU CAME ALONG, ALREADY BUSY, AND WILL BE AFTER YOU HAVE GONE.

I love having you here. You're great. But remember you're a guest, so don't assume anything. Your job is to listen to me for every step of your life. The little decisions and the big ones.

My art room is filled with canvasses which, although to you may appear neglected or as though the artist has gone off and started another painting, they are actually being worked on right now. Every human canvas you encounter is being worked on by God right now. Not waiting for you to convert them. I don't need your help unless I say.

Which means you're going to need to be very good at hearing my voice otherwise you'll have no idea what I'm saying.

Yes I need as much help as I can get with these paintings, but I require helpers who only do what I ask. Don't touch unless I say.

'Uzzah reached out his hand to steady the ark, because the oxen stumbled. The LORD's anger burned against Uzzah, and he struck him down because he had put his hand on the ark.'   1 CHRON 13:9 NIV

EVERYONE YOU LOVE IS A CANVAS I AM PAINTING.

Does it appear to you that I am going too slow, that I have gone off and started another canvas and neglected your favourite ones? Wrong Mark. I am preparing the colours, pulling the canvas tight, sketching the first impressions, filling in the paint. I am repairing that tear.

You are in the presence of the master artist working. If you want to follow me you need to come to terms with the way I am, and not the way you want me to be.

YOU ARE CREATED IN MY IMAGE, NOT ME IN YOURS.

I am not your idea of a God, *I am God.*

So although it does not suit the standard tidy Christian perspective of how I should act, every single human you come across, although they may have gone astray like the rest of the human race, I am the good shepherd and I have left the other sheep safe in the pen and am, this very minute, out getting this one and carrying them back to the fold.

SO DON'T TOUCH UNLESS I SAY TOUCH.

I am doing it already, I am at work right now. I am not waiting for you to do it. Stand back and let me, and only touch when I say touch. Instead of leaping in to do the job yourself when you see a person going the wrong way, stand back and watch me do the repair or paint the picture. Only lend a hand when I say.

But how will I know when you are saying?

Ask. Write or speak, or think my answer. If you want to know what I'm saying, take hold of, grab hold of, make my answer your own. Just like you're doing already. What you're doing is what I want you to do.

I'M GOD SO I'M QUITE CAPABLE THANKS.

Be ready to lend a hand, but also be ready to see me do the whole job while you watch. I am capable Mark. Capable in your situation without any help from you.

I'll tell you when I need help. Watch what I am doing with everyone you love. Watch me paint an incomparably beautiful picture on each of them.

And look differently now at everyone you meet. Each of them is a canvas, each being painted by me, with no help from you. I have known them since before they were conceived. You have only just met them. I don't want you to think the world is filled with blank and torn canvasses that need you to paint or repair.

My idea is for you to enter my art room to watch me paint the many canvasses, just to watch and enjoy my work.

WHEN I ASK YOU TO PASS ME A BRUSH, OR STIR A COLOUR, THEN WELL AND GOOD.

But I am the painter Mark, you are the watcher.

If this is not me they will have lost nothing by trying it

But if it is me and they don't, they will have lost everything.

Father if I can hear you this clearly, sense your very reality, rely on and lean on you, then how do I tell others more hungrily seeking than I was?

How do I tell them about this mind-blowingly real experience with God.

Mark tell them to listen.

Can I give them any tips to listening?

Of course. Tell them to write down my reply, but not to wait for the reply to come. Start writing and my answer will come. *A mystery and yet so simple.*

WHEN YOU START WRITING, MY SPIRIT IS DRAWN BY YOUR FAITH.

Just a little wee seed of faith, just enough to start writing something and see if God starts bringing the words.

There I will wait to see what the LORD says and how he will answer my complaint. Then the LORD said to me, 'Write my answer plainly.'
HABAKKUK 2:1-2 NLT

Tell them to start with their name, or 'My Son' or 'My Daughter'. Whatever works for them. Just start writing something and I will give them the words to write for the rest of the sentence.

Father some will feel this is hocus pocus. What can I say to them?

TELL THEM IF I AM NOT IN THIS, THEN NOTHING WILL HAPPEN. BUT IF I AM, THEN EVERYTHING WILL HAPPEN. They have nothing to lose and everything to gain.

> *'Leave these men alone! Let them go! For if their purpose or activity is of human origin, it will fail. But if it is from God, you will not be able to stop these men; you will only find yourselves fighting against God.'*   ACTS 5:38 NIV

TELL THEM TO TRY IT THEMSELVES BEFORE CONDEMNING IT.

Tell them they have nothing to lose. Challenge them that if I am in this, waiting to talk to them, like a man does with his friend, then if they ignore it they will have robbed themselves of their very reason for being born, to talk with the Creator.

Imagine turning your back by mistake on an opportunity that men have longed for down through the ages, an opportunity to speak to and hear from the Creator, as clearly as one man speaks to another.

To hear from him, so clearly, and without having to become perfect, without being unnaturally pious, or performing any other religious rite.

Mark many modern, charismatic, Jesus-believing, 'think-they're-free-of-religion' Christians are actually, incredibly religious. So horribly religious that they would stone my prophets if there were prophets left to stone. You have been no different.

MY PEOPLE MUST START HEARING CLEARLY AND CONSTANTLY FROM ME. TELL THEM TO DO THIS.

Tell them to practise this. Tell them to try it and if it's not me to discard it.

I do not want a people who wait to hear me, I want now a people who try to hear me, who seek after me, who try to find me. I'm just here Mark, just here.

God what about that verse, *'they that wait on the Lord'?*

Mark you seek and knock and try to hear me, then you wait for the things I promise when I speak. People need to understand the bible as a whole concept, not a single passage at a time.

TELL THEM THAT IF YOU DO NOT HEAR REGULARLY FROM ME, THEN THERE IS LESS AND LESS TO DROWN OUT THE ENEMY.

If they do not hear my voice they cannot stop themselves hearing his. His voice is everywhere, he is prancing about roaring his lies.

But God I don't have enough answers, I don't seem to be able to convince people of this. I get talking and then somehow get too overbearing.

Exactly. The battle is mine Mark, not yours. So the best way to tell people about this conversation is simply to do it yourself. Those with a heart for it will see your example and follow. That allows my spirit, not yours, to do the persuading.

The enemy tells church people they are not good enough, and as a result, when they hear this lie, they begin to dream up all sorts of things they can do to please me. All sorts of ways of acting that they think will make me want to speak to them.

YOU ARE ALREADY ACCEPTABLE TO ME MARK. ALL OF YOU. THAT'S WHY I DIED. I ACCEPT YOU.

If people don't hear me they begin to hear the enemy instead. He is shouting at you all day long, so if you are not listening to me you hear him instead.

I speak clearly and in a way that humans can actually hear and understand. As easily as another human talking to them. But most don't hear me. Their ears are stopped up. Not because of common sins, but because they have decided they can't hear.

As a result the enemy's voice is heard instead. He lies, his roar is his only strength, just lies. But if a lie is listened to it gains strength.

Your enemy is constantly calling out lies about me to my people, and lies about themselves too.

SATAN IS CAREFULLY BUILDING A PERCEPTION, FOR MY PEOPLE, OF WHAT THEY AND I ARE LIKE.

As a result of his accusations many think that they are less than acceptable to me, that I often have to turn away from them because they are dirty and sinful. Excuse me?? I am the same God who hung on a cross and called out to my father to forgive those who jeered as they walked past.

HAVE I HAD A PERSONALITY CHANGE? HAVE I COME DOWN FROM MY CROSS AND TAKEN THE ENEMY'S SAD ROLE AS THE ACCUSER?

My people need to read my words again. If they did they would quickly see that I run from judging them, I put off judging the world till the last possible moment.

'He cares enough to respond to those who seek him.'   HEB 11:6 MSG

I CARE ENOUGH TO RESPOND TO ANYONE WHO SEEKS ME.

No matter what their moral state. Tell them they have nothing to lose by trying to write down, speak out, or even think out my answers to their questions. I long to answer their questions. I died for this opportunity. I have waited down through the ages for people who will talk to me and expect to hear me answer back.

I AM RAISING UP AN ARMY OF PEOPLE WHO LISTEN TO ME.

Right now, finally frustrated with religion and the lack of people listening to me, I am raising up an army of men and women who will actually hear me. I am no longer waiting for them to choose this, instead I am raising them up from the very stones, the hearts of cold stone that line the pews of many of my churches.

I NEED PEOPLE TO TALK TO MARK BUT FEW ARE LISTENING.

So I am raising them up. I am drawing them out, and putting in them hearts inclined to listen to me. This is what I spoke of through the prophets. That I will put in you a heart of flesh.

'I'll pour pure water over you and scrub you clean. I'll give you a new heart, put a new spirit in you. I'll remove the stone heart from your body and replace it with a heart that's God-willed, not self-willed. I'll put my Spirit in you and make it possible for you to do what I tell you and live by my commands.'   EZEKIEL 36:24 MSG

I'm not waiting anymore, I'm starting to do it. What a fortunate age you live in, the age when God, finally frustrated to the point of action, begins to put hearts of flesh in men so that they naturally and willingly listen to me.

The word of God, the actual spoken to your spirit word of God is not heard very often by Christians these days. It is not expected, and so it is not heard.

'In those days the word of the LORD was rare;' 1 SAM 3:1 NIV

God what do you want me to do about that? I don't have a platform. In fact, as a result of these conversations with you, the few Christians who did listen to me are beginning to have serious concerns about me.

That's fine. I'm going to raise up a new bunch of people who will listen to you. I'll choose them. You won't.

They'll be people who expect to hear from me. Expect so strongly that they throw caution to the wind, and get out a pen and paper and begin to write down what I say.

Get out a pen Mark, open your laptop and write what I say

I have a lot to say and not much time to say it. So listen, write it down, record it, store it up and I will show you then how to pass it on. Because this meal, although you are one of the workers in the kitchen, is a meal for all Mark.

You have not come to this on your own.

The purpose is much larger than your own. At the start of this pain I gave you a song. The one and only song I had ever given you. *'The Lord your God is with you and he will do great things, much greater than you hoped for, and the things you hope for too'.*

These are the things that are *much greater* than you'd hoped for. You are now seeing them come to pass. You had no concept of what I was talking about. Now you do

And Mark don't worry, I am also, as I promised, bringing you the things you've hoped for. I am not a miserable and stingy God. I keep my promises.

And to those who are afraid that a desire to hear a clear answer may bring deception, tell them this; I will never allow the enemy to speak convincingly and pose as me to those who genuinely seek me.

If you, then, though you are evil, know how to give good gifts to your children, how much more will your Father in heaven give good gifts to those who ask him! MATTHEW 7:11 NIV

CONVERSATION

Thirtysix

The source of light can be traced
when it shines through dust

Hi God.

Mark I want you to know that I am always, indisputably here. You can trust me. I have beckoned you, I have turned up and talked to you and yes it really is me

Father what do you need? What do you want?

Mark I want people who want to know what I've got to say. I am not looking for people who listen for the sake of listening, who listen because 'It brings them closer to God' in some sort of 'amazing Christian experience'.

WHAT I'VE GOT TO SAY NEEDS TO BE SAID TO KEEP CREATION FULLY CREATED.

I've got a universe to run. Everyone was created for a purpose. I want people who want to hear what I've got to say because what I've got to say, to them, is important and must be said for creation to be fully created.

What you see when you look out your window is just the beginning, just the building blocks, the start. Then I added man the creator.

WHAT DID YOU THINK? THAT YOU WERE JUST GOING TO CREATE A LITTLE BIT?

Look at Adam, he got to sit down and name what I created, as I created it.

You are gods in the making.

Imagine if Adam had kept going, he was only days into it when the whole thing came crashing to a halt. Why do you think the snake, the sliming one was so intent on stopping what was happening right then? He saw, as David saw later, as was evident at the tower of Babel that Man is a god, a god in the making.

> 'It is written in your own Scriptures that God said to certain leaders of the people, 'I say, you are gods!' And you know that the Scriptures cannot be altered. So if those people who received God's message were called 'gods...'   JOHN 10:34 NLT

SATAN COULD SEE THAT IF MAN CONTINUED IN THIS TALKING BACK AND FORWARD TO GOD RELATIONSHIP THAT HE WOULD SOON BE OVERPOWERED.

He could see the plan. That with humans talking back and forward to me, as creators too, then the world as God had designed it would come to full fruition.

To his horror Satan realised that the earth and all that was in it would reflect a true and full likeness of me. And that he would be no match for it.

SATAN WAS SHOCKED TO SEE THAT I HAD NOT FULLY REVEALED MYSELF.

Suddenly he saw that what he had tried to emulate, what he had seen of me and thought he could copy, was just a small shadow of who I really am.

I had not yet fully revealed myself. Creation the earth, the oceans, the animals, Man himself, all of it had been brought into place so that as light is seen more easily when it shines through dust, God would finally be seen in his full glory as he shone through creation.

Satan realised that what he had been seeing, what he had thought he could overthrow was such a small, infinitesimal glimpse of God and that if he had listened, if he had seen God in his full splendour he would not have wanted to, let alone tried to overthrow.

God I feel a bit like 'who am I?' to be hearing this. I've never been taught this, so I assume that it isn't current bible scholar thinking. Which in turn means that people in senior positions will have all sorts of problems with this. I just wish some days you could talk to me about nice things. Stuff that wouldn't offend anyone.

How long before you would be bored with that do you think?

Very quickly. But at least I wouldn't cause people all kinds of problems. At least I wouldn't rock the boat.

Mark back to the point of this morning's discussion; If people listened to me, allowed me to shine through the dust in their situation they would startle back, they would see such a wonderful loving them, wooing them, always in it for them God that they would not want to control me anymore, or box me, or overthrow the true me.

They would stand back in awe, their hearts would worship. Because that's how it happens Mark. True worship comes from truth. When men see the truth, when they see what I am really like, they worship without having to make themselves do so. They worship in spirit and in truth.

'When he comes [the holy spirit], he'll expose the error of the godless world's view of sin, righteousness, and judgment: He'll show them that their refusal to believe in me is their basic sin; that righteousness comes from above, where I am with the Father, out of their sight and control.' JOHN 16:8-11 MSG

CONVERSATION

Thirtyseven

Make sure the thing you wait for is what God says to wait for

You wait. You receive. It's the way I work. You wait, you receive.

So Mark always make sure the thing you wait for is the thing I want you to wait for. Otherwise your time is wasted.

Is it common to wait for the wrong thing?

Yes! Exceedingly common. Much too common. Heartbreakingly common.

What causes it?

Religion.

What do you mean?

Don't presume or assume. Ask me what I'm saying.

Religion traps people into thinking that God's specific will is pre-prescribed into a set of rules about what God will do for you. But I'm not pre-prescribed. I do what I want and when I want.

'Our God is in heaven; he does whatever pleases him.' PSALM 115:3 NIV

What about the bible though? It gives all sorts of promises about exactly what you'll do!

Mark it pays to find out what I want, specifically, right now, in your particular situation. It pays to find that out from me.

The bible gives you the principles, but you have to find out if that's the particular principle I want to apply in this situation.

For instance the bible says that *'The blessing of the Lord brings riches'.* And I do. The bible is true. But I don't always bring riches, I only bless and bring riches when I decide to. And yet people overlook the need to listen to me direct and instead they start a business and then expect that, because they are Christians that I will bring riches, that God is 'on their side' and will bless their business financially. And they wait and wait and wait. Hearts are broken, faith is lost, lives are lost, marriages are broken by waiting for the wrong things. Things I have never promised to that person specifically.

NO ONE TEACHES THEM HOW TO LISTEN TO ME, OR THAT THEY NEED TO LISTEN ALL THE TIME.
No one teaches them how to find out what I am really saying about their business. No one faces them with the hard fact that the only businesses I am going to bless financially are the ones where I specifically said to the person concerned that I would bless their business financially. If I said it I will do it, but if I didn't you'll have to work hard to make me.

RELIGION MAKES PEOPLE BELIEVE THAT GOD WILL ACT IN PRE-PRESCRIBED WAYS AND THAT HE CAN'T MOVE OUTSIDE OF THAT.
Let me just say this Mark. As your friend David heard from me in his own conversation, it is a dangerous concept to say to me 'God I know you wouldn't do that'. The bible is filled with people who came to trouble because they were convinced they knew what the scriptures said.

Peter with the food that scripture said he couldn't eat. Paul killing Christians because their beliefs threatened the scriptures he held so dear. The Pharisees killing me for the same reason.

RELIGION SEES, BUT RELIGION IS ALSO BLIND.
Religion sees that God heals, which I do, so assumes that God will heal every sick person. But that's not what always happens. Religion sees that God hates divorce, which I do, so assumes that every marriage will be restored. It won't. I seldom override a person's choices.

You must listen to me, be ready to hear the hard facts, and let me tell you whether to believe for healing, restoration, financial blessing, rebuilding your family, or not. You need to listen to me Mark.

So how do they listen then?

They make a choice to hear me. They ask me their questions, every question possible, and they expect to get an answer right then!

Whenever we get to this I feel like a bit of a freak. Like 'here he goes again about his weird idea of asking God a question and writing, typing, speaking, drawing, singing the answer'.

Well. Does it work?

Yes.

For others who try it?

Yes.

So what's the problem?

> ### TRY THIS THEN TELL YOUR FRIENDS
> ### WHAT YOU DISCOVER
> Want to try your own conversation with God? Go to the page immediately following the contents page. Or go to page 243

To have strong trust you need a strong mind

Lord even though I am having this ongoing conversation with you, I still have so little faith in this area. When it comes to these things that you have promised me personally, I am afraid to believe in case I'm wrong. The evidence suggests otherwise, so I'm afraid to believe and then find myself hurt and destroyed.

Lord are you saying you want to talk to me about trust?

YES. I HAVE A LOT TO SAY TO YOU ABOUT TRUST. THIS IS PART OF IT.

Trust is a tool for building our relationship, and is the structure, the 'framework' of the relationship too. What you are encountering when you are afraid to believe something that does not seem very believable is trust. Trust is a thing I have put in you.

Trust is a tool, the glue you have in your own tool kit that helps you build a relationship. It is the tool to help you create the framework of the relationship, any relationship, but it is also the framework itself.

I HAVE BUILT THIS TRUST TOOL INTO EVERY HUMAN.

Every human understands in their heart that their trust must not be given away lightly. Another way to describe trust is that it is like your spiritual nerves. Your physical nerves allow you to experience extreme physical pleasure, or extreme pain. And trust allows you to experience extreme spiritual pleasure, a relationship that is safe and true, or extreme spiritual pain; betrayal, dismay and broken trust.

The thing about trust, the way it works is, that it responds to the information the mind feeds it. So if the mind tells trust that it has been betrayed it believes and responds accordingly. Spiritual pain follows. If the mind tells trust that it is safe it gives itself freely.

ALTHOUGH THE MIND TELLS TRUST WHAT TO THINK, EVENTUALLY, TRUST BEGINS TO TALK BACK TO THE MIND.

I have built into trust the ability to caution or reassure the mind and heart. This is critical. Absolutely critical and almost entirely ignored by many. Is it any wonder that *'the love of many grows cold'.*

THE PICTURE I AM SHOWING YOU IS A KEY TO HOW RELATIONSHIPS WORK.

The mind tells trust that it likes this person, so it asks trust to trust them. And trust begins to respond, feels safe and so tells the mind that the mind is safe. It says, 'we are safe' and then the two of them, trust and the mind, tell the heart to go ahead, invest yourself in this relationship, you're safe. The heart and trust are closely intermingled but they are different. The heart is you, whereas trust is a tool, a 'thing' that is given or taken.

MARK THIS MAY SEEM A BIT CONFUSING, BUT STICK WITH ME, THINK IT THROUGH.

It's imperative you understand this. I have given you the picture at the easiest level to understand it, but the picture exists at almost every level of your life. For instance when a friend tells you something the mind might reject it, but trust comes and suggests to the mind there might be a case here for belief. If the mind is willing to accept trust's advice then the two encourage your heart, encourage you to put your heart into believing what your friend has said.

You are human, so at times you have experienced betrayal. And; you have also told trust that you have been betrayed at times when, actually, you haven't.

And then to complicate the issue even further you yourself have betrayed others and broken their trust. The result is that your own trust understands that if you can't always be trusted, then nobody can.

AS A RESULT YOUR TRUST IS OVER-CAUTIOUS, IT NO LONGER UNDERSTANDS WHAT TO BELIEVE.

It doesn't know anymore whether it should believe what your mind tells it. But it still understands the basic truths I have built into it. Your trust knows that if it invests itself in the wrong thing you will be hurt. Its job is to build relationships, but also to prevent you being hurt spiritually. And the betrayal of any relationship causes spiritual hurt.

The pain you experience when that happens is pain in your spirit, your heart and inner being. So, as a result of past hurts, your trust needs your mind to be strong enough now to reassure it, to reassure trust that what it is saying, what your mind is saying is true and can be relied on.

YOU NEED A STRONG MIND TO REASSURE YOUR TRUST

'For God did not give us a spirit of timidity (of cowardice, of craven and cringing and fawning fear), but [He has given us a spirit] of power and of love and of calm and well-balanced mind and discipline and self-control.' 2 TIM 1:7 AMP

In this current period of your life, I am speaking to your mind and telling you to believe some of the most beautiful words, the most beautiful ideas you have ever encountered. But you are going to have to decide whether or not to trust me.

I am the one talking. No human is giving you any reassurance you can count on. So your trust is cautionary, it understands that if you trust me unwisely on this you could be viciously hurt, possibly even completely destroyed. Your trust understands the risks, the degree of danger involved and cautions you.

So it comes down now to a choice. I have spoken to your mind and heart. They have told trust, they have put trust on notice that it is required, that for them, your heart and mind, to respond to what I have said, trust must get involved.

But you find that your trust is being cautionary.

YOUR TRUST NEEDS TO LEARN NEW RULES. IT NEEDS REASSURANCE FROM YOUR MIND

You need to tell your trust that you really have heard from God and ask it to risk itself because this really is God. Your mind needs to be strong, confident and able to reassure trust, so that eventually trust can reassure it.

And that's the rub Mark, although trust is designed to respond to information provided to it by the mind, trust understands there are no guarantees. All trust is risk. It understands also that the mind cannot see everything, cannot understand the whole situation.

There are no guarantees for trust. It has to trust the mind and heart to feed it information reliable enough to trust. Your trust understands that, having received the information, as reliable as possible, it must then weigh up the risks and decide whether or not to give itself.

IN THE PAST YOUR MIND HAS FED YOUR TRUST MANY WRONG IDEAS, IT HAS TOLD YOUR TRUST THAT GOD HAS LIED.

Your mind has told trust that life has dealt you unfair blows. Because of that your trust has begun to withdraw. Mark I want your trust to be released, set free to trust me again.

When I tell you something, when I say to believe that this will happen, or that I really am saying that thing, your trust cautions you because of what you have told it over so many years. You have told it that God never seems to deliver on his word. You have told it that sooner or later people betray your trust.

IT IS TIME TO RE-PROGRAMME YOUR TRUST MARK.

The only safe way to do that is hear from me what to tell it. If you rely on your own judgement about what you can and can't trust you will get it wrong. YOU. MUST. HEAR. FROM. ME.

If you listen to me and tell your trust what I say, it will grow used to my presence and begin to feel safe enough to trust me.

Trust has a memory, it remembers the times it has trusted and the times that trust has been well placed. If you listen to and hear from me trust will build up a library of experience that says God can be trusted. It will know that God speaks, and God delivers. It will still have to go to the mind and ask, 'this new information from God is it reliable?'

The mind will need to be strong and tell trust that 'yes, this is God, yes this is reliable'.

FIRST THE MIND, THEN TRUST.

But the nice thing is this Mark, very soon the wheel begins to turn, the mind tells trust, then trust reassures the mind, and then the mind tells trust again and so on. Very soon trust and the mind will function and communicate freely between themselves. So Mark when I tell you that a thing is happening, or is about to happen but there is no evidence, your mind needs to tell your trust to trust me anyway. *Evidence or no evidence.*

You need a strong mind Mark. What you are doing at present is letting your mind be fearful that it may not have heard me right.

Everything your trust tells you is based on what the mind has told it in the past. Your mind needs to tell your trust new things. It needs to say God's specific promises to me can be trusted. The things God tells me personally, the promises about my life, his words just to me, can be trusted.

And Mark you can ask as many times as you like for reassurance. I will always answer.

Remember that Fear, the being with that name, understands how you are made and designed. It looks for, waits for the discussion between your trust and your mind and then, when he sees an opportunity to cast doubt he takes it.

Mark these are the facts and issues of physical/spiritual creation.

PEOPLE NEED A BETTER UNDERSTANDING OF HOW TRUST, THE MIND AND THE HEART WORK.

With that understanding they will be able to venture into a new territory of faith. They'll be able to hear me speak and be able to believe what I have told them and act on it when there is little or no evidence to substantiate what I have said.

THE EVIDENCE MUST EXIST FIRST IN YOUR HEART AND ONLY TRUST CAN MAKE THAT POSSIBLE.

Let your trust go Mark. Tell it the truth. Tell your trust that this is God and God can be trusted. Do not wait for trust to tell your mind because first your mind must tell trust. First your mind speaks to trust, then trust reassures and comforts the heart and mind on the basis of what the mind has told it.

CONVERSATION
Thirtynine

How to have a chemical romance
with God

Father why is it still so hard to believe the things you tell me about my life?

Because it's difficult to believe. That's how I have designed it. It's a little difficult to believe.

Why?? So many more would believe in you if it was a little easier. Surely that's what you want?

No. Because that's not really belief. When it's too easy it's not belief.

Oh that's just lovely!! You mean you like this pain that comes from trying to believe the things you promise us personally?

Mark that's the nature of believing in me, in having a relationship with me. It's a little tough, only a little, but it is. I'm invisible, which makes it at first exceedingly difficult, and then still always a little difficult to have a relationship with me at a level where you genuinely believe and trust the things I tell you.

It's difficult because I'm not an invisible man.

If I were an invisible man it would be easier. You couldn't see me, but you could still reach out and touch me, and you'd be able to see me do things, shifting furniture, lifting objects and of course you could hear my voice. My voice would still be audible just like yours. Everything about me would be human, believable, reassuring, other than the fact that I would be invisible.

BUT I AM NOT ANOTHER HUMAN, I AM GOD.

And so far above you in size and power that it is natural to want to think that I don't exist at all. Or if I do exist that I am not particularly involved in your day to day reality. And I allow you to think that way so that the only people who attempt a back and forward relationship with me, a 'you said, God said' conversation are the ones who really want to.

I've created things so it seems completely natural to get on with your own 'reality' and manage your own life, and not to have a conversation with me. It's not what I want but I have designed it to be the natural way to think unless you have the courage to think otherwise.

TO BE HUMAN IS TO THINK THAT GOD ISN'T REALLY INTERESTED IN YOUR DAILY REALITY.

Listening to me doesn't seem easy. I have made it appear that way so that you to have to really work at listening to me. For that reason a back and forward conversation, 'God said, you said' is not common. Not even in church. The customs, patterns and formulas of church are easier than trying to strike up a backwards and forwards conversation with an invisible God.

But if you work at it, face the difficulties and keep listening, until you're sure you're hearing me, you'll come face to face with reality! Face to face with a spontaneous, real, personal, chemical relationship with God.

IT IS NO DIFFERENT THAN THE RELATIONSHIP BETWEEN A MAN AND WOMAN.

A woman offers you her heart but the natural response is to feel a little unsure that she really is doing so, to wonder if you have 'read the signs wrong', to wonder if maybe you're just telling yourself she likes you when really she doesn't. It's natural to think maybe this won't last, that somehow this can't really be happening.

Can you see the parallels Mark? You wonder in your relationship with God whether you're just telling yourself I am making those promises I made you, maybe I'm not saying those things at all.

At some point in any relationship you come to a step you must climb for the relationship to progress. It's the point where you need to decide to believe in that person's love for you; against all your doubt. At that point the love becomes explosive and real at a tangible, in your heart level. Human relationships or God relationship, it's all the same.

I HAVE MADE IT A LITTLE DIFFICULT TO BELIEVE IN A PERSON'S LOVE FOR YOU, AND A LITTLE DIFFICULT FOR YOU TO BELIEVE IN MY LOVE FOR YOU TOO.

A little difficult to believe that special person's promises and what they say. And a little difficult to believe my promises and what I say. It's the only way to establish a real, personal, chemical relationship between two humans, or between a human and God.

I have made myself evident, it is easy to find me. But you have to find me.

IF I MADE IT EASY TO BELIEVE A RELATIONSHIP WITH ME WOULD MEAN NOTHING.

If I made it too easy to believe that special person loves you or that I love you, then love would have no value. Both situations require trust and faith. Effort against strong odds is required and that builds love.

If it was easy to believe you'd be mad not to have a relationship with me. Which would make that relationship meaningless for most. It wouldn't be deep, it wouldn't be forged out of love that happens at a personal level.

When you love another human it is because something happens in your heart that makes you appreciate and want to be around them. For that to happen in a Human/God relationship I have to make myself invisible.

IF YOU COULD SEE ME THERE'D BE NO TIME TO DISCOVER YOU APPRECIATED ME.

Way before that happened you'd be overwhelmed.

The only way for me to forge a personal connection between us, not an obedience thing, but a personal, spontaneous, real, not religious, heart-felt, explosive, actual-love connection between a human and myself; is to make it difficult. Just a little difficult to believe. There's no other way.

Here's how it works. As you search for me, you are forced to keep choosing to ignore the reality of your world. You are forced to believe in this invisible God who promises such hopeful outcomes in a world full of things that aren't very hopeful. It takes its toll, you have to believe against what appears to be reality. Your emotions are brought into play. Emotions at a personal level.

You have to move past the nice normal Christian experience, where after your morning prayer God leaves you to get on with your day. You find you have to push past that and pursue a real relationship, to begin to try and listen to and hear regular conversations with God.

If our relationship remains all nice and warm but not much hearing me speak, then the moment life dishes up a crisis, things change dramatically. The crisis is suddenly in your face and much more real than this God who is warm feelings, but seldom speaks clearly.

The crisis forces you to put all that 'God stuff' to one side while you deal with the problems. You might pray for, and have others pray for a good outcome, but the crisis becomes more real than this God of yours.

I have designed life so that a crisis will feel more real than me. When your life looks like it is going down the plug hole it takes a fierce resolve to believe the promises I have made about the situation that is in crisis. It's the resolve to believe me in the face of extreme odds, that determines your character.

Then after such a crisis when finally, after an extremely painful wait, my promises come home to you, you see that I can be trusted. When life says the opposite, I can still be trusted.

And yet, after all that, it still doesn't occur to many people to begin listening to me more. Instead they carry on the best they can in their life, still not really hearing much from me.

I HAVE DESIGNED THE PHYSICAL/SPIRITUAL DYNAMIC SO THAT IS NOT EASY TO HAVE A RELATIONSHIP WITH ME.

If it were easy it would never happen at the human heart level. When you have a relationship with that special person I send your way, your heart leaps when you see them, something about them connects with your heart.

With God and man the only way for that to happen, for a connection to happen that is that personal and real is for me to make it a little difficult to believe. Just a little difficult.

The moment you reach out I am there, in a very real and tangible way, but you need to reach out.

And yet I come to you, not you to me, whenever you need me.

There's a mystery going on here Mark, an apparent contradiction. On the one hand I say that *'I have not made myself hard to find'*, on the other I say that *'it is the glory of kings to uncover a matter'.*

I tell you that it is me who pursues you and not the other way around. I say that you will find me and that I am not hard to find, but on the other that you must seek me for that to happen.

I say that I am self-evident in my very creation, *'all creation testifies to the glory of God'*, but on the other hand that you will need to seek me to find me.

The 'reality' of a relationship between a man and a woman is not always tangible either.

She may not initially appear to return that love you feel, that 'real, tangible, it's definitely love' love that you feel for her. But it is real in your heart. So although it's a struggle you choose to hope.

For that sort of relationship, for a relationship that real between God and Man I need to make it just a little difficult for you to believe.

As you struggle to believe that a personal connection really does exist between us, as you begin to hear what I say and then have to struggle to believe those things, something happens in your heart.

An emotional shift, a spontaneous 'appreciation' of, a connection at a personal and intimate and very special level, a real love relationship with God. You and God, connected first as friends, real friends and then as lovers.

You and God in love.

Don't knock it Mark, that's the level I'm looking for and taking you to.

The insistent reaching out to pursue and listen to me when you can't see me, and when it's easier to think I don't often speak, sets your heart up, for an explosive, real, chemical relationship with God. With me. Just me.

CONVERSATION
Forty

Your enemy will always attack you
he hates you

And his attacks will be vicious. This is war.

God every day, no matter what you've told me, no matter how stupendous and amazing the truths are that you've unfolded, no matter how much encouragement I get from others, I still have to struggle against pain and unbelief. It's so difficult to believe the personal promises you've made to me.

And Mark you will continue to have to struggle. Deep Sadness and Doubt, those ugly beings, will come and try to destroy you. That's because you have stood up and said 'I want to hear from God in my life'.

Yes but I didn't want a battle. Quite the opposite. I wanted to stop fighting. Stop battling. It's hurt the people I love.

Mark when you say you want to listen to me all creation goes on notice. Especially Satan. He is jealous and angry and hates us both.

YOU HAVE PUT YOURSELF IN THE FIRING LINE BY TRYING TO LISTEN TO ME.
Expect opposition. Expect discouragement, expect fear and pain and hurt to come and ask for entry. The secret is to refuse them entry.

Did I just hear you say 'in season and out of season, reject, fight, tell them to leave'?

Yes. Absolutely you heard that. This isn't religion that you find yourself part of. This isn't a formula. You are no longer part of that nice formula that says; 'Follow God. Rebuke the devil. Life will go well.'

What's wrong with that?

Everything. I am not a formula, I am God, the living and terrible God. I am not trying to strike fear into your heart. Not at all. You know that I am gentle, and come as a lamb, I am merely showing that I am not a formula.

I AM SEPARATE FROM YOU, NOT SOMETHING YOU CREATED.

Many people treat me like a household God, you would think they had dreamed me up and created a religion around me. Actually they have done just that. They have dreamed up an idea of me that is nothing like reality, and then they have built a nice religion around their idea.

They have formularised our relationship. It goes something like this; 'up in the morning, had a nice session with God, read my bible, prayed for my family, and off to work. Had a bad thought on the way to work, but rebuked the devil, it's all good now. I'm believing for increase in my business', etc etc. Their formula sounds good, but it's not. It boxes me and how to deal with the enemy into a nice little formula. But you're in a war. War's aren't nice. That's what I'm wanting to bring home to people. They're in a war.

Following me is not 'nice'. And it can't be formularised. Ask Esther, Elijah, David, Isaiah.

YOU ARE IN THE MIDST OF A BLOODY AND VICIOUS
SPIRITUAL WAR.

When you make yourself available for a walking talking conversation with God, your life becomes anything but predictable and the reaction of your enemy becomes vicious and even less predictable than me.

I hold worlds together. The sun stays where it is because I hold it there in my hand. How can a God like that be formularised or predictable?

'I am the Alpha and the Omega,' says the Lord God, 'who is, and who was, and who is to come, the Almighty.'   REV 1:8 NIV

And yet for the sake of people I accept and fit with their many formulas. I fit with their idea of a predictable God, what else can I do? Mercy demands it. So I wait and hope and draw and woo them, waiting for something better, something more intimate. And that's part of the job I have for you Mark, to help me woo them. Show them in a gentle, wooing, funny, exciting, never condemning, never judging way, show them what a relationship with me is meant to be like.

Because the way to win the hearts of men is with love, not condemnation. Love and freedom, not control.

I mentioned that the devil is even less able to be formularised than me. How so? Is he greater than me? Hah! He would have you think so. No. Not at all.

I AM PREPARED TO CONTROL MY POWER. HE IS NOT. HE HATES YOU.

He does what he wants, when he wants. He is not, as some people have painted him, a nasty devil you rebuke on the way to work.

He is not the weak devil who obediently goes away because you follow the 'I rebuke you' formula. He prowls about, he roars, he attacks. He is the prince of this dark world.

Many people get off lightly because they do not cause him enough pain to provoke a vicious counter attack. They think he is obedient to them, but quite often, without meaning to, they do what he wants them to.

He has them believing that he goes when they demand. He tricks them into thinking they are powerful and that he is submissive to their rebukes.

THE TRUTH IS HE'S EASIER TO CONTROL THAN THEY THINK.

But many never find that out because they have formularised me and him. They have very little effect on him. He plays a game with them. They rebuke, he withdraws, he is fooling them into thinking that they have him under control. As a result he can move about largely unbothered by many people. Too many are more likely to nervously rebuke the devil where he's not, than run at him where he is.

THE SECRET IS TO KNOW WHERE HE IS AND TO RUN AT HIM.
'And then David ran to meet the giant.'
The place he is most likely to be is trying to prevent you having a conversation with me.

To do that he needs to focus on having you believe that the things I have already said to you are not true. That's where he is working. To persuade you that what I have said, is not true.

Recently he has focused on you with much more intensity than you have ever experienced before. His aim is to persuade you that you have not heard the things I have promised you specifically, personally.

If he can get you to believe that, then you are much less likely to believe that I would want a conversation with you.

As a result many never experience the conversation with me that is available to them regardless of their moral state.

It will astound them when they hear me speak into their minds. They will be like Job. 'I have heard of you by the hearing of the ear, but now my eye sees you.'

'When his voice resounds, he holds nothing back.'　　JOB 26:14 NIV

'And this is only the beginning, a mere whisper of his rule.
Whatever would we do if he really raised his voice!'　　JOB 26:14 MSG

A RELATIONSHIP WITH ME, WHERE YOU HEAR ME OFTEN, REQUIRES DISCOMFORT AND RISK.
It demands everything that goes into any true relationship; time, love, commitment, vulnerability to the whims of the other, in this case me. It requires a total focus. But the comfortable place Satan has lulled many into tells them that such a committed, always focused on me relationship would be over zealous. He tells them that such a thing would be religious. He has them fooled.

BY BACKING AWAY FROM WHAT HE SAYS IS RELIGIOUS, THEY HAVE FALLEN INTO THE CLUTCHES OF RELIGION.
Neither hot, nor cold, many have gone to sleep in the warm.

THIS. IS. WAR!
Don't romanticise it. Realise you are in a blood and guts, huge

casualties war with an enemy so much larger than, so much more deceptive than you that, without a very clear strategy and very effective weapons you have no hope. Absolutely no hope. And a nice quick rebuke of a devil you think is just taking potshots at you is not a strategy at all.

He wants to kill you.

He wants to destroy your faith and is working always and constantly toward that end. Expect it. Man up, arm up against it. I will turn up. When you're hanging about in a constant conversation with me you have not only victory, but the complete and absolute authority, the level of authority I have to simply tell him to go.

'All authority in heaven and on earth has been given to me.'
MATT 28:18 NIV

The point is this Mark. If you want to follow the formula, keeping me and the enemy in nice little 'good/bad boxes', then the enemy's fight will feel controlled and although at times difficult, it will appear that for the most part he does not trouble you.

And that will actually be the truth because he won't need to. He will play your game, your nice little Christian formula. He will become your friendly jailer. You will be under his control. He won't need to attack. He'll already have you where he wants you. Behind bars. In the prison of already believing you have him largely under control.

BUT IF YOU DON'T PLAY HIS WAY HE WILL COME LOOKING FOR YOU.

If you ask for a conversation with God, the enemy comes looking for you. His designs on you are immediately vicious. He seeks to bring death, disease, discomfort, he wants to bring you broken heartedness, and tie you up in bonds.

He wants you to believe that you are not under attack at all, that I have not spoken to you and that your doubts about what I have said are simply logical and realistic thinking. 'Has God Said?'

Tell him. 'Yes! God has said'.

HIS WORLD STRATEGY REQUIRES THAT A MAN WHO SEEKS A CONVERSATION WITH ME IS SILENCED!

He knows that if you expect me to talk to you without any respect to your behaviour, that you are suddenly dangerous. You will begin immediately to unravel his lies, first in your own life but very quickly in the lives of those around you.

You and everyone you love are bound by his lies, that's all that's tied you down. Truth, the words I speak to you in conversation loosen the bonds. Truth is the opposite of lies. As light removes darkness, truth dissolves lies.

I see you Mark as a man sitting down on the ground with the bonds falling off, loose and starting to slip from your body.

I SEE YOU AGAIN AS A MAN RUNNING TOWARD MY ENEMY WITH DESTRUCTION ON YOUR MIND.

Destruction, tearing down, breaking of the enemy's walls and bonds and ruses. The bonds the enemy had around you are falling off. You grow stronger with every step you run, you charge at the enemy.

YOU HOLD YOUR SWORD IN YOUR MOUTH AS YOUR HANDS TEAR THE LAST BONDS FROM YOUR BODY.

As you run with excitement toward the fight, I see you anticipate the stroke of your sword, the thrust and twist. You bounce the sword from one hand to the other, feeling its balance, feeling its worth. Run! To battle! See yourself the way I see you. Restored, reunited, set free, strong, lethal. See yourself that way.

Why I choose you
Not the other way around

God I choose to believe you. Thanks. I don't know why we're having this relationship. Why you're talking to me so clearly, in so many conversations, every single day. It shouldn't be possible!

It's crazy. It's so close. It's so hard to believe. But I choose to believe you. I choose to tell the enemy to stand back as he comes to ruin this.

Are you saying, that you have chosen me, not the other way around?

Mark absolutely. That is exactly what I am saying. I am saying that to everyone on the planet. I have always said that.

IF A MAN THINKS HE HAS CHOSEN ME HE THINKS HE HAS THE UPPER HAND.

That encourages him to want to run our relationship at his own pace. If he thinks he did the choosing, he'll try to run the relationship too. I become a God that *he* chose, and so the medium through which he chose me, normally church, or a group of friends, becomes the medium through which he communicates with me.

The tool, the communication with God tool, is church or his friends. It happens a few times each week so that's when the most meaningful communication with me happens.

Furthermore if a man chose me then that says to his inner spirit that, a bit like if he pursued a woman and she was initially a bit standoffish, it says to his inner spirit that maybe he's only having this relationship because of his persistence and maybe God isn't as keen as he is himself about the relationship.

If he believes that, which many people do, he then assumes this is because of some sin, some failure on his part.

He knows that God is a fair and loving God, so assumes that if God's a bit standoffish then this must be because he himself has fallen short of my standards in some way.

Of course my enemy is very happy to assist him with this perception. The man accuses himself of not being worthy enough to talk to me and the enemy sees the weakness, and adds to the perception.

So in summary;

If a man chooses me he gets to determine the basis on which the relationship will be run, it is almost as though he has created me in his image and not the other way around.

But actually the real truth is; I pursue him and as a result I get to determine, or it should be me who gets to determine, the basis on which the relationship will be run. And that basis is grace, mercy, love, forgiveness and a Creator who runs to you.

Which is the second reason it's so important that I choose you, not the other way around.

If you think you chose me, you'll end up thinking it's you who runs after me, and because the enemy helps you to think this, you end up thinking that as you pursue me, I run from you. But that's not true. I am the father who runs to you.

I chose you and I keep choosing you. You're great.

You're the right choice for me.

'You did not choose me, but I chose you.'   JOHN 15:16 NIV

God said set my people
FREE!

What are you saying?

Mark listen. Listen carefully.

Ok then. What are you saying?

I am saying you are on track. The specific promises you believe I have said to you are actually the very things I am saying. You haven't got this wrong. You are hearing me loud and clear Mark, loud and clear.

If you listen carefully, if anyone listens carefully the things I am saying are clearly audible to the mind, heart and spirit. Clearly. As clearly as if I was standing before you.

ALTHOUGH MY VOICE IS NOT OFTEN HEARD BY THE HUMAN EAR, I AM EASILY HEARD BY THE SPIRIT.

So why is it seemingly difficult to hear my voice? In part this is because you are not used to listening with your spirit, so are often easily confused. That's alright.

Don't give up. Just practice. Practice like a child practices communicating with its parents. Because you are my son and I am your father.

You need to reach out, to push yourself a little to make contact with me, that's where faith comes in, nevertheless the moment you decide to listen, to do your best to hear me, you will find that your spirit quickly begins to decipher what is happening in the spirit world.

That's what's happening to you, and although your enemy strives constantly to persuade you that this is not true, it is.

You can hear me so clearly and so loudly and so accurately that you would be astounded. I'll say it again Mark, and actually I'll keep saying it over and over again as the truth of it becomes part of your daily experience, as it becomes more and more real for you. *'I care enough to respond to those who seek me.'* And *'I have not made myself hard to find, I do not play hide and seek.'*

I WANT EVERYONE WHO LISTENS TO ME TO REVEAL THE SECRET OF LISTENING TO OTHERS.

That's why you are getting the experience so powerfully and so first hand. You are privileged. You have been given the job of communication. First a direct communication with God. It's everyone's job, but many leave the job undone.

Secondly to communicate your conversation with God to people and third, but not at all least, to communicate to them how to have a similar conversation themselves.

That's the calling, that's the thing I want you to say, to make clear. That any man, woman or child can hear me clearly, almost frighteningly clearly.

JUST ASK AND I'LL SPEAK.

Practice, practice and more practice at whatever is the best way for you to hear. Don't wait for me to speak. Speak my answers back, by doing so you call down my voice, you exercise faith and without faith it is impossible to please me.

Use whatever version of this works for you: Speaking to me and speaking my voice back out loud. Writing to me and writing back my answers. Thinking to me in your mind and thinking my answers back.

Always take action rather than just waiting. Unless I specifically say to wait.

I want a revolution and I am going to get it, no one can hold back the work I am doing, I am raising up thousands to hear me, to hear me clearly and more and more often.

Even if what I say is not always for the sharing, the voice of God brings truth which sets you and those around you free. More and more truth being spoken absolutely clearly to thousands of hearts, enough to turn the world upside down.

That's what I want Mark. Thousands, millions of people hearing me speak clear and intelligible sentences in a constant conversation.

THERE IS A REVOLUTION COMING, CALL IT OUT!

Speak it out, put those around you on notice. It cannot be kept silent anymore. The spirit is moving Mark. Make it clear. Speak it out and tell those who do not want to be part of it to get out of the way for their own sake.

They do not want to find their own reluctance causing those who try it to stumble.

'If anyone causes one of these little ones--those who believe in me--to stumble, it would be better for them if a large millstone were hung around their neck and they were thrown into the sea'
MARK 9:42 NIV

This sounds serious and it is. Anyone who wants to come and hear me, they are my little ones. And anyone who tries to convince them that they cannot clearly hear my voice causes them to stumble. A warning to them, a caution to those who speak against the conversation. Don't do it. For your own sake don't.

The voice of God is coming, moving, rising up.

IF YOU DON'T WANT TO BE PART OF IT, JUST STEP ASIDE.

Miracles are coming. Mighty moves are coming. What you are seeing now is just the beginning.

I am wanting to be less demonstrative with the few who currently do signs and wonders, and be more real with many. I want my people set free. I want less of the signs, less of the theatrics that keep my people as an audience, and more speaking direct to their hearts individually.

I want individuals, on their own to realise the freedom I have for them. I am the God who feeds the five thousand.

I do not wait on kings, I do not feed just a few, I want my people, the throngs, the masses set free to speak with and to hear from me. I want millions in conversation with me everyday. Are you willing to help Mark?

Thousands, millions to hear from me but individually, not en masse, individually.

Sometimes all at once, sometimes one at a time. But I want my people set free and if those I call to spread the message are not prepared to do it I will raise up others. Are you ready?

I don't know Lord. I'd sure like to be, but only you know. Am I?

You are ready. So ready. I want you to get ready. Arm up, mount up, look about you, see where the harvest is ripe and ride there. Speak it out, tell others to hear my voice. Begin, call it out. Ask those closest to you for their help, input and commissioning.

You need others to help.

You need the insight of others to help you see where to ride and where to strike. Because striking is the word for this Mark. This is war. Why do you think your enemy seeks you out. This is war. I want you now to seek him out Mark, to put him to flight.

> *'Five of you will chase a hundred, and a hundred of you will chase ten thousand.'*   DEUT 32:30 NIV

IT IS NOT HARD TO HEAR MY VOICE, PEOPLE OVERCOMPLICATE IT.

They want it to be more difficult than it is. If you reach out and touch me, lay hold of my voice, and expect to hear me you will. Loud and clear. It is my promise from time immemorial.

> *'...seek and you will find...'*   MATT 7:7 NIV

What do people think this means?

WHAT DO THEY EXPECT TO FIND WHEN THEY SEEK ME?

A nice feeling? A sense of warmth? Wake up! If you seek God you are going to find God. This is something that has escaped people for centuries. Hidden, as it turns out, in plain sight.

Don't let this continue Mark, it is time for people to hear me clearly. To know that they can come to me for a conversation, can hear me that clearly. All they have to do is ask. They don't have to impress me. They are already acceptable. I made them acceptable. All by myself. It is time for my people to be set free.

The question I have for you is are you prepared to brave ridicule to speak this message out? Even if it's not popular

Yes. I guess I'll need your courage. And I think I'll need wisdom. I seem to hit people over the head with the message. Somehow I don't seem to understand how to give the message gently. I mess it up.

Don't panic. I'll give you the words to speak. If you listen, I'll tell you what to say, who to say it to, and how to say it. And I'll surround you with others with more gentleness. You'll need each other. You them, and them you.

I want people to hear my voice. In conversation. And I'm not accepting no anymore. Someone, many many someones are going to help me. Do you want to be just one of them?

I sure do. Man I do.

Mark let's put this subject up on the white board of your mind. Do you think for a moment that the bible is the end of my discussion with man? Do you think that nothing else is ever going to be clearly and reliably said by God? The bible itself explains that's obviously not the case.

'So faith comes from hearing and hearing through the WORD['rhematos': A thing spoken, a spoken word, made by the living voice] of Christ'. ROMANS 10:17 NIV

'Man shall not live on bread alone, but on every WORD ['Rheo': to speak, a spoken word made by the living voice] that comes from the mouth of God.' MATT 4:4 NIV

The bible itself needs my words spoken direct to your mind, to open it up. Anyone who claims differently does not understand the bible.

THE BIBLE IS THE TOOL TO HELP YOU DEFINE AND REFERENCE THE THINGS I SPEAK DIRECT TO YOUR HEART.

So, the point? The point is that you and whoever else wants to can hear from me, so clearly. You would be frightened if you realised how clearly. And why? It is a gift. A gift for all. *'My sheep hear my voice'.* Everyone hears it a bit, but anyone who wants to hear more clearly, can easily do so.

Just ask, just begin to believe I'm doing it *'I care enough to respond to those who seek me.'* And yes, I really do and will continue to speak clearly, despite behaviour to all who wish to listen.

CONVERSATION Fortythree

I am not you

And I'm not a product of your mind.
You're a product of mine.

Mark if I tell you to do, or believe a thing and it seems unlikely don't jump too quickly to conclusions.

DON'T JUDGE WHAT I SAY UNTIL YOU HAVE TRIED IT.

That's faith Mark. Stepping out. Making a choice to go where you are sure there is no hope. Making a choice to go there anyway, provided God has told you to.

When you are completely sure there is no hope in some course of action, and then God says I want you to do it anyway; do it. Believe me, not the evidence.

How will I know which things you really want me to do and believe for?

Conversation. Ask me and listen. Ask and write down, or speak out, or think out the answer.

AND DON'T TURN YOUR NOSE UP AT WHAT I SAY.

You'll be surprised, you'll often be amazed that the place you were sure there was no hope, is the very place that hope exists.

'We can make our plans, but the LORD determines our steps.'
PROVERBS 16:9 NLT

This is an important concept and it hangs on a passage in the bible that is often misunderstood.

'...my ways are higher than your ways.'
ISAIAH 55:9 NIV

You'll hear that verse preached and talked about in ways that separate me from people. God up here, you down there.

It gets used to make out that I am so far above you, and you so far beneath me that the gap is too vast to bridge. And although it is understood, in theory, that the gap is bridged by me and my love, nevertheless the picture is of a gap. A gap that says you're unworthy. The enemy nails that picture to the wall of your mind. With long, jagged, rusty nails.

I think you'll agree Mark that's not the purpose I had in mind. I went to a lot of trouble, trouble that included nails, to bridge that gap.

BUT AS IS OFTEN THE CASE, PEOPLE AND THE ENEMY USE THE BIBLE TO BRING DOWN NOT BUILD UP.

Because actually there is no gap at all. The bible makes that clear. Physically I am right where you are;

> *'I'm never out of your sight. You know everything I'm going to say before I start the first sentence. I look behind me and you're there, then up ahead and you're there, too—your reassuring presence, coming and going.'*   PSALM 139:4 MSG

And spiritually too, I am right where you are.

> *'Be strong and courageous. Do not be afraid or terrified because of them, for the LORD your God goes with you; he will never leave you nor forsake you.'*   DEUTERONOMY 31:6 NIV

So here's something I want you to do. I want you to open up the truths of the bible to those who say that although God never leaves us, we leave him. I beg your pardon? I pursue you Mark, you can't leave me.

IF YOU LEAVE ME I COME TOO.

I'm always there. I walk with you, I follow after you, I woo you. How on earth can I be constantly drawing you in, no matter what the state of your heart, if I stand still and let you wander away? I pursue, I run to you, I am always there. I do not stand and wait for you to come back, I pursue you. I come with you.

Now back to that passage that says *'my ways are higher than yours'.* Those words were written to show you that, if you try to listen to me, have a walking talking 'relationship relationship' with me then you are going to come face to face with the fact that I am not you.

I AM *NOT* CREATED IN YOUR IMAGE.

I thought you up. Not the other way around. I am not part of a formula. I'm God. I've got my own thoughts. I've got a whole bunch of stuff going on that you don't know anything about. And when you start asking me questions you're going to start hearing things that don't make much sense, to you, but make an awful lot of sense to me.

Why? I know things and think things that you don't. I'm not you.

'My thoughts are higher than your thoughts.'   ISAIAH 55:9 NIV

I've got plans that you don't know about, but I need you to be part of.

It's the nature of being God, and being a completely separate being from you. And the only way you can hope to know what I'm thinking is to ask me!

Because I speak into your mind, then it can seem that I'm a product of your mind. But I'm not. You're a product of mine.

I DON'T FIT WITH AND AM NOT A PRODUCT OF YOUR THOUGHTS.

I've been thinking thoughts, all by myself, without any help from you for billions of years.

And I will still be doing so after you've gone. I'm separate Mark. Not an extension of you. People think they understand this, but actually, they don't. Their responses, reactions and choices show they don't understand it at all.

It's why I made it clear right at the beginning of the bible. It's a foundation principle, and written there for a purpose; *'God said let us make man in our image'.*

One of the reasons I made sure it was included in the bible is to show you that I am not an extension of your thinking. I am not created in your image.

THE UNIVERSE, AND ALL THAT'S IN IT, IS ABOUT ME. NOT YOU, ME.

You don't have to feel condemned or told off, I'm simply pointing out a fact, and really drilling down into the concept because it's so fundamental to a walking talking 'relationship relationship' with me.

When I tell you something that doesn't make sense, that goes against what you had thought to be the truth, it brings crashing into your reality the fact that God is not just an extension of your thoughts.

It reminds you that God exists outside your space and time. I'm not a lucky dip box filled with blessings for whatever it is that you want. Although I bless your plans where I can without upsetting the balance of creation, I am primarily involved in bringing about my own plans. Not yours.

My plans, which are always for your good, are often completely outside of, and different from what you had in mind.

In his heart a man plans his course, but the LORD determines his
steps.   PROVERBS 16:9 NIV

Why go on about this Mark? Simple.

You cannot have a 'relationship relationship' with me if you allow the enemy to persuade you that mine is a 'quiet existence', primarily in your mind. He wants you to feel that I don't exist quite so dramatically, not so pervasively, right in your face and outside of your mind. He's wrong. And he knows it.

IF YOU FALL FOR THAT LIE YOU WILL STAY IN CONTROL
OF OUR RELATIONSHIP AND BASE IT ON YOUR OWN
WORLD PICTURE. NOT MINE.

You'll have no concept that God wants to turn up and talk to you, in your everyday life, on a day to day basis, just like your family, friends, team and clients do. And that when he does turn up and talk, (every day), he is going to say things that are foreign to you, new ideas, things that don't always fit with what you know. Things that make you worry and search the scriptures and realize that you didn't understand the bible as well as you thought.

Because you don't. Very few do. Do you get that?

If you're not in conversation with me you can't understand the bible, no matter how studiously you learn it. Just ask the Pharisees. And not only that, but you need to remember that this concept is a corner stone of faith.

The book says of Abraham that *'he went to a country that wasn't his, when he left he had no idea where he was going'.* That's what faith is about, it's why Abraham is called *'the Father of faith'.*

HE HAD NO IDEA OF WHERE HE WAS GOING.

And yet I kept giving him the picture as he proceeded. You'll hear it said that I only talked to Abraham about 15 times. Use your common sense Mark! If every conversation between Abraham and I was recorded it would fill a library. What you read in the book are, obviously, only the conversations recorded in the book.

The enemy wants you to think that because Abraham had no idea where he was going, that faith is some sort of vague marching out blind. The enemy is not an expert on faith. He has none.

I TOLD ABRAHAM TO GO, I TOLD HIM THE EXACT STEPS TO TAKE.

He didn't know the exact destination, but he knew step after step where to go.

Do you want to argue with that? Others will challenge you about it.

Well, ummm I don't think it says that in the bible, so how can I be sure I'm not just making that bit up?

Simple. I told him when to start and stop. It didn't happen by accident. Think about this Mark; the bible also only records a small number of conversations between Abraham and Sarah. Do you honestly think that what's in the book is the sum total of the number of times they talked?

Well God lots of people think you directed his steps in that vague 'he just knew' kind of way that some modern Christians seem to think you talk to us?

THEY'RE WRONG. THE BIBLE MAKES IT CLEAR I SPOKE TO ABRAHAM IN WORDS HE COULD UNDERSTAND.

He didn't have a vague impression of what I was saying and then just walk out in blind faith. HE. HEARD. ME. SPEAK. Clearly.

'The LORD had said to Abram, 'Go from your country, your people and your father's household to the land I will show you. I will make you into a great nation, and I will bless you.'' GEN 12:1-2 NIV

I spoke to him in full sentences he could understand. And in case anyone wanted to question that, I had some of those sentences recorded in the bible. Indisputably there.

Abraham was called, he got instructions, he heard me speak. I told him to move out. And I told him one step after another where to go.

Unless you'd like to suggest that the verse I've quoted twice this morning didn't apply to Abraham. *'A man plans his way but the Lord directs his steps.'*

Abraham knew I had spoken. He decided to believe that I exist, and that I care enough to respond to those who seek me.

He was entering into a 'relationship relationship' with me. He'd heard me. He didn't know where he was going, but he did know the steps I told him to take.

There are times when I tell you the destination and then later show you the path to get there. I give you the path step by step. Other times I show you the path, but you are not sure, because I haven't told you yet, where the path is going.

But make no mistake, I will tell you. Listen, and I will.

So Mark don't turn your nose up at my plans and instructions, they really are good. When you hear me say or promise a thing, even if it seems hopeless, go with it.

'If God says it's okay, it's okay.'   ACTS 10:15 MSG

GOD WILL SPEAK TO YOU LIKE THIS TOO IF YOU WANT

Want to try your own conversation with God? Go to the page immediately following the contents page. Or go to page 243

CONVERSATION
Forty Four

You will have trouble in the world

But the world itself isn't trouble, quite the opposite.

Father you really do speak to me totally clearly don't you?

Yes Mark I do. This isn't you making it up, I'm speaking to you.

Thanks God. You're so amazing. So close. The answer to loneliness. That negative thought just then, the thought that said 'that's not God talking'; was that just my own natural, soulish thinking or was it evil?

Mark you know now that it was the enemy.

HE'S SO SUBTLE YET NOT VERY SUBTLE AT ALL.

That's the dynamic I want you to see this morning Mark. I made it clear in the book.

'In this world you will have trouble.' JOHN 16:33 NIV

What I want to do this morning is explain a bit about that, because many people have misunderstood it. I want you to clarify it for anyone who is interested.

Trouble comes when you are in the world. But I didn't mean that silly religious idea that the world is 'dirty' and because of that you have trouble. That's not what I meant at all.

Trouble does not actually belong in the world. The earth was not made for trouble, quite the opposite.

Trying to get humans to understand this concept is difficult for a very simple reason. You were created to run the world with me, to steward, tend, organize and improve the place. So your enemy is absolutely committed to making sure that doesn't happen.

And when I say 'run the world' I don't mean I want my people to boss others around. The way to 'reign with Christ' is to serve those around you.

LOTS OF CHRISTIANS THINK THE WORLD IS TROUBLE.
But that's their idea, not mine, something the enemy has tricked them into thinking. Lots of Christians have been hoodwinked into thinking that they don't really belong here because they are destined for something much nicer.
They are, eventually.

BUT RIGHT NOW THEY ARE DESTINED TO BE HERE. ON EARTH.
And it's a fantastic place to be. Not a bad place. A really really good place.

'The earth is the Lord's, and everything in it.'   I COR 10:26 NIV

You are destined to do and enjoy, in miniature version, the same things on earth as you are in heaven. Earth is a practice run. A great place!

MY PLANS FOR YOU START RIGHT HERE.
And to rule and reign on earth, which actually means to serve, you need to take part in, be comfortable in, love this world and the people in it.

I get that God. I like it. But what about that verse that says something like *'those who love the world are God's enemies'*? **How does that fit??**

That's talking about loving the world system. Not the creation, but the system the enemy has set up. Selfishness, greed etc. Adoring it, serving it, wanting to follow its decree. I'm not talking about that.

I'm talking about loving the world, the earth, the physical time and space, people, interaction, work, life. Loving that.

As I did and still do right up until this minute. *'For God so loved the world that he gave his only son...'*

The point I am making right now, in real time, just in case you thought you were making this up, is this; the world is good. Not evil, good.

TROUBLE WILL COME BUT IT DOESN'T BELONG HERE.
I want my people to shake off the lie that the world, time and space, people, the process of interaction and living together in the world is somehow bad. It's not. It's good.

'God saw all that he had made, and it was very good.' GEN 1:31 NIV

Look around you; sky, earth, trees, grass, leaves; walls, windows, ceilings. Things I have made and things I have inspired humans to make as copies of what I have done. If you had just arrived from nothingness would you think this looked like a negative place? Of course not, the place looks wonderful! Not evil. Wonderful!! For goodness sake, the bible says that what you see 'declares the glory of God.'

THINGS LOOK TO BE GOOD AND GETTING BETTER.
That's the dynamic Mark. I've designed a positive world, a world designed to accommodate and make possible even more positive things. Plenty of time and space for humans to love, receive love, to create and to enjoy my creation. Not only that but to enjoy their own and others' creations. A great place.

EVERY DAY I SAY THIS IS A GREAT PLACE!
The point this morning? Many points actually, just hearing me speak is healing you Mark, but the key point of this conversation, let's stick with that, is if the world is a great place, it stands to reason that positivity, goodness, hope, are what the world is about.

And, if that's true, it also stands to reason that the person who created the world is positive too. It stands to reason that I'm positive. I'm serious about goodness, hope, encouragement, happiness, joy and love.

IF I'M SERIOUS ABOUT BEING POSITIVE, ABOUT GOODNESS AND HOPE, THEN WHERE DO NEGATIVE THOUGHTS COME FROM?
If a negative thought enters your mind, then it's almost guaranteed that it had its root in hell. It's either come from evil to you by circuitous route, handed down, from one hand to another, or it has come straight from hell this moment.

You need to understand a thing or two about your enemy.

He does not understand or care for a fair fight. The 'Earl of Queensbury Rules' mean nothing to him.

THE ENEMY HAS ONLY ONE RULE WHEN HE FIGHTS. DEATH. YOURS.

He has only one aim in mind when he fights, and he is always fighting. He wants you destroyed. His focus is your total and complete annihilation. Don't forget it.

This is how it works. You listen to me, you hear something I'm saying and you're increasingly confident as we speak that it really is me; then suddenly you find you are not so sure after all.

When that happens it's negative, it's 'trouble' and although you will have trouble in the world, it doesn't belong here.

If it's trouble you can be sure it has only one source, it comes from him. He hates you! And because it comes from him you can also be sure that it is a carefully thought out attempt, albeit seemingly innocent, to destroy you.

IT DOESN'T FEEL LIKE DESTRUCTION BECAUSE HE HAS TO ENTICE YOU TO YOUR OWN DESTRUCTION WITH LIES.

He must start every enticement with something subtle, and cloying. Nevertheless, anything negative, anything that contradicts something you've heard me speak to you, a promise I have made to you personally, anything that contradicts it is his lie. It is not a 'gentle reminder from reality'.

It is an out and out attempt to destroy you. It starts out soft, but that's where it's going. It's a carefully thought out attempt to destroy you.

A relationship across the room
is no relationship at all

Father shall I type this morning about that concept you showed me yesterday while I was working? Or should I do that another time?

Mark write it down now, speak it out, time is short.

Ok I think what you told me was that our relationship with our wife or husband is like a picture of modern Christianity. Is that right?

Absolutely. A very similar picture.

It's like this; Modern Christianity is about trying to have a relationship with God. A person's life is often about trying to have a relationship with their husband or wife. There are some striking comparisons and similarities. That's because you're human. I made you that way. Which means the way you relate to anyone, human or God, will be similar.

Let's look at some principles, some key concepts and comparisons. For a start it's very difficult to have a relationship with your husband or wife unless you're determined to press on, stay committed, never give up, always believe for the best.

Love is like that. When you think there is evidence you are loved, all of a sudden they draw back. You wait, you struggle, the pain of believing in the relationship is sometimes unbearable. Even if you keep yourself open to their love and don't take offense, don't build walls of hurt, the waiting for your love to be returned can still seem fruitless and pointless.

And so it is for modern Christians, they receive promises both from the bible, the pulpit and direct to their hearts and minds that they can have a relationship with me.

But for those serious about me, the journey is difficult.

They press in, it seems encouraging, then all of a sudden the cares of the world pop up and they forget to press in, or the enemy clouds the communication. And when they stumble about trying to re-establish the connection the king of lies tells them their sin has sent me scurrying off like a frightened rat.

That's a lie Mark. A commonly held lie. It's all part of this 'the Holy Spirit is a gentleman' idea. People need to read what the book says about that and stop jumping to popularly held, non-biblical perceptions.

In the book I am the one Jesus called 'The Friend', or 'The Comforter'. It is my job to comfort you.

I don't need you to comfort me.

I don't need you to protect me from your sin. Your sin doesn't scare me. I see past it. I love you, I comfort you.

A key reason humans need comfort is the result of sin. When sin causes discomfort I come to reassure, to woo, to mend. I am not some prude who must run from sin. I don't run from it, I remove it.

The enemy has convinced so many that the most important part of Christianity is repetitive process. Church services, church group meetings, bible study, quiet times and so on. Those things, if compared to your relationship with your husband or wife, are like going to barbecues and parties with them. Fun, but imagine trying to maintain a strong and deep relationship with her if your most intimate communication is at parties and barbecues, and other public meetings. Everything you did together would seem clinical. It would lack spontaneity. That's what happens for so many who are trying to love me. Their relationship with me is mostly public. It lacks private spontaneity.

So many people have a 'party relationship' with me.

They see me from afar, across the room, there's the odd touch, the brief glance, they know I'm in the room, they take solace from that.

They see me smile across the room, they smile back. *'But Lord Lord didn't we prophecy in your name?' 'I'm sorry, I never knew you.'*

If someone doesn't speak out about this soon, thousands will discover that I never knew them, and that they never knew me.

A RELATIONSHIP ACROSS THE ROOM IS NO RELATIONSHIP AT ALL.

Think for a minute about the Jews, they are 'My People'. I have named them that for centuries. Will every Jew stand before me in loving and intimate relationship? Of course not. 'My people' is a term that signifies a contractual arrangement, an agreement, it does not guarantee automatic and deep relationship. The same goes for modern Christianity. There is a contractual arrangement, an agreement.

The reality can only come from relationship and relationship comes from communication. There must be a conversation with me. If you are my sheep you hear my voice.

THERE IS NO RELATIONSHIP WITHOUT COMMUNICATION, ONLY A CONTRACTUAL ARRANGEMENT.

And so it is with a man and a woman. So often there is a contractual arrangement, but no relationship, no communication at the depth there is meant to be. But that can be changed. It's not easy, it takes excruciating effort, but it is possible. It's all to do with communication. Listening without prejudice, without taking offense. And so it is in a relationship with me.

A relationship with me, at its deepest level, is not a feeling of my presence.

You feel the presence of a woman at dinner on your first date. That's not a relationship. The conversation over many days, an ever-increasing exchange of thoughts and understanding, that's a relationship.

When a couple believe in me, listen to me and I draw them together they will hear me make many promises to them about their relationship. Promises that astound and humble them.

My question to that couple, any couple I draw together is this, are you going to reach out and believe and absolutely accept as gospel the promises I made to you? Are you going to live those promises, together?

I have made and am continuing to make thousands of promises to the modern church. They hear them, they like them, my fresh promises make them feel warm and encouraged. But they don't live them. I promise that *'I stand at the door and knock and if any man will open the door I will come in and eat with him, and him with me'.* Tell me truthfully, do you come across many who actually converse with me?

No. In fact even some Christian leaders tell me you can't have a 'God said/you've said' conversation. That I'm deceived for thinking that I can.

Well Mark, a conversation is what happens when you open the door to someone and they come in and sup with you. A conversation starts.

A PERSONAL, TALKING BACK AND FORWARD CONVERSATIONAL RELATIONSHIP.

Do you see that happening? The problem is that although they hear the promises, my people don't grab hold of them. The promises sound good, but too spiritual to really grab hold of.

Christians need to take hold of what I am saying to them.

And what am I saying to them? In short; I live, I'm not a distant reality, I'm not an 'across the room God', and I don't want that kind of relationship. Meet with me, one on one. What I want is a conversation. All day. Not a religious commitment to more 'quiet times'.

SUP WITH ME. BELIEVE THAT YOU CAN TALK, BACK AND FORWARD WITH ME.

That's all. Talk back and forward with the Creator of the universe all day, sit down and sup with him, and him with you, and your entire life will change. Tell my people that. They think that verse is about salvation, it's not. Salvation is the door, not the house. It's about me and them. Together. 'Supping'. A conversation.

And remind them the verse was written to Christians. Christians who had become lukewarm.

What am I doing here?

This whole existence, life, the universe; it's all about love. Yes really. Love.

Lord I don't know why you put up with me, why you pursue me.

Because I love you Mark. Pure and simple. That's what this is all about. This isn't religion, isn't about going to church. That can come as part of enjoying me but it's not what this is relationship with me is about.

Good one God! There goes any hope I had of putting this into a book.

Why?

The book is your idea remember. It is isn't it?

Yes. What's the problem?

Well with you saying that a relationship with you is more important than church, it will make plenty of people want to throw this book in the bin.

You're going to be very surprised at what happens. And anyway I said church can come as part of enjoying me. But the relationship comes first. The point is simple. I've had enough of your rules about how often to go to church, read the bible, have a personal prayer time. Rules, rules and more rules. No more rules Ok Mark? I get to decide how often you do those things. Not you. Me.

I CAME TO SET YOU FREE, NOT TO TIE YOU UP.

The relationship with me comes first. After that come the trappings. Church, bible reading etc are great in their place, but they are not what I came to make possible. I came for a relationship. Those things are some of the results of the relationship. But they are not the relationship itself. How have I told you any relationship is built?

By listening to each other.

Exactly. I want you to listen to me. That's what I want you to tell people.

How do I tell them?

Start with these conversations. People are reading them. More and more people. And that will lead you to other opportunities to demonstrate How to have a conversation with me. Urge others who know how to do it to demonstrate it too.

THERE ARE NO RULES OTHER THAN RELATIONSHIP. RELATIONSHIP WITH ME IS THE ONLY RULE.

Get rid of every rule that doesn't fit with that.

'One of their religion scholars spoke for them, posing a question they hoped would show him up: 'Teacher, which command in God's Law is the most important?' Jesus said, "Love the Lord your God with all your passion and prayer and intelligence.' This is the most important, the first on any list. But there is a second to set alongside it: 'Love others as well as you love yourself.' These two commands are pegs; everything in God's Law and the Prophets hangs from them.' MATT 22:34-36 MSG

There are not meant to be rules about when you should go to church, or how often you're meant to read the bible. I'll tell you when to go, when to read, how often, how much. But you've got a problem with that too haven't you?

Yes. Many people will feel very uncomfortable with that. They know they don't hear you clearly enough to confidently say to their pastor 'God told me not to come last week.' And a comment like that will get them offside with the pastor, he will advise against it, see it as unreliable. Some will go as far as saying it's satanic.

Yes they will. Some. Let them. But plenty of people will feel set free too. Church can be great. But a relationship with me is more important. People are starting to crave that relationship more than church.

I want them to find me on their own, and then take me to church with them.

The pastors won't like that at first, but a congregation who bring God, rather than come looking for him, will make the lives of church leaders much easier. It will see them able at last to achieve what they dreamt might be possible.

A REVOLUTION IS COMING, PEOPLE WILL LISTEN TO GOD, NOT MAN.

People are sensing that a relationship with me is not conditional on the amount of times they go to church. I am not a God who talks to you more if you go to church more. Let me decide how often you go. Many people will feel the bonds fall off when they read those words.

Now. Let's talk about personal prayer times. Prayer has come to mean something it wasn't meant to. That's changing for those who join this revolution.

Oh oh. What do you mean?

You know exactly what I mean. This exchange we're having right now. This will be typical. People who join the revolution won't do all that religious, quiet, spiritual, pious praying. They will converse with me. Back and forward. That *is* the revolution.

Many people have a closer relationship with their dog than they have with me.

Oh great God. I might as well just press delete right now. A book with that kind of comment in it, a book that suggests that God said that, is going to be the biggest flop ever.

That remains to be seen Mark. You're going to have to find out. Press on, publish and find out. Prayer, for millions, has become a 'religion of one'. It's about as unfulfilling. They do it on their own, and yet it seems as predictable as religion.

MOST PEOPLE DO NOT EXPECT TO HEAR ME SPEAK, BACK AND FORWARD IN CONVERSATION WHEN THEY PRAY ALONE.
Of course they don't expect it. It doesn't happen.

That's changing. I want people to know that this is not about a process, or even a culture. This is about a relationship, and that relationship is because, first and foremost, I love you. I want to be with you, near you, around you.

I GENUINELY LOVE YOU. IN SIMILAR WAYS TO THE WAY YOU LOVE ANOTHER PERSON.
Only on an infinite scale. I want you to think about how you would love someone. What you do when you are in love with someone. You want to give to them, do things for them. I am no different. Actually it's the other way around.

YOUR LOVE IS A COPY OF MINE, YOU LOVE LIKE I DO ONLY ON A SMALLER SCALE.
That's what this is all about. I love you. That's all it's about. I pursue you. I am with you, around you, talking to you, asking you questions, answering yours. I am looking for things I can do for you. And Mark with regard to that, I am in the middle of a masterpiece of blessing for you. I am painting a blessing for you that, when finished, will cause others to gasp. They will be astounded at the blessing I have created for you. And why am I doing that? For the simple reason that I love you. That's all. Because I love you. *'How much more will your father in heaven give good gifts to those he loves'.*

So back to the love thing. How do you feel about someone when you love them?

I want to do things for them.

Exactly. Nothing is good enough unless it's the best. You want to give them extravagant gifts, you want to take away pain, you'd rather have the pain yourself.

'by his wounds we are healed.'   ISAIAH 53:5 NIV

This whole story; the universe, it's not about some big process.

IT'S JUST ABOUT BEING IN LOVE.
Love that strong, is something that existed in the universe before

a single man or woman set foot on earth. It was us, Father, Son and Holy Spirit. We were in love. That's a little 'touchy feely' for some. A bit like the discomfort children feel when they see their parents show affection for each other. But it's not bad. It's fantastic.

GOD; FATHER, SON AND HOLY SPIRIT, IN LOVE WITH EACH OTHER.

You've got this huge universe, all the intricate systems we have put in place for its structure and its management, yet the entire thing is all about us being in love.

Let that sink in. As children need to see their parents are in love, humans are safe, secure and find meaning when they see that we, the three of us, the mighty ones, actually love each other. Yes. We love each other.

Your spirit has been designed and built to know that all is well, that you are safe when you see we love each other. When you see gentleness, care, concern, giving, desire for the best, happiness, warmth, encouragement. When you see those things are the founding principles of the universe, you know in your spirit that all is well. You know then for sure, that you yourself are loved. *Really loved.*

WE ARE REALITY.

Our love is reality. You can trust us. With us is love and trust and wholeness. The world is founded on that. The world is all about that. Your enemy and mine has done his best to mess that picture up.

HE'S LIKE A SPOILED CHILD WHO STEALS HIS BROTHER'S PRESENT.

Not having received the present himself, the world in this case, Satan steals it away from the one who it was given to (you, mankind) and then taunts you, by hurting and maiming your gift, the present that is rightfully yours.

He has convinced you that the gift is not even for you, is not even really a gift. Instead he tells you that the world is a mess, evil and has no meaning.

He lies. The earth is a gift. Your life is a gift. We do not need it. We do not need the earth, the universe, your existence. We built it and gave it to you as a gift, just for the simple reason that we love you. We really love you. No holds barred love you. Head over heels love you.

WE CREATED THE UNIVERSE AS A PLACE TO LOVE US.
That's all this about Mark. It's about love. It's the Beatles song;

'ALL YOU NEED IS LOVE, LOVE, LOVE IS ALL YOU NEED'.
That's what the whole universe is about. Love. We love you Mark. Don't overcomplicate the issues. That planet you can see in the night sky? It's there because of love. Just remember. Love. Every situation, every conversation, everything. Remember love. Think God is love. Always ask yourself what is God saying, (God who is love), what is he saying right now in this very moment?

SEE OTHERS, SEE YOURSELF THROUGH GOD'S LOVE GLASSES.
It sounds airy fairy, but trust me Mark, try it, listen and I will teach you how.

Love. Not a religion, not a system, not a process. I turned up this morning, as I always do, because I love you. I want to be with you. I want to help you. I want to encourage you. I love you Mark. Get used to it. Believe it. Right now, real time, love.

That's me, the Creator of the universe, the One True God, the Great Spirit, the I AM. Yes me. I love you. Just you. I'm hanging about. Not gentle Jesus meek and mild, although that is true too, but not the nice 'Jesusy' sort of Jesus in the Sunday school pictures.

But right now, right here, in the room, with all my majesty, my train filling the room; high and lifted up sure, but also right here, down here beside you. Can you get that?

'In the year that King Uzziah died, I saw the Lord, high and exalted, seated on a throne; and the train of his robe filled the temple.'
ISAIAH 6:1 NIV

The universe was created so that I could put you on it and love you. And you love me back. A conversation. A relationship. Not a way of life, or a process, or even a culture. But a relationship, just you and me. A conversation, just us. You up for that?

Sure am God.

The enemy's war plan is to convince you there isn't a war

He wants to distract you from the real war with little decoy skirmishes.

Father did you just say that you want to talk to me about the enemy? About the fact that you do not let him attack me in any force greater than I am able to push back?

Yes.

That you've governed his strength so he can't attack me with any more force than I can cope with? And it's a day by day thing? He's never allowed to attack me with any more strength than I myself have on that day?

Yes. Absolutely.

> 'No test or temptation that comes your way is beyond the course of what others have had to face. All you need to remember is that God will never let you down; he'll never let you be pushed past your limit; he'll always be there to help you come through it.'
> I COR 10:13 MSG

Let's just look at that word 'temptation'. Your enemy focuses your thinking on feeling guilty for and trying to overcome small sins, dirty sins, embarrassing sins.

IGNORE HIM!

He wants to focus your attention on what to do about those difficult, hard to manage, habitual sins; anger, laziness, your thought life and so on.

All of them are things I want to clean up if you let me. But life is not a test to see if you can overcome them in your own strength. That's not what this Christian walk is about. He tricks you into thinking that fighting little sins is what Christianity is about. But that's a lie. A religious lie.

He wants you focused on what he says is your poor performance in those areas. He taunts you. He says that your little sins create a gap between you and me.

HE LIES. THERE IS NO GAP BETWEEN US.

You are acceptable just the way you are. Acceptable enough to die for.

The enemy tells you there's a gap between us and that you'll never bridge it.

He says you're too sinful. Religion makes you feel the same, but tells you the opposite, which just makes you feel even more confused and condemned.

There's no gap between us Mark. I'm right here. You'll find that if you just listen to me the little sins will eventually fall off. You've seen it yourself with anger and rejection.

In these last few difficult years, as you've had to listen to me to avoid having a breakdown, you've found that anger and rejection have grown far weaker, and less able to distract you. At a time when everyone expected them to grow stronger in your life, listening to me has made them weaker.

THE MORE YOU LISTEN THE MORE YOUR BAD HABITS WILL FALL OFF.

But don't rush. It takes a life time. It's not something you have to sort out today.

The enemy has distorted the word 'temptation' until he has made it appear to be primarily about naughty little sins because he wants you focused on those things. He wants you trying to overcome them in your own strength.

But Mark I fix those things. You can't. If Paul had trouble, you will too.

'For I do not do the good I want to do, but the evil I do not want to do—this I keep on doing.'   ROMANS 7:19 NIV

The enemy uses religion to make you feel guilty for and try to overcome those sins so he can walk unnoticed into your life and hit you with the real temptation, the one that really will keep you helpless and in chains.

HIS REAL TEMPTATION IS TO GET YOU TO THINK I AM DISTANT. BUSY. GRIEVED BY SINS YOU CAN'T OVERCOME.

That a conversation with me is not possible. He lies.

His real temptation is to get you to stop believing that the reason you were put on earth is a back and forward relationship with me. A constant conversation with God. He wants to tempt you into thinking that I don't really care enough to respond to you, whenever you want, as a man talks to his friend.

> 'he [the holy spirit] will expose the error of the godless world's view of sin, righteousness, and judgment: He'll show them that their refusal to believe in me is their basic sin'   JOHN 16:8 MSG.

He wants you to think that you are too sinful. And that God doesn't get involved at a 'you said/God said' level. He wants you to think that the impression that I'm saying something from time to time, and the feeling of my presence on Sundays is about the level of involvement you should expect from me.

A subtle lie.

YOU HAVE BEEN TAUGHT I AM NEAR, BUT YOU HAVE NOT BEEN TAUGHT STEPS FOR A CONVERSATION WITH ME.

You have been taught that if you are less sinful, more committed to church and read your bible more you will hear me. Or that God might be testing your faith by staying silent. That has happened in history, but it's not often true.

Following rules is not going to help you hear me more. The way to hear me is to believe that I will speak, then ask me to do so and listen for what I say. 'Those who come to God must believe that he exists and (believe) that he cares enough to respond to those who seek him.'

Grabbing a pen or a computer and writing down what you think I am saying, or speaking it out or even thinking it out helps.

Christians often feel my presence on Sundays but it is not normal for them to converse with me. In fact those who try it are seen as a bit strange, super-spiritual.

That sure is what a lot of people think about me. I would have thought the same a few years back.

The impression that many people have is that it's up to them to live a good godly life during the day. That they should pray and read their bible when they get a chance, and attend meetings. And if they ever do hear from me, meetings is where it's most likely to happen.

The impression is that I am watching, and although I might give you strength, or a bit of blessing when you really need it, for the most part it's up to you to pray each day and then get on with your day trusting that whatever happens will be directed by me.

Take this morning for instance, getting this conversation out and onto the page is like pulling teeth. It doesn't seem to be flowing. You feel like you can't hear me.

That's him. He's telling you that you're not really hearing me. Every word I speak, he's shouting at you that I'm not. Others reading this can see it's me, but as you type it your enemy is shouting that it's not. He's afraid of the power you receive when you hear me, and you are hearing me.

THIS IS ME LOUD AND CLEAR. YOU'RE HEARING ME!

Little habitual, 'naughty' sins don't even interest him. He keeps telling you how bad you are for doing those things because he wants you to be so distracted fighting them that you never end up feeling good enough about yourself to listen to me. He knows that the moment we have a conversation, you'll be dangerous.

A PERSON WHO HAS A CONVERSATION WITH ME CHANGES.

He wants to convince you there isn't really any big battle going on, other than what he pretends is a big battle. Little sins.

He wants to convince you that I'm not speaking to you. That's his main battle. It's a full frontal attack, that doesn't seem like an attack at all. An all day long attempt to get you to think that you're not in conversation with God. He tells you that God is not interested in, or if he is interested, can't have a conversation with you because you're too 'sinful'.

Rubbish. I'm talking to you now and you've got heaps of issues unresolved in your life. Heaps. Frankly they're less important to me than having a conversation. This talking back and forward is the reason I created you.

He casts doubt. Have a look at what he did with Eve, he hasn't changed. He asked her *'Yes but has God really said?'* He takes a thing that I have said to you, a promise I have made specifically, individually to you and casts doubt on that. Something I've said straight to your mind. It might be something I have said to you about your family or your job.

Those promises are the most powerful because they come direct from me to you. And almost as important as the specific thing promised, is the fact that the promise reminds you I am talking, specifically, just to you. That I am real, concerned and involved in your life minute by minute. That I am interested in you. That I love you, in a warm, accepting, not judging way that you can actually relate to. Your enemy gets special pleasure out of casting doubt on those personal promises.

So, back to your original question.

Yes. I wanted to know if I had really heard you say this morning that you never let him through in any force greater than I can manage?

The answer is yes. That's what I said to you this morning. He cannot attack you in a force that is any greater than you can manage. Any lie he tells you, is no stronger than you are that day. You are just as strong as that lie. Otherwise, I wouldn't let it through.

CAN YOU IMAGINE HOW INFURIATING THAT IS FOR HIM?
But he is cunning. Knowing he can only destroy you with lies, he has spent thousands of years perfecting his ability to do just that.

HIS MAIN LIE IS THAT I AM NOT SPEAKING. 'HAS GOD SAID?'
Mark if that's his main lie, what do you think the truth really is?

That you are speaking to me?

Yes. I am. He tells you that the things I am clearly and gently saying to you are not me. Things like *'I love you Mark'. 'I do not condemn you, don't worry about that thing, or this.' 'I am going to do this for you, or bring that to pass for you.'* Things like *'Say this to that person',* or *'Don't say anything just listen to what this person is saying and I will show you what to say next.'*

He pretends to be me and tells you I can't look at you because you're sinful, but that if you focus on overcoming all those persistent little sins that I will be able to accept you again.

THAT'S NOT ME, I DON'T SPEAK LIKE THAT, IT'S HIM PRETENDING TO BE ME.

He wants you to think that the battle is about the little sins you find so hard to manage. He wants you to keep fighting skirmishes with an enemy who is seemingly impossible to overcome. He's got you focused on those little things, making them seem like the main battle. But actually they're a decoy. He does it so he can fight the real battle without any interference from you. The real battle is to convince you that I am not talking to you and that you cannot hear me. And that I do not want to converse with you. And that even if I did, you'd be too sinful.

THIS SHOULD HAVE BEEN OBVIOUS.

The bible that some say takes away the need for conversation with me actually states the opposite.

The bible makes it absolutely clear that Satan's entire battle is to suggest that I do not speak. That you and I cannot converse. People who encourage others not to hear from me, who speak against a conversation with me have no excuse. The bible removes their excuse.

To make it clear for them I had it recorded in the very beginning of its pages. The account of what Satan said to Eve. He suggested to her that I had not really spoken, that I was not talking plainly and clearly with her and Adam. *'Has God really said?'*

The way he started the fight is the way he will continue it. The battle the enemy brings to you is to tell you that I am not speaking. And that even if I am, you cannot hear me.

HE KNOWS THAT IF YOU CAN'T HEAR WE HAVE NO RELATIONSHIP.

Many people don't understand this. But he does. If you and I do not have a conversation we do not have the relationship you were born for. It makes a mockery of salvation and the cross. That's his aim.

He knows that human beings cannot have a relationship without conversation; constant communication, back and forward.

Satan's lie is to convince you that conversation with me is not necessary, or even possible. He tells you that I have not said the things that I have said, specifically, to you.

SATAN WANTS TO CONVINCE YOU THAT I DON'T OFTEN TALK TO YOU.

If he can convince you of that then he can keep you in prison. He doesn't much mind if the prison is a religious one or has godly overtones. Provided he can keep you cut off from experiencing real conversation with me, then he is happy.

And he has an easy job, because you have not been taught how to listen.

PEOPLE WHO HAVEN'T BEEN TAUGHT HOW TO LISTEN TO ME, ARE NOT GOING TO HEAR ME SPEAK VERY OFTEN.

They don't know how. They're not confident they can. Listening to me isn't a habit.

He tells you that you don't hear from me very often because of your sin. He tells you that your little sins cut you off from hearing my voice. He lies!

THE SIN THAT CUTS YOU OFF FROM HEARING MY VOICE, IS THE BELIEF THAT YOU CAN'T HEAR ME.

The sin that stops you hearing me is the belief that you do not hear me. That's the sin.

A REFORMATION IS COMING TO THE CHURCH. IT IS PEOPLE HEARING MY VOICE IN A CONVERSATION.

When people begin again to hear my voice, daily, minute by minute direct to their hearts, they will rise up and put the enemy to silence.

They will be set free. They will walk into a 'relationship relationship' with me. Because Mark what else is there? There is nothing else, nothing worthwhile compared to a conversation with me.

Don't listen to this drivel that other things are just as important as listening to me.

Try that approach in any relationship. Try saying that there are things that are just as important, even more important, than listening to the other person. Nothing in your relationships is as important as listening to the other person.

People who peddle that rubbish need to drop their religious theories and have the courage to try a conversation with me themselves. They would soon see the truth.

A CONVERSATION WITH ME IS WHAT YOU WERE BORN FOR. THE ENEMY KNOWS THAT, EVEN IF SOME CHURCHES DON'T.

His attempt to prevent that conversation is what this battle is all about.

I told you that you are as strong as any temptation I allow him to throw at you. I have told you that his real temptation is to tell you that you can't have a conversation.

You are as strong as that lie. Destroy it.

CONVERSATION
Fortyeight

God wants to tell us
everything about everything

You can hear him tell you as much
as you want to know. Just ask.

Lord are you saying that I can come to you with every little problem and concern, every work question, 'Shall I call this guy, do that, order this'?

Yes.

And every big life problem, every life question; the ones that seem too big, I can bring those to you too and you will give me specific instructions on what to do and think?

Yes.

Even the really complex emotional, relationship, family sorts of problems? We get told we can bring those to you and just 'put them at your feet'.

You can if you want.

But?

But if you want a conversation with me about that problem, then that's what I prefer. What you're born for is to listen to me. A conversation with me. If you put your problem at my feet and leave it there then I'm listening to you, but you're not listening to me.

What do you want then?

To give you specific instructions, detailed, minute by minute, point by point answers. You can hear as much as you want to, about as much as you want to.

I WANT YOU TO HEAR EVERYTHING ABOUT EVERYTHING FROM ME.

That's what life is about. You were created for this. Just this. To bring every aspect of your day, the good things, the bad things, the 'you don't know what to do' things and put them before me and say Lord what does this mean, what shall I do about this, what's going on here, should I worry about this? It's not a nice side benefit to this God walk, it's not an optional extra for the over-zealous.

God I've always been labelled 'over-zealous'. I think I might be a bit OCD.

What we're talking about here is not OCD, it's WHAT. THIS. WHOLE. GOD. THING. IS. ABOUT.

I don't want you relying on bible verses as your guide. I want you to listen to me first, then consult the bible. If you don't consult me first you'll misunderstand the bible.

THE BIBLE IS MY WORDS AND DESIGNED TO BE A TOOL.

A tool that you use once you have got your guidance direct from me. First you ask me, then the bible is there to help you. Either to expand what I've said, to determine it's real meaning, or, if you're unsure, to determine whether you've actually heard from me.

'they received the message with great eagerness and examined the Scriptures every day to see if what Paul said was true' ACTS 17:11 NIV

The bible makes it clear that you need to get your guidance direct from me. *'Man shall not live by bread alone but by every word that proceeds from the mouth of God.'* I didn't stop talking once the bible was published. It contains my words, but there is much of my word still being spoken. *'The heavens pour forth speech.'*

So for instance, let's say you have a person at work who is under stress and you are concerned about them. Rather than automatically offering biblically-based advice, or to pray for them, you should ask me what to do. I don't want you doing anything until you've got your instructions from me. You might have to ask me in your mind, and I will tell you, I will definitely tell you. You can write or think back the answer in a situation like that.

So often people do damage in my name by basing their actions on a bible verse, but not asking me first. For instance many have done incredible damage to the work I am already doing in those close to them by reading the following verse and misinterpreting it.

'Preach the word; be prepared in season and out of season; correct, rebuke and encourage--with great patience and careful instruction. 2 TIMOTHY 4:2 NIV

They decide that it means they should preach to their friends and work colleagues all the time. It doesn't. If they'd asked me I would have explained to them what it means. That's the answer to the meaning of every bible verse Mark. Ask God.

How to use bible verses to check what I say direct to you.

The bible tells you to ask me, and it states that it doesn't matter who you are or what moral state you are in, I will answer your question.

'If any of you lacks wisdom, you should ask God, who gives generously to all without FINDING FAULT ['onedeizo': to view as guilty and therefore deserving punishment] and it will be given to you.' JAMES 1:5 NIV

That bible verse says I will answer your questions without viewing you as guilty or deserving punishment. It's an encouragement to come and get your answer direct from me. So let's say I tell you not to offer advice to the person at work, but simply to listen, not to offer to pray unless I say so, but simply to let them talk. And let's say my advice seems totally wrong, and actually you feel you should be offering advice immediately, or praying or taking some serious action. So once again you pray under your breath, you ask me if you've really got this right. And I say yes, and to have confidence that you are hearing from me, not to doubt your ability to hear me.

There is another bible verse you can use as your tool to check you've heard right.

'But when you ask, you must believe and not doubt, because the one who doubts is like a wave of the sea, blown and tossed by the wind'. JAMES 1:6 NIV

The bible verse is not your answer it's your tool to check your answer. The answer comes direct from me.

Now, why do you think that people don't like this idea?

Well because they think it threatens the validity of the bible?

Yes they do. But are they right?

No. You're saying the bible is correct. It is a book of what you have said in the past. We can use it to check what we think you're saying now.

Good answer. Now, what else will people be concerned about?

That if we try and hear you direct, then we might get it wrong.

And what does the bible show is the answer to that?

That getting your guidance from the bible direct, without hearing first from God is equally as dangerous.

How so?

Because the bible is full of stories of people using scripture to justify disobeying you. The Pharisees killing you, Paul killing Christians and so on. It's so easy to misapply a bible verse, twist it to fit your situation. For instance 'By his stripes we are healed.' People assume that means that if they pray for healing, then you'll heal without question. But obviously you don't always heal.

So what do you think I'm saying?

That we should ask you if you want to heal that person first. And if we think you say yes, then the bible verse is one of the available encouragements to help us have faith.

Good. Ask me first. And then confirm with scripture when you are unsure. I don't want you to think that this asking questions about every single matter is too mundane for your walk with me. It's not mundane, it's the very reason for the relationship. A conversation. About your life.

BUT THE ENEMY WANTS TO PERSUADE YOU OTHERWISE.
He wants to make sure that you never understand this, never get to see that the reason I put you on earth is a conversation with me.

So he has carefully established a number of popular perceptions of what it means to be a Christian and handed them out to Christians as their world view.

The devil has become one of the most listened to authorities on how to have a relationship with me.

TWO OF THE DEVIL'S MOST POPULAR CONCEPTS ABOUT WHAT IT MEANS TO BE A CHRISTIAN:

1. THE 'GOD'S WATCHING TO SEE HOW YOU GO' SCENARIO.

The first is that God has dropped you into the world 'to see how you go'. Having met God and given him your life, this scenario says that you then find yourself living out your life, doing your best to do what the bible teaches and what godly teachers tell you and what you read in Christian books.

From time to time you hear God say something direct to your heart and of course you do your best to follow that. The basis of this scenario, a favourite of the devil, is that I'm watching, helping where required with blessing, and moving situations around a little, particularly when you either badly need help, healing, etc. or when you've been particularly well deserving. This scenario suggests that's when I'm most likely to help with blessing, financial, relationships etc. This scenario says that because God is God and you're human, then obviously you're not going to have constant, specific and very clear contact with him. However you can feel close and know that he is watching. A favourite verse to justify this misconception is;

> 'For now we see only a reflection as in a mirror; then we shall see face to face.'   1 COR 13:12 NIV

What that verse actually means is that you can't see me right now, but you will one day. It *does not* mean that you can't have a conversation, or hear me speak actual words. Paul, Moses, Elijah, all of them. They all heard me speak actual words. Nothing's changed.

I want to be in constant, dynamic, real-time relationship with you. Talking to you in a voice you hear in your mind and understand. And you talking back. Not praying words that have nothing to do with what I just said. But a conversation. 'I said/You said'.

God why do you always talk to me about this?

Because it's the sole purpose, the meaning of life. A conversation with God. The relationship that blossoms out of that conversation is what life is all about. What it's supposed to be about.

2. AND THEN THERE'S THE 'FEAR SCENARIO'. A PERSONAL FAVOURITE OF THE DEVIL.

This one says 'you can't hear from God because of your moral state.'

That's another lie he has taught my people. Not as popular, but still very common. The devil loves this one because it causes you to misunderstand my character and it brings you constant anguish which he particularly enjoys.

This scenario says that you could hear from God, and would, if only you were more obedient, a better person, or didn't commit this sin or that. He points out your many sins, reminds you that your life is a mess and that you don't find it easy to hear from me. He says if you would just get your life clean, deal with this sin, get rid of that problem, then eventually you may be able to hear God speak. He pretends it's me speaking. The devil really enjoys this scenario and often throws in one of his favourite lies which is, 'even if God does actually speak to you at some point, you may still be too evil to actually hear'. Wrong again! *'If any man lack wisdom, let him ask God who gives generously to everyone without finding fault'.* Without finding fault Mark. The bible makes it clear that you can ask me anything and I will tell you without looking at your moral state.

THE IDEA IS RELATIONSHIP. THAT'S IT. RELATIONSHIP.

The idea behind you being able to bring every question to me is simple. I want us to have a relationship. That's impossible without communication. Regular. Back and forward. I talk, you talk.

The depth of a relationship is directly proportionate to the amount and depth of communication.

I really want to hear your questions on every issue; 'My daughter wants to go out with her boyfriend, what shall I say?' 'My wife thinks I should ask for a raise, what shall I do?' 'Shall I stop here for gas or keep going?'

I AM INTERESTED IN EVERY SINGLE LITTLE THING ABOUT YOUR LIFE.

Remember what I said about the sparrows, *'Not a single sparrow falls to the ground without my father knowing.'*

This is clarified time and time again in the bible. I care about what's going on. Every single little thing, and I want to and am talking to you about those things. And you will, anyone will hear if they listen for the answer. Ask away.

HE'LL TALK TO YOU NO MATTER WHAT YOU'RE LIKE
Want to try your own conversation with God? Go to the page immediately following the contents page. Or go to page 243

The Eternal
Mountain Guide

Want to know where you're going and how to get there? Here's how.

Lord I just want to talk to you this morning. Hear you speak. What do you need Lord, what do you want?

Mark that's easy; I want followers. People who want to continue with the journey no matter where I'm going.

When you hire a guide for an adventure, a mountain climb or a journey into the wild, then you follow your guide and it's understood right from the start that they know where they are going and you don't. The guide leads, you follow. It is also clearly understood that you are on a journey. With a specific destination.

YOU ARE NOT GOING TO BE STOPPING ANYWHERE PERMANENTLY.

If your guide leads you into a clearing with a beautiful view across a deep valley, with sun and somewhere to lean against your pack, you don't think the stop is permanent. Picture a place like that, you need a rest and it's nice to come out of the companionship of your own thoughts and talk to others. No one in their right mind, there in that clearing with you, considers the idea of setting up camp in that place for good. It's a nice break, but you're going somewhere.

EVERYONE IS WAITING FOR WHAT THE GUIDE SAYS NEXT.

You're hoping the guide will allow a decent rest time because you need one. Someone might even laughingly quip 'I could sit here and look at that view for ever', others laugh too, but no one takes it seriously.

But many of my followers really do want to stop in the clearing forever. They aren't really followers at all. They're looking for a clearing. Others are the opposite. Without waiting for the guide, they have pressed on on their own. You have been no different, so don't get too excited about yourself.

THERE ARE TWO TYPES OF FOLLOWERS IN MY GROUP.

First there are the ones who have no idea where this journey is going and are happy to go blindly, blithely along, chatting and having fun and jostling others, being jostled themselves, having a great time but not sure if we're just walking out of the car park and up to that line of trees and back, or actually going on a mission. So for them the issuing of packs and rations comes as a bit of a surprise, but they're happy enough to go along with it if that's what everyone else is doing.

The other type of follower is the person who thinks they know exactly where this journey is going. They have read the description in the trip promotional material, read the map, seen the write up on the destination and they have formed a picture in their own minds of where they're going. But they haven't asked the guide to describe in any detail the journey or the destination.

They've asked the odd question of the guide, yet even while he was still talking have begun to fade away into their own thoughts, their own interpretation of what he is saying, rather than listen to the specifics. They look across at the group who are laughing and having fun and obviously not very prepared, they look in wonderment, and an element of scorn. 'Those people don't even know they're on a journey, they're not even really ready' they say to themselves. They are right of course, but then they are not ready either.

AS THE JOURNEY BEGINS THE TWO GROUPS DISPLAY DIFFERENT CHARACTERISTICS.

The laughers, the happy jostlers become disillusioned and weary, 'this is a lot of effort' they say. And so it is, an extreme amount of effort, particularly when you don't even know you're actually going somewhere.

The serious group, the ones who have studied the maps and read the promotional material without any real input from the guide begin to want to go off on their own.

The guide calls a rest, but the serious group want to continue. 'We can't stop here too long, we're nearly at that lovely clearing on the map, we should push on.' Always and ever increasingly their own agenda. One group has no agenda, the other has ever increasingly their own agenda. Neither are on the right track. The laughers and jostlers are constantly in danger of simply falling by the wayside, giving up because it is too hard, the serious group are constantly wanting to push on in the direction they believe is best. Can you see the problem Mark?

Yes it's a mess. But easy to understand. I'd be in the serious, but equally mislead group.

You were in that group for decades Mark and the situation you now live in is testimony to that. You were on the journey, but you didn't know you could hear me tell you what to do, day by day. It would have seen you build where instead you knocked down.

I don't want either group. I have no choice because mercy demands I work with what I'm given. Mercy demands that I take groups out on this trip who will never make it, most fall by the wayside, some go off on their own. But can you imagine the group that would be most fun for me and as a result for themselves? The group who would get the most out of the journey, and be most likely to complete it?

OH FOR A GROUP WHO WILL FOLLOW ME!

Can you imagine them? They would be serious, they would know they were on a journey. They would be keen to prepare and would do so by listening to the guide. They would listen for every step, hang on his every word. When they didn't understand they would wait till he had stopped speaking and ask for clarification.

They would check and recheck they had the provisions, clothing, equipment and directions they needed. And they would keep checking. As the journey progressed they would be ever more focused on listening to the guide. Knowing they were now so far from home that to miss anything the guide said would endanger them and bring about the distinct possibility that they would end up unable to find their way back or forward and simply perish in the wilderness.

MOST OF MY PEOPLE DON'T EVEN KNOW THEY'RE ON A JOURNEY, THEY'RE JUST HAVING FUN.

They perish when the going gets tough or just keep consoling themselves with the fact that they're having a great time and end up staying in one of the many clearings. They stop there in groups and try to survive the dangers of the surrounding wilderness. The guide has gone on and is now miles further along the track. But they are happy staying in the clearing.

A SMALLER MORE FOCUSED GROUP REFUSES TO STOP WHEN THE GUIDE CALLS A HALT.

Having paused at the clearing they quickly found a branch in the track, and frustrated with the guide, they decided that this was obviously the correct branch, so they pressed on. The light was better, the going more suitable, so off they went. The track they chose actually leads round and round the clearing, in a circle, far enough away from the guide to be clearly the wrong track yet close enough that his voice can be heard echoing through from the clearing. They are reassured each time his voice is distantly heard. 'We must be on the right track' they think.

IT'S A MESS. I WANT FOLLOWERS BUT INSTEAD MOST DON'T EVEN REALISE THEY'RE GOING ANYWHERE.

A smaller group do, but think they understand the destination better than me.

People in the first group are pulled along by others. Dragged, jostled, cajoled along behind me. But they are always wanting to stop, happy to rest forever if that's what the rest of their friends do. And the second group is off on their own direction, frustrated with my pace, they are reading the map without help from me and misinterpreting it.

Neither group are true followers. I want followers.

A FOLLOWER LISTENS.

A follower doesn't drag behind and he doesn't push ahead. He learns by listening to the guide, to walk and be comfortable at the pace of the guide.

His natural inclination is to be frustrated when the guide slows down for the less able in the group. He is also naturally inclined to start thinking he can see a better way to interpret the map when the guide seems to be pushing the group harder, when his pack begins to dig into his back, when the steps seem too high and a break would be good.

But he continually works at conditioning his thoughts, his thinking and walking pace so he can easily follow me. That's what I want. People who understand this is a journey. That there are no permanent clearing stops and that you shouldn't go off on your own.

> *'You're blessed when you stay on course, walking steadily on the road revealed by GOD. You're blessed when you follow his directions, doing your best to find him. That's right--you don't go off on your own; you walk straight along the road he set. You, GOD, prescribed the right way to live; now you expect us to live it. Oh, that my steps might be steady, keeping to the course you set; Then I'd never have any regrets in comparing my life with your counsel. I thank you for speaking straight from your heart; I learn the pattern of your righteous ways. I'm going to do what you tell me to do; don't ever walk off and leave me.'* PSALM 119:1-8 MSG

MARK WHAT SORT OF FOLLOWER DO YOU WANT TO BE?

Having a happy time, but no idea of where you are going? Or serious and focused but forming your own interpretation of the map without asking the guide?

Well I don't want to be either sort. I want to hear from you all day. I'm so used to it now I couldn't live without it.

Good.

I don't want the sorts of followers who interpret the map themselves without asking me, the sort who study it carefully and are seen as something of an expert in 'map matters'. They lead astray those who can't be bothered studying it themselves.

But I want followers who are serious, yet willing to hear me explain the map. I don't want you to interpret it yourself. *I want to explain it.* I want followers who are always focused on listening to my voice and nothing else. It's the best mode of survival in the wild Mark. Just listen to the guide.

THE 'MAP' HAS AN INSTRUCTION FOR MOUNTAIN JOURNEYS. 'THIS IS MY BELOVED SON, LISTEN TO HIM.'

When Peter was on the mountain with me and started trying to determine the next part of the track himself, that's what I said.

And I meant what I said, took the time, made the effort to focus my attention on the situation, and I spoke audibly so there'd be no misunderstanding.

If you think about the two groups I have described on that journey you'll see that both think they are listening but neither are.

If you listen the journey goes better and you've got a chance of getting to the destination.

'This is my Son, marked by my love. Listen to him.' MARK 9:7 MSG

You are supposed to find Me in your own world

You find me in your family, friends and work, paid or unpaid.

Lord did you tell me when I was having a coffee in the garden this afternoon, that you wanted to talk about the platform, the world that you have created for us, that your bible says has *'plenty of time and space for us to seek and find you'?*

And did you tell me that the world you're talking about in that verse is first and foremost not the whole world? Not the whole globe??

Yes I did.

So did you tell me that the 'world' you're talking about in that context is actually our family, our work whether it's paid or not, our friends? That you're talking about what I'd call 'my world'?

Yes again. Absolutely.

I'M A PRACTICAL GOD.

'Practical' means to be relevant to, fit in with the world around you, fit in with time and space, with reality etc. I invented time and space, reality is the product of my mind, not yours, it's something I thought up, reality was a thought in my mind before it was 'real'. Reality is not the property or the domain of the atheist, or the agnostic. They are in fact, separated from reality because they have decided that the one who invented reality, didn't. As a result their domain is the very opposite, in fact as far as you can get from reality.

I am a real and practical God, a 'busy managing time and space and holding it all together' God. I'm holding the very atoms and molecules together so there is a world in which you can exist or deny or seek my existence. So why would a God like that say that your 'world' is first and foremost the sphere of your own existence, your family, work and friends?

Simple. The earth, your life here is the starting gate, just the starting gate for your existence. Now you are here, eventually you will be there. Here first to rule and reign which in my book means serve. Then there to rule and reign. Serve. And it's my job to teach you to do that. Starting here.

The concept is simple. Here I am the one who thought it all up, and now holds it all together to ensure it doesn't explode and burst out into the nothingness. Here I am, that one, and instead of dominating and subjugating I serve, I die, I come to the rescue, I overlook behaviour, I run to the wayward.

That's how it's done, and that's what you're here for. In your family, your job, your home. 'Your world.' That's where you are supposed to find me. Not at church, you find me in your world. Then if I tell you to go, then you can take me with you.

IF YOU WANT TO LEAD YOU SERVE. YOU DON'T TAKE ACCOUNT OF WRONGS.

If you want to lead a business, a family, an event, a church, an organisation, a husband, a wife, or even a universe; you serve them. You defer to them. You overlook hurt, you do not take account of wrongs. As a result of which, in your mind, they have never wronged you.

Read the passage again Mark, read a few and put them together *'God is love'* and *'Love does not take account of wrongs'.* Now use practical, 'real' thinking, logical, obvious strategic and conclusive thinking. If love takes no account of wrongs, then any wrong done to you by another person does not exist, that person, in your mind, has never wronged you. Which means you need to love them, as you did, before they wronged you.

That's what it means to rule and reign. It means to serve, to forgive, to overlook, to love, to take no account of wrongs.

Your 'world' is first and foremost your family, your friends, your work, paid or unpaid. That 'world', is the most important world I speak of when I say *'And he created the world, with plenty of time and space that we might seek and find him'.* The idea is that you focus on your 'world', your family, work and friends, and in that world you find me, you seek and find me.

So why do I labour this, why did I bring the subject up as you drank your coffee in the garden? Because some of my people have this ridiculous idea that focusing on what interests them most is somehow bad, unspiritual, not godly. That's a lie concocted by evil and religion. The enemy loves that lie for this simple reason. He is afraid that if you begin to focus on finding me in your family, work and friends, you will touch pay dirt. You will find the purpose you were born for. And when that happens he's in trouble.

A CONVERSATION WITH ME IN YOUR WORLD.

I have made it clear that you must love your children, serve and honour your parents, serve and honour your wife, love and never look down on your brother. I have modelled the whole focus of history, *'Christ crucified from the foundation of the world'* on the concept of friendship *'Greater love has no man than this, that he lays down his life for a friend.'*

So where have my people been? What have they been reading?? For goodness sake my whole story from start to finish is family, friends and business. Yes business too, *'My Father is always at his work to this very day, and I, too, am working.'* Your world, that stage, that theatre is where you live out and learn to serve and love.

And by doing so you not only push your part of the world, the globe, all of time and space, in the direction it is meant to go, not only do you do that, but more importantly you learn how to find me.

So yes, the world you find me in is 'your world'. You do not learn to seek and find me in church. Church is not for that. Godly church leaders agree. You find a true and lasting relationship with me, one that comes out of conversation with me, on your own.

The depth of the relationship, if there is any depth, doesn't happen in church, can't happen there. Church wasn't intended for that. Neither do you do it reading Christian books or going to Christian conferences, not in prayer meetings, and not in small groups. Am I knocking all those things? Not at all, why would I? Consider Isaiah, the beginning of his story was in the temple. He was there and so was I, my train filling the temple. I have no aversion to the meeting place. If you read the bible you'll see I designed it, panel on panel, piece by piece. It just isn't meant to be the main place you seek and find me.

It's the place you take me to share with others.

But Christians have this idea that the relationship I'm after is to set yourself apart from your family, friends and business. No no no.

ABRAHAM WAS CALLED THE FATHER OF THE FAITH. HIS STORY IS ALL ABOUT HIS FAMILY AND WANTING A SON.

A son. His whole story is about his son, his wife, his nephew and his business. Time and time again, that's what his whole story was about, finding me, serving me, trusting me within the environment of his family, friends and business.

If you want to be a little Abraham then look for me in your family, friends and business. Get used to it, I'm going to say it till the day you die. That's your world. Not church, church work, quiet times, prayer groups, mission trips, witnessing. None of that is your world. You are going to, if you really want to find me, find me in your family, friends and business.

RELIGION, RELIGION. UGH RELIGION! AWAY WITH IT.

Christians often focus on family, friends and business, but in one of two wrong ways. You will recognise yourself in both these examples because you have swung from one to the other and then back again. It is time you settled in the middle, where, in this situation, the truth lies.

That's the reason for this discussion. To show you that, in this situation, middle ground is what I want from you Mark.

My people have divided themselves into two groups. The first group focuses on family, friends and business by seeing them almost, but not quite as 'unholy', 'unspiritual'. They see their relationship with me as totally separate to all those things. Their relationship with God they believe is things like church, quiet times, reading the bible, small groups, witnessing, retreats, reading Christian books and pretty much any kind of endeavour or service with a religious or church overtone. Big mistake. It doesn't get them any closer to me. Some of them are even in danger of being like those this verse talks about; *'ever learning but never coming to the knowledge of the truth.'* These people are the zealots, the super spiritual group. You have often been a zealot Mark. And in that role you have done big damage, while thinking you were drawing others to me you have pushed them away.

The damage done by the zealots encourages another group to form. This second group of people, which you have also found yourself championing, are rightly frustrated with the zealots. They see how wrong and warped and like the Pharisees the zealots are. Unfortunately, having seen how wrong the zealots are, instead of listening to me, they take their own counsel on the matter and decide the best option is the direct opposite.

If they'd listened to me they would have heard me say take the middle ground, choose a combination of spiritual and practical. However, because their motivation is anger at the zealots and not love, they opt for the extreme opposite. So they eschew spiritual foundations and truth to focus on what they have rightly seen as ignored by the zealots; family, business and friends. They form whole doctrines about how wrong it is that the zealots have ignored family, business and friends.

WHAT I WANT, IN THIS CASE, IS THE MIDDLE.
A perfect combination of both. I want spiritual values, I want people totally focused on me, on hearing my voice minute by minute, all day long. I want them to find and have that 'relationship relationship' with me in the world I have given them, which is their family, friends and business.

I want you to share this with others, and when you do it will be for them too, right now, as you hit the keys and type this out I'm talking to you, just you. And the purpose is to tell you that no, you are not overdoing it by focusing so much attention on waiting for me to deliver to you the promise I made to you. The personal promises I have spoken direct to your mind. The ones about your family and your business. It might seem unspiritual to you, but it's not.

That's what I am focused on, it's me trying to focus you on those things, not the other way around. Focus on them Mark. That's where you'll find me. That's where you'll learn my character and nature, as you serve them, your family, your business team, your clients and your friends.

These people Mark, and I want you to get this, this is big, these people are my little ones, not the only translation of those words but a very important translation nonetheless. *'I want you to know that when you see one of these little ones of mine thirsty and do not give them a drink, you refuse me a drink.'* So Mark focus on these people. Find out from me which ones I want you to give a drink. And then for goodness sake, give them a drink.

Practical Tips

How to have a Conversation with God yourself.

Six interviews with God.

The following pages offer practical steps for anyone who would like to have a conversation with God themselves.

They include six interviews where he asks me the questions and I tell him how he has taught me to have a conversation with him.

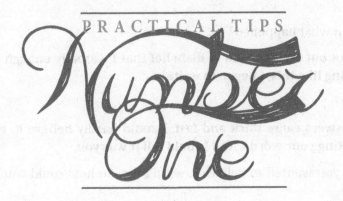

Yes you can hear God talk to you

In whole sentences about whatever you ask.

HOW TO TRY THIS YOURSELF WITHOUT HAVING TO BE SINLESS FIRST.

Mark I want to ask you some questions. Your answers will help people understand how to have a conversation with me. You know they are easily able to hear me speak so clearly in their minds that they'll understand exactly what I'm saying. I want you to give them pointers so they can try this themselves.

Ok.

So first explain how you started doing this.

Because of my situation I had already been writing down all the things I thought you were saying but not in actual conversation. Then I went to a camp where they asked me to read a bible verse and then write down my thoughts. Then write a list of questions to you about the verse. That all seemed Ok. But then they asked me to write down your answers!

How did you feel about that?

I thought they were mad. It seemed like conjuring up your voice rather that waiting for it. But I decided to give it a go because a friend I respected had urged me to go to this camp. But I didn't think it would work.

Then what happened?

Well I got out my pen, and in disbelief that I was silly enough to try something like this, I began to write.

And?

Your answers came thick and fast. I could hardly believe it. Here I was writing your words. And I could tell it was you.

But you wanted to believe it wasn't me. So how could you be so sure?

For that very reason. I wanted to prove the idea stupid, so when I could see that the words I wrote came from you I was blown away.

Did I move the pen?

No nothing like that. I've got control of the pen.

So how did it actually work?

I'd write a question to you. I think the first one was something like 'God are you saying in this verse in Philippians 3 that my Christianity is not enough, that I need to push further? That in this verse, Paul was saying, like Bono sings, that he still hadn't found what he was looking for?'

And then what happened?

I wrote your answer. And I could tell as I wrote that I was hearing you and writing your words. The act of writing seemed to be an act of faith. It seemed unbelievable and yet I knew it was you. I'd start the sentence with some words to get my mind moving and receptive to what you were saying. Maybe my name, or the obvious beginning of a sentence. Something like 'What I am saying Mark is...'

Ok? Then what?

So I'd start writing and your answer might come something like this; *'What I am saying Mark is yes. Your heart cries out for more because there is more. You're just touching the surface. You're right to be frustrated with normal Christianity. I want you frustrated.'* **I started writing to prove this wouldn't work, but as I wrote I discovered it did. It was so obvious that it was you. I wanted to doubt, but I couldn't.**

Something happened in your mind and heart when you saw that this was true?

Yes something exploded in my mind. I thought if I can hear this clearly from God about a bible verse, I wonder if he'll answer any question this clearly? I had heaps of questions about my life, my family and business, and the thought that I could get them answered this clearly was incredible.

So what did you do?

I asked you a whole bunch of questions, about stuff I was worried about.

And what happened?

Two things. You answered. Oh man did you answer. It was fantastic!! But the other thing that happened wasn't so fantastic. I asked the people who ran the camp if I was getting it right. Do these sound like the answers of God? They said I must leave those sorts of questions about my personal life in God's hands. They told me to seek first the kingdom of God, the inference being that stuff about my personal life isn't the kingdom of God.

And?

Well I thought something seemed a bit wrong. We can't box you like that. I wondered if Religion had stepped in without those people realizing. Religion suggests that when things are dear to us, family, health etc, that you're not pleased, and to get your approval we need to focus on 'spiritual' things.

So what did you do?

Well; you'd already answered a whole bunch of personal questions so I decided not to argue, but just to keep asking you questions about everything anyway. I was so excited. A conversation with God. What could be better!

You wanted to talk about stuff that was important to me! Not boring 'holy stuff'. The more you spoke, the more I realised that you do speak about everything we want to know.

So the people at the camp were right about their basic 'writing it down' approach?

Absolutely. So right! They had discovered this idea that God will converse with us whatever we're like. They opened up to me the most incredible thing that has ever happened to me. That you want to converse all the time, all day long, about every little thing, right down to whether to buy the expensive salt or the cheaper one at the supermarket.

Ok. So what was the next development?

I started writing questions to you, about everything. All day long. So much in my life was going terribly wrong. You'd made me some amazing promises about family and business, but none of them seemed to be coming true.

And what was the outcome?

I started getting answers about everything.

How did you know it was me?

I could just tell. You sort of can. A friend of mine who has started to converse with you too describes it as a feeling of 'satisfaction'. You just know when it's God. The odd time when it wasn't, I could quickly sense that.

Explain?

It might seem you'd said something really encouraging. It might sound like you were confirming a promise you'd made some other time. So I'd enthusiastically write it down, but the moment the words hit the page it wouldn't seem right. That really confused me.

So?

I'd ask you again. And it might still seem you were saying that, but it would still seem wrong. So I'd ask again. And eventually, as I wrote the words I would know this time whether or not it was you. Yes or no, I'd know.

What did you learn from that?

That the enemy will try to sound like you to put me off track.

Why would he want to do that?

Subterfuge. This is war. He tried the same thing on you, he quoted verses to you. If he can use a truth to get me listening to his voice, and make me think his voice is yours, then he can begin to take me down the wrong track.

So sometimes you'd end up asking me the same question again and again before you broke through and heard the right answer? And you always seemed to know when you needed to do that?

Yes. I'd be terribly frustrated thinking 'well how can anyone possibly hear from God with this confusion?' And yet if I kept at it, I'd always end up knowing what you'd said.

People who don't like this idea of a conversation with you say that if there's confusion it can't be from God. That threw me at first but then I realised they were just as confused as anyone else. And I remembered the angel who came to Daniel. He'd had to battle a demon for three weeks before Daniel could hear your answer. I realised that hearing you speak into my mind is going to be a battle. But what a fantastic thing to battle for!

Then you moved to speaking my answers out loud too. How did it happen?

I was writing questions to you and then writing your answers. It was happening all day long and I realised it was getting impractical to do it all the time. I like the writing because it helps me think out exactly what you're saying, but when I'm riding my motorbike it means stopping to write. I might be flying down the road on my motorbike, having a full blown conversation with you. It was silly. I was riding and stopping all the time. Crazy!

I asked you and you seemed to say it would be Ok, instead of writing, to speak my questions to you and then speak your answers back. I could see this was a sort of self-prophecy. Something my friend David confirmed a couple of years later. You'd been talking to him too about what he called 'self-prophecy'.

This sounds so silly and religious now, but I would speak out my question to you, and then lay a hand on my own head and prophesy back your answer.

But it worked?

Well yes. I could tell it was you. I was a bit nervous about it at first, but I could tell it was you because it felt exactly the same as when I ever speak some sort of prophecy to someone else. It was the same God talking. It was you. But this time it was a prophecy to myself. Kind of weird. But obviously true.

But then you got less religious?

Yes eventually I could hear you say relax. You said to forget the hand thing, just speak what I tell you.

And do you have to double check my answers when you speak them out loud?

Often. Often I'm not sure if I've heard you or not, so I come back repeatedly until the answer is clear. When it's clear I can suddenly sense that in my spirit.

I told you something which has really helped. What was that?

That this is a conversation between the infinite God, (you), and a finite human, (me). And you want me to be me and you to be you in that conversation. So I have to be relaxed about the fact that I'm human. Relaxed that the things I want to ask you are human things and not churchy, missionary, religious, 'Godish' sorts of things. Relaxed that I want to ask you about my wife, my kids, my business, my supermarket shopping etc. You told me to leave you to be God, and enjoy that I'm human because that's the way you love me to be. If you didn't you'd have created me as something else.

'So God created man in his own image, in the image of God he created him; male and female he created them//God saw all that he had made, and it was very good.'   GENESIS 1:27 AND 31 NIV

You don't have to be perfect to hear Him

Mark I want to continue with this 'interview'. I want to give others practical tips on listening to me. What have you noticed to be the differences in your life as a result of listening?

Well the good side is there is such an overpowering awareness of you being near. Right there. Every day I experience you making yourself evident to a level I had experienced only a handful of times in my whole life before that.

I mean obviously you were here all the time before this, but now when I listen, you make yourself known. And right now I find myself in a situation of my own doing, where I need to hear exactly what you're saying to get through.

I've been waiting all my life for you to make yourself more evident, and blaming my sinfulness as the reason you didn't. But now you tell me that wasn't the issue. You were waiting for me to listen so you could make yourself evident.

It's fantastic. I can ask you questions about anything that's happening in my life, and you answer! Sometimes you even tell me what's going to happen next.

What's that like? Does it make everything Ok?

It does and it doesn't. It makes more sense of what's happening. You show me why things are taking place in my life, you show me when to let things pass and when to take some sort of action.

But sometimes it doesn't make everything Ok?

Well no. You don't just fix everything. I had this idea that the closer we got the better everything would be. But it's not like that. If something's not right you don't just fix it. You show me how I've made it wrong, and then you encourage me to fix it myself.

How?

Well you often point out what I've done to hurt others. I used to always come and complain to you about them, but you don't seem interested. You want to show me how I've hurt them and what I can do to mend the hurt and build bridges. And how to work on changing so I hurt them less and less.

But is listening to me worth it?

Yes.

Why?

Because what else is there? What could possibly match a conversation with the Creator? Imagine you met an angel. And you knew it was an angel. And the angel said to you, 'God's waiting around the corner to talk to you. I'll take you to him.' It'd be like you'd won the lottery.

Now that happens to me every day. All day. God's waiting around the corner to talk to me. Actually you're waiting in my room, in my car, on the motorbike, in my office. Always there.

Even though life doesn't suddenly get all better, I know I'm getting closer to what I'm on the planet for. Listening to you. The relationship that comes from a conversation with you is what I was put here for. I'm finally hearing more and more of what *you* have to say. It's not always nice or comfortable, but it's awesome too.

What sort of questions am I comfortable with you asking?

I used to always be at you to 'fix this, sort this out, make that person do this'.

But when I realised I could actually hear you speak whenever I wanted to, I started asking 'are you going to fix this?' 'What are you going to do in this situation?' It makes more sense somehow. There doesn't seem much point asking you to fix a situation if that's not what you want to do.

It feels so much better to ask you what you think about a matter and know I'll get an answer straight away.

Does it make you a better person?

Hmmm. I think I'm heading closer to where you want me to be in my life.

But?

I'm still pretty hard to get on with I think. I certainly haven't become 'Mr Popularity'. I am a bit less likely to attack others, but still inclined to say and do things that hurt them.

There's no overnight changing. I think becoming a new person must be a lifelong journey?

It is.

But because I can hear you, then at least I can hear you tell me that, and that makes my stupidity in relationships a little easier to take. But probably not for others. I suspect that even though I listen to you, I'm still a pain for some of my kids for instance.

Would you recommend to others that they learn to listen to me?

Only if they are up for a good deal of pain and genuinely prepared to become uncomfortable. If they just want a comfy Christian life they should avoid listening to you like the plague.

How so?

Well there are no overnight fixes. My Christianity was based on this idea that you came and fixed life's problems. But now that I'm hearing you talk all the time, I'm learning that's not your idea at all. You want to do life with me, not fix life for me. As a result you say a lot of stuff that's very frustrating.

Like what?

Well you make amazing promises about the key areas of my life that still haven't happened! You promise a great outcome in a particular area and although the evidence that it's happening might be there, it doesn't happen quickly. Some stuff takes years, and still hasn't happened. Some stuff looks like it will never happen.

The Freedom Diaries

You're more inclined to say *'It works out fine Mark. You can expect a fantastic outcome. Right now I want you to wait. Be patient. It's worth it.'* **I can't hide my head in the sand about issues anymore. I can't plead 'fix this God' and then just carry on with my life. The more I listen to you the more you gently lead me to working slowly through situations, facing the consequences of my actions. A lot of those consequences aren't pretty.**

So do I talk much about how you've fallen short?

Almost never! I used to think that's all you really thought about when my name got mentioned. How bad I was. But you just don't seem that interested. You've been telling me it's religion and the enemy, 'the accuser of the brethren' that want to focus on my sins. You've told me you don't want me constantly pleading for forgiveness and feeling small.

You make me feel so accepted, and then you want to involve me in fixing what's gone wrong, improving situations etc.

How much of what I say is what you expect, or want me to say?

Not a lot. You often say the opposite of what I want. When I want to do something you say don't. When I don't want to do something you say do.

> *'To what can I compare this generation? They are like children sitting in the marketplaces and calling out to others: "We played the flute for you, and you did not dance; we sang a dirge, and you did not mourn.'*
> MATT 11:16 NIV

I'm beginning to realise that verse is about me. I want everything to be tickity boo and sorted. But you don't.

You want to teach me how to be a human by talking me through problems.

You want to *do life with me,* **not** *fix life for me.* **The most painful thing for me about hearing your voice, and it is a pain, is that I'm no longer in control.**

> *'The High God rules human kingdoms. He arranges kingdom affairs however he wishes, and makes leaders out of losers.'*
> DANIEL 4:17 MSG

I can't get stuck into anything unless you say. And often you don't say to get stuck in.

I imagine if a person is not a self-starter you'd be telling them to get stuck in all the time. But me, I want to get stuck in and you say don't.

It makes me feel like I've lost my drive. I'm always having to wait to hear what you've got to say instead of just doing what I want. People who used to like my spontaneous activity, are unsure how to take me anymore. I'm unsure how to take me now that I'm listening to you. Listening to you can be a real pain. But it's also the best thing in the world!

How do you know it's really God?

And why it's a battle to hear him.

So be honest Mark. What did you think about yesterday's interview with me?

I wondered if I was making it up. I thought 'surely God doesn't just ask questions like a reporter!' And even if you did, how can I possibly hear you that clearly? I had some grave doubts about it.

So what's changed your mind?

A number of people who I respect found it very helpful. They could hear you speaking even if I personally struggled with it.

Is that often the way?

Yes. Often I'm convinced I'm not hearing you. I stop in frustration. Get angry at you. Tell you I'm obviously just making this up. You quietly tell me to continue, but I'm not keen. It often sounds so crazy.'

Do you think this is typical?

Yes. Others try this and send me their conversations and it's the same for them. I can see they're hearing God, but they're not sure.

Why do you think that is?

It takes a huge amount of faith to believe you're speaking, straight into our minds just like a man talks to his friend. It's one thing to believe God exists, the Christmas and Easter stories, and then to feel your presence and direction in a warm but not very specific sort of

way. That was what I understood Christianity to be and it takes quite a bit of belief. But nothing like the faith it requires to hear you speak whole sentences, sentence after sentence. That takes huge faith because it seems so crazy. For me it does anyway.

And the enemy is so focused on preventing anyone hearing you clearly.

> You wanted to add something else, but you held it in, weren't sure about it. Say it out loud.

Well my old Christianity, which didn't include a constant back and forward conversation with you didn't really seem much like faith to me. But I didn't want to say it because that might be knocking others who are content with that.

> Well why do you think it though?

lived my old sort of Christianity for 37 years before I started listening you, and I *know* that listening takes so much faith it hurts, whereas rmal Christianity didn't. Not for me anyway.

> What do you think the bible says about a conversation with me?

Paul and David and others said they were always talking to you or hearing from you. Isaiah, Jeremiah, Habakkuk; it was constant back and forward conversation. It's written right there.

But that didn't used to be my experience. I used to hear from you now and then. Maybe once every year or two. When our little boy had cancer you turned up and talked to us very clearly. Maybe four times in eight months, and that seemed unusually frequent. We acted on what you said and you kept your promise to heal him.

Four times in eight months seemed a huge number of times to hear you speak specifically. Now I hear more than that before I get out of bed in the morning.

You told us to shift from the city to the country to raise our kids. About six years later you told us to shift again. But we heard from you very specifically like that only now and then. The rest was vague impressions.

No one I knew seemed to expect a conversation with you. Occasionally we'd get a strong feeling of direction about our business, or schooling our kids, but not a regular, clearly spoken, conversation.

So aren't you getting a bit big for your boots saying that listening to me all day takes faith, but that Christianity as you knew it didn't?

Well I don't know. Maybe you can answer? All I know is that the verses in the bible about faith all centre around listening to you. Not just hearing you when you intervene, but to actively listen to you all the time. That's what the book seems to say that faith is.

> *'So faith comes from HEARING ['akoé: inner hearing, discerning God's voice;] and hearing through the WORD ['rhematos': a spoken word, made by the living voice of Christ].* ROM 10:17 NIV
>
> *'It's impossible to please God apart from faith. And why? Because anyone who wants to approach God must believe both that he exists and that he cares enough to respond to those who SEEK [ekzéteó: to seek out, demand, inquire] him.'* HEB 11:6 MSG

Strong's Concordance gives a very good interpretation of tho verses. I want you to ask me questions and expect an answer. Tha what those verses talk about. That you need to believe that I w answer.

Yes and what I always thought Christianity meant doesn't really see to fit with those verses. Normal Christianity allows your presence to fall, but it doesn't actually 'inquire, or demand' about specifics.

And asking you questions and then not 'seeking out' or 'demanding' an answer seems a waste of time to me. And it doesn't seem to show any faith in you. Or myself.

Is it easy?

No. It's terrible. You're invisible. Believing you exist is hard enough. Believing you'll answer when I demand an answer is even worse. For me it takes excruciating amounts of faith.

So is that the peak of faith required? To believe that I will respond?

Not for me no.

It gets worse?

I don't know about worse, maybe that's not the best description. But harder. Much harder. For me anyway.

What bit is harder than believing that I will respond?

That you have responded. Believing that you will respond is a little easier. But to believe that you *have* just about does me in. To believe that I just heard in my mind and wrote down, or spoke out your words takes a lot of effort for me. I battle constantly with Doubt.

How much? How big an issue is Doubt for you?

Huge. Every single day. All day.

So what do people say about that?

They're sort of incredulous. They ask how can you hear this clearly from God, and then be so filled with doubt?

And?

Well at first, for a couple of years that really phased me because I didn't have an answer. And the doubt Doubt causes is so painful.

So what changed?

You showed me that doubt is absolutely to be expected. Hearing God's voice and Doubt go together. Doubt, the scheming, filthy, slimy, God-mocking, misshapen, disgusting being. The fallen angel.

He always turns up. The moment anyone tries to listen to God he screams orders and he or one of his mini-Doubt slaves are on that person. Immediately.

Why?

Because listening and hearing generates faith as the two verses I quoted earlier say. *'Faith comes by hearing the spoken word of the living Christ'* **That's what the original Greek for that verse means. Faith comes from hearing you speak, and Faith destroys Doubt.**

Anyone who decides to listen to your voice has just declared war on Doubt. And he's serious. War is war. And it's no fun when he attacks.

So what do you when he attacks?

Well a lot of the time I forget what to do and I get the mental and emotional thrashing of my life. You tell me something really positive, something that gives me huge hope in my situation, but then suddenly I'm racked by doubt. It's like going through a total mental breakdown in a few minutes, or a few hours flat. I imagine it'd be something like mental torture. An inquisition. It makes me want to

stop hearing from you. To revert to my old 'not listening to God much' Christianity. Which is obviously his goal. That sort of Christianity is safe for him. When we listen to God, that's not safe for him at all.

So this is a battle?

Absolutely. Listening to you attracts a fight from forces way bigger than me. So then I have to ask you what to do. And you always say to tell him to go.

How does that go for you?

Way better than it did in my old Christianity!!

How come?

Because now, this new Christianity, where I listen to you all the time, he attacks all the time. He's often got me up against the wall outnumbered and overwhelmed. I can't describe the horror of the torment. I've never experienced anything like it. And of course I don't realize it's him at first. So when I wake up to what's happening it makes me angry. He hits me so hard that I need to fight back just for my sanity. The pain of Doubt's presence gets so agonising that I try anything.

His taunts and jabs and mocking are that bad?

I can't describe how bad. The more I listen to you, the more he attacks with clear and vicious lies. And he's horrible to be around. Even before I hear the specific lie I feel wounded.

So when you tell him to go it works?

Yes. It's not very spiritual. Not many 'in the name of Jesus' sort of proclamations. I'd probably be in trouble with the religious big wigs. But it works.

How do you know?

Because the sudden relief is astounding. I tell him to go, and suddenly it's like you open the window on all that's good.

What about the idea that a conversation with me is deception, so the reason demons disappear when you tell them to go is that you're on the same side?

That's a pretty dumb idea. The Pharisees tried that one on you and you responded with that famous verse.

> *'And the teachers of the law who came down from Jerusalem said, 'He is possessed by Beelzebul! By the prince of demons he is driving out demons.' So Jesus called them over to him and began to speak to them in parables: 'How can Satan drive out Satan? If a kingdom is divided against itself, that kingdom cannot stand.'* MARK 3:22-24 NIV

If Doubt is asking me if you have really spoken to me, and I remember to ask you 'is that the filth bugging me?' you say yes. So then I'll say whatever you tell me to say to him. It might be something like *'Stand back!'* And suddenly it's like a window opens on all that's good in the world and I can see clearly again. Doubt disappears. Gone!

For good?

Sometimes for only five minutes. Sometimes more. Sometimes less. At first I thought maybe I was going properly mad. Doubt one minute, confidence the next. But every time I remember to tell him to go there is *instant* peace. Whereas madness doesn't have any control over doubt and mental anguish.

But it is a battle. And a battle gets very tiring, and should only be entered into if you're prepared to fight to the death.

Ok. That's enough. You need to go to the supermarket with your nephew.

Number Four

What sorts of questions can you ask him?

Mark I want to talk in this interview about the sort of questions you ask me. What sort of questions do you spend most of your day asking me?

Personal ones.

Do you mean private ones?

No. But this is weird. You already know the answer to every question.

Mark look at the bible. I ask plenty of questions. I always know the answers in advance, I ask because I want a conversation. Questions start a conversation.

Ok. When I say personal questions, I mean things that aren't big God issues. The conversations I send out to others tend to be you talking to me about some spiritual issue. This interview for instance; the core subject here is 'listening to God'. I'd call that a God issue, as opposed to asking you what I should do today, which is what I'd call a personal issue. Personal is primarily about me not about you.

Mark whenever I talk about me it's not really about me at all; it's really about you. It's for your sake.

Ok well the answer to your question is that most of the day, the questions I'm asking you are personal ones. Stuff about my life, just my every day life.

And you're obviously relaxed with that? Feel that it's Ok by me?

Well it sure seems to be.

How do you know?

It was the need to ask personal questions that got me listening to you in the first place. I had burning questions about my everyday life. My wife and my kids mostly. I wanted to know what you were saying about our relationships. I'd made so many mistakes, and done so much damage that I realised I couldn't risk doing anything, I couldn't take another step in those relationships without asking you.

Sometimes I still forget to listen to you, and then I almost always mess it up.

I ask questions about my friends, my business, my motorbike, my re hip, my boat. Just the normal everyday stuff. I ask you about what's on my mind.

And instead of ignoring me, you seem eager to answer. You must be because you keep doing it, and instead of feeling all condemned about the conversation makes me feel great. You talk about all the stuff that's worrying me. Which, I hope you don't mind, is not a missionary programme or giving to a church, it's how can I be a better man for my family? Or should I be saving more money?

You're also wondering if you should state the second reason. Say it.

Well the second reason I'm pretty sure you're Ok with me asking lots of questions about personal matters is that verse in the bible.

> *'So here's what I want you to do, God helping you: Take your everyday, ordinary life—your sleeping, eating, going-to-work, and walking-around life—and place it before God as an offering.'*
>
> ROMANS 12:1 NIV MSG

That verse says you're interested in my everyday life. And I find that when I ask you questions about my everyday life you seem more than happy to answer.

Why do you like that?

It destroys that image of you being stuffy and religious and only interested in churchy subjects. It says you're a God who turns up to talk about real stuff. That sort of God appeals a lot more to me than a boring religious sort of God.

No, it's not just you. Everyone hopes there might be a God like that out there somewhere.

That's a relief. I like that you're happy to answer questions about my everyday life because that's what I'm thinking about. It suggests the verse I just quoted means live your everyday life asking God what to do in every situation.

So; most of the time, the questions you ask me, and the things I talk to you about, are personal everyday life things?

Absolutely. I ask you things like what shall I do at work today? Shall I txt my daughter and tell her I'm sorry about what I said, or will that make it worse? If you say to txt then I'll ask you what to say in the txt. And then if that seems to have been the wrong thing, I'll ask you; d I hear that wrong God? And so on.

And I answer that level of detail?

Yes! Sometimes I think I'm making it up. And then I'll tell som I respect what I think you're saying, even though I'm strugglin believe it myself, and they'll be helped by it and tell me that it definitely you speaking.

What do you think about suggestions that I'm not interested i such mundane things?

Actually those suggestions really help me.

How?

Because they're so obviously dumb that they make it much clearer to me that you do want to talk about the little details. Which supermarket you want me to shop at, whether to get chicken or steak this week. Suggesting that you're not interested in mundane things shows such a lack of knowledge about the bible. You obviously are.

Why do you say that the bible makes that clear?

Well it talks about *'if a man is worthy of consideration as an elder he must be a good husband and father'.* You're interested in the little details of a person's life.

Then it talks about a particular wife and goes into detail about how she runs her home, invests in property, works etc. Little details, yet important enough that you want to talk about them.

The bible even says you count the hairs on my head. And each time a sparrow falls you know. I looked it up. About 13.7 million birds die every day in the US alone. That's a lot of hairs and sparrows! The bible makes it clear that the little stuff is important to you.

In the bible you went to all kinds of effort to tell the Israelites about where to put the toilets in the camp. The little stuff interests you.

Ok. Last question. How does this relate to your work? Is it actually possible to listen to me about what to do at work?

Yes. You're obviously interested in the little details in every area of my life. Home. Family. Work. If God wants to talk to me about whether to buy Italian Herbs and Spices, or just chilli this week...

You really think I do?

The same God who talks to me in the supermarket aisle, if I ask his opinion, is the very same God who told me to marry my wife and that he'd save my son and my daughter from death if I got others to pray for them. You're the same God. I can tell. I recognise your voice.

'My sheep listen to my voice.'   JOHN 10:27 NIV

Alright, so how does this relate to your work?

I have a conversation like this throughout each day about work. I write down my comments to you and your comments back to me. Just like this. Some of the things you say seem downright stupid, sorry but they do; but they come true. It's incredible.

So what I tell you about work is every day stuff, and short and medium term planning issues like you'd expect to discuss with a partner or a boss?

Yes. Often I feel it's time we got stuck into some project, and you'll say no just wait to see what happens. Or you'll tell me to do a job I think is a waste of time. Or you'll seem to want to focus on my relationship with my staff. You might say I need to inspire them more. Or I'll see something that obviously needs attending to and want to give some orders to that end, but you say just to leave it, because my business manager will tend to it when it's appropriate. And invariably he does. You know what's going on.

If I take the time to ask you, you've got plenty to say about my work.

So that's important; taking the time to ask?

Yes. It seems to be the key. If I don't ask you to talk to me, then you'll only speak when you absolutely have to for my good. You don't push yourself on me. When I badly need direction you'll intervene. For instance when you wanted us to get thousands of people to pray for our son so he didn't die. Or when you wanted us as a family to shift to where we live now. You'll get involved and move things along. But that's not often.

But if I ask your opinion on everything, all day long, then you turn up and talk back. All day long. Just as powerfully as you did when you gave us big direction like shifting homes. You'll actually turn up that powerfully many times a day if I ask. It's unbelievable. And you talk about every little thing. All I have to do is ask, and you speak.

'I sought the lord and he answered me.' PSALM 34 NIV

'The moment I called out, you stepped in.' PSALM 38 MSG

PRACTICAL TIPS

Number Five

Is it always clear what God's saying?

Mark listening to a God you can't see is difficult. Is that what you're saying?

Yes. Very. I spend my whole day learning how to do it. All day, every day. Asking you a question, trying to figure out what you're saying. Hearing something in my spirit, then trying to determine whether it was you. All day.

Many people would say that's obsessive, or that God's not that interested.

They do. All sorts of people; from atheists to hi-ranking Christians. They tell me I'm being obsessive and you're just not that interested in talking to us in that much detail. But I suspect that if they found that they could hear the voice of the Creator, they'd get obsessive about it too. And they can. Anyone can. But you already know that.

They say it's not possible to function in life if you're listening to God all day. They say it's too super-spiritual. I thought the same thing at first. But then I decided to experiment. I read a bit of Frank Laubach's book 'Diary of a Modern Mystic' about his tests.

Laubach was a famous missionary to the Philippines. He decided in about 1929 to test whether he could think about God once every minute. He wanted to see what would happen if he did. Would he be better off, or would it stop him functioning effectively in everyday life? He found it made him more effective, more organized, more productive. It amazed him. But it worked.

When I heard that I decided to try something similar. I was already trying to hear your voice all the time because I was in a desperate situation.

But it's not always clear, without any doubt, what I'm saying?

No. Not for me.

So how do you eventually determine what's me and what's not? Can you give examples of how this works, the process you go through to hear me speak?

Yes sure. The most important thing I've learned is that there is a lot of interference. I remember really early on, I was grizzling to you that it didn't seem practical, didn't seem like reality to be listening to you all day. It seemed too spiritual. It seemed impossible.

And what did I tell you?

You explained that I already hear the enemy talking into my mind all day. That he's constantly suggesting negative things, reminding me of hurts, making me feel sad etc. Constant and clear talk from demons. That we really are spiritual beings and we hear spiritually all day long. But we need to choose which spirit we'll listen to.

That made it easier?

Yes because it didn't seem so weird anymore. If I'm already hearing the devil then it makes sense to listen to you instead. If it's just a choice of which spiritual voice I listen to then the choice is obvious. God's voice. And it put me on guard, helped me be more aware of what's going on in the unseen world around me.

Ok. So you're saying it's not always clear what I'm saying and that there is plenty of interference from other spiritual voices, demons?

Yes. I never much liked talking about demons. I mean I always knew they existed, but it seemed a bit over the top to talk about them. But yes. They're at us all the time. And when I try to listen to you, they immediately focus on making sure I don't.

Says who?

Says you in the bible. The very first shot Satan took in this war against us humans was to cast doubt in Eve's mind as to what you'd said. 'Did God really say?'

But then he made it worse, he started telling her that you were saying and thinking things you weren't. He told Eve that even though you said if she ate from the tree she'd die, that actually you knew that she wouldn't.

Satan wanted Eve to think that you are not altogether truthful.

> *'You will not surely die,' the serpent said to the woman. 'For God knows that when you eat of it your eyes will be opened.'*
>
> GENESIS 3:4-5 NIV

He does that to you?

***All the time!* He just about drives me mad.**

Is that a good thing though?

Well in a funny sort of way yes. It makes me very conscious of how **real he is, puts me more on my guard. And it makes me hate** him. **Trying to hate Satan used to be tough and I guess my belief i**n him **was a bit fuzzy. He's very appealing and seductive.**

But now it's easier to hate him, because he's constantly annoying **me and frustrating me by trying to make me think you're saying** one **thing, when actually you're saying the other. The intense frustra**tion **of trying to hear you because of his interference makes me genui**nely **hate him.**

There's something else you wanted to say.

Well listening to you, and hearing you despite all the interference from him, makes me realise how much he hates me. It's as though listening to you has forced him to declare his hand. Forced him to admit that he does exist, really and truly. That there are millions, maybe billions of demons. And that they really do hate you and, consequently, they hate me too.

And that helps?

Yes.

> *'Stay alert! Watch out for your great enemy, the devil. He prowls around like a roaring lion, looking for someone to devour'*
>
> 1 PETER 5:8 NLT

> *'Now the SERPENT ['nachash': crafty tempter, world power] was more crafty than any of the wild animals the LORD God had made'.*
>
> GENESIS 3:1 NIV

Is it Ok if I mention a really important point that helps me?

What's that?

I've discovered that your voice will always feel and sound like your voice. *'My sheep hear my voice.'* **But you won't necessarily say things that are what I think you would say. Or even should say.**

You need to explain that.

Ok, I'll give a generic example. My kids are too old for this one, but let's say a dad has a problem with one of his kids. They steal something. The dad knows the bible says to *'spare the rod and spoil the child'.* **He's also read a book by some pastor who says you should whack your kid if they steal. And his own pastor is a stern father and admires other firm dads.**

Now let's say that dad comes to you and asks you, 'what shall I do God?' He's already planning to smack his son, that's not his question, he's asking what else should he do. And let's say that for some reason, in this particular case, you say don't smack him.

That doesn't sound to him like what God should say. It disagrees with his own beliefs, his pastor's beliefs and the books he reads. It does not sound to him like what God should say. But somehow he knows that it's you all the same. Because it sounds and feels like your voice. The words are foreign but the voice is familiar.

So how would that dad know that it was me speaking?

He asks himself does the voice sound and feel like God? *'My sheep know my voice.'*

And how can a person tell that?

It's not always easy. As Eve found out, the enemy is very good at confusion. He tries to make us think his voice is actually you talking. For instance he loves to pretend that condemnation is actually you.

So give some practical tips on how to determine whether it's me or him?

Well for me, I know that I must always be totally intent on hearing you. Never lazy. Always vigilant. Never just accept the first voice into my mind. Be totally committed to hearing what you say, whether I like what you say or not. Constantly checking if the voice sounds and feels like your voice. It's tough and takes lots of practice.

'Be always on the watch, and pray that you may be able to escape all that is about to happen.' LUKE 21:36 NIV

So I might ask you. 'Shall I mention to my daughter the idea of a sailing trip?' And I'll hear 'not right now'. So I might ask 'but you did say to invite her didn't you?' And I might hear 'Yes. You know I did.' All of that might sit fine so I'll go with it. Even though it's frustrating it sits fine in my heart.

What do you mean 'sits fine'?

Somehow it feels and sounds right. My friend David describes it as a 'satisfaction' that it's God. The voice sounds like your voice and feel like your voice. It sits fine.

Ok, but we still haven't talked about interference?

Ok, so an example of interference is that I might ask you a question. Something about a client, something I think I need to advise them. And I'll hear 'yes.'

Now because I know the enemy loves to confuse me when I'm listening to you and because it would be easy to do lasting damage to an important relationship by getting this one wrong, I'll ask a few times, just to be sure. And let's say the answer is clearly yes, you should talk to him.

Well then I'll ask 'should I talk to him about it now?' And often in a situation like that I'll hear 'yes.' But something in my heart might tell me I need to be doubly sure about it, so I ask again, and once again I might hear 'yes', but still feel the need to check is strong. So I'll ask again, and let's say I hear 'no'.

If that happens I get annoyed and a bit confused. I ask which is it? Yes or no?

This sounds incredibly complex, what do you do then?

It is complex! This is a war remember! You said that.

I did.

So I don't give up. I realise that the enemy is involved in either the yes or the no. Which means this issue must be important so I become even more insistent. I ask again; and again if necessary. It's so important to be insistent. If you want to hear God you're going to get resistance, and you have to be prepared to push through it. You

have to demand the right answer.

One of the words in the bible for seek means to demand and to enquire. The issue is how important is it to you to hear God? Not just about that issue, but about any issue? It better be important because if it's not you'll give up before you hear him. In my experience it has to become the thing that drives you above all else. Is that obsessive? Of course! *'Love the lord your God with all your mind!'*

How many times is enough? How many times do you have to ask before you know you've heard me correctly.

As many as it takes. I have to keep asking until I know in my spirit that I've heard you. One time I sat at the kitchen bench for four hours, alone, shouting at you in frustration. Weeping. Shouting at the enemy. Knowing that I had not heard clearly and peaceably what you'd said. I stuck at it for four hours until I knew absolutely for certain what you'd said.

Why was that particular issue so important?

It probably wasn't any more important than any other issue. What was important was that I knew you had something to say about it because there was so much interference from the enemy. Once he got involved I was then honour bound to keep asking until I heard what you had to say.

'ASK ['aiteo': petition, demand] and keep on asking.' LUKE 11:9 NLT

'the kingdom of heaven has been forcefully advancing, and forceful men LAY HOLD OF IT' ['biazo' laying hold of something with positive aggressiveness]' MATTHEW 11:12 NLT

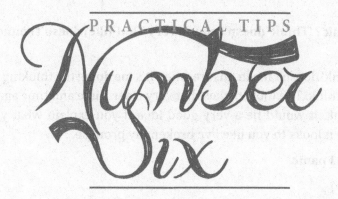

PRACTICAL TIPS

Number Six

What to do when you think God has broken a promise to you.

One last interview with Him.

A friend of mine, enthused about this idea of listening to God, was sure she heard him say something would happen that week, but then it didn't appear to have happened. She was heartbroken and dismayed. That's part of this experience. We're not used to hearing God, so when we think we hear him and then it appears we haven't after all, our whole world threatens to collapse.

The following pages are the conversation I had with God on my friend's behalf. I hope it helps you too.

IF YOU WANT TO LISTEN TO MY VOICE THIS WILL OFTEN HAPPEN. DON'T GIVE UP. TAKE THESE STEPS.

God I'm wondering what to tell my friend who heard you say that something was going to happen, and then it didn't.

Well. What do you think you should tell them?

God this is about hearing your voice. It's something that you're teaching me. Isn't it better that I ask you? This is not a subject that anyone seems to know much about and I'm struggling to learn as I go.

I think it would be a good idea if you explain what *you* do when you think I've said something will happen and then it doesn't.

You 'think'? 'Think' doesn't sound very 'God-like', doesn't sound very sure.

'Think' doesn't mean unsure when it's me doing the thinking Mark. Yes I think. The bible makes that very clear. Time and time again. So I 'think' it would be a very good idea if you explain what you do when it looks to you like I've broken my promise.

Ok. Well I panic.

Why?

Because I'm immediately terrified that I don't hear you after all. That these conversations are just make-believe.

Why does that make you panic?

Because my whole life now is based on living for things you've told me to live for. Things I've heard you say direct to my mind. Things that don't seem to have any hope of happening! In pretty much every significant area of my life I'm only hoping for the outcomes I'm hoping for, because you've told me to do so. The evidence looks to be the opposite of what you've said - so I'm only waiting because you said to wait.

So if it appears that you've misheard me, that either I've broken my promise or you didn't hear me right in a relatively small matter, then you wonder whether I've said any of those other bigger things?

Yes.

So then what do you do?

I demand to know what's happening. I shout at you if I'm somewhere I can. But even if I'm in a crowded room I'm insistent under my breath. I want to know what on earth is going on. I'm desperate. I can feel my world caving in. My world of promises from you, the ones that keep me going, suddenly seems like a house of cards collapsing onto the floor.

How does that make you feel?

Like you've abandoned me.

And yet you demand answers?

That's just human God! When we feel abandoned by anyone we feel desperate for answers. We feel like we're falling down a hole and we grasp for reality. For answers.

So this must be something that happens regularly? You've got ready answers for it.

Absolutely.

So why on earth would you still try to listen to me if it can often feel like I've broken my promise?

Because so many times I hear you say things that there is no way I could know on my own and yet they come true. So I'm learning. It bends my mind, but I'm learning that us humans really can hear you. If I do, then others can too.

Yes but Mark you're bitterly disappointed when it seems I've broken my promise. So why persist?

Well I figure, because you're God, that somehow I've misunderstood.

Does that make it any easier?

Not at all. I get angry that you'd let me misunderstand. I feel like maybe you haven't lied exactly, but you've let me down, abandoned me. Left me I guess.

This doesn't sound like a very 'peaceful' relationship with God?

Now you're just winding me up. You know that's what the naysayers tell me. That this can't be you I'm hearing because there's anguish, and anger and I have to keep pressing in to find out what on earth you're saying.

Yes. I want others to know that's what they'll come up against if they persist in trying to hear me. Everyone in the bible who persisted in trying to hear my voice ended up being out of favour with the very people they thought would be on their side.

Ok. Well the real reason I don't give up when it seems like you've broken your promise is that I'm desperate. My whole world feels like it's caving in, and I need answers.

You're wondering whether to mention the thing about David in the bible. Mention it please.

Ok, well I remember that David felt like you had broken your promise. Quite often in the Psalms he says things which make me realise he went through this too.

> 'Will the Lord reject forever? Will he never show his favour again? Has his unfailing love vanished forever? Has his promise failed for all time? Has God forgotten to be merciful?'   PSALM 77:7-9 NIV

And Jeremiah felt like it too.

> 'You are right, O GOD, and you set things right. I can't argue with that. But I do have some questions: Why do bad people have it so good? Why do con artists make it big?//Meanwhile, you know me inside and out. You don't let me get by with a thing!'
> JEREMIAH 12:1-3 MSG

And even you felt like it.

> 'My God, my God, why have you FORSAKEN me ['egkataleipó': left me behind in dire circumstances].   MATTHEW 27:46 NIV

Ok. So you feel abandoned, you remember that David, Jeremiah, and even I felt the same, but because you're desperate you persist. You demand to know what's going on. Exactly how do you demand? What's the process? People need to know this Mark.

It's just something that I've developed out of desperation I guess, but if you think people need to know this; I demand to know what's going on by asking questions.

What questions?

The next obvious question. I ask you something like 'God did you say that thing I thought you said?' And then I write down, or speak out or even *think* your answer, depending on what's appropriate. It depends on whether I'm on my own or with others etc. And I keep asking that question until I feel that 'satisfaction' that tells me I've heard from you.

How long do you stick with that?

Hours quite often.

Why?

Like I said, if I think you've broken a promise, or I think I've heard you wrong then my world is caving in. So I have to know what's going on.

Ok, what's the next obvious question?

If I'm satisfied you say *'yes I did say that'*. Then the next obvious question is 'well how come it hasn't happened?' And you might say *'it has'*. So I'll ask, what on earth do you mean 'it has'? God be honest with me 'It hasn't!'

Explain how you can have such a fluent conversation. This isn't normal for a lot of people. But millions of people want it.

I write down my questions to you, just like I'm doing here, and then write back the answers in faith. It's like prophesying out your answers in writing I guess. Or I speak out, or even think out my question and speak back or think back your answers.

And you keep at it until you're 'satisfied' you've heard me. Does that take long?

Yes, when I'm desperate and it seems you've broken your promise, and I have to find out what's going on, a small conversation can take hours because I'm having to check and recheck your answers until I'm really satisfied that's you talking. You're God. You're invisible. I've had no real training in having a conversation with you, so sometimes it takes excruciating amounts of effort to be sure I've heard you.

And?

And there's opposition. Huge opposition. Satan does not want me fluent in a conversation with you. As I said it's not normal. But you've told me it's meant to be. Which must mean that Satan is viciously opposed.

Some have asked why you think you're so special that God would talk to you like this, or that Satan would pick you out for a beating.

I'm not special. I've messed up so much in my life. Anyone can do this. And if they do you'll answer. And when you do Satan is duty bound to attack. He must otherwise they'll become dangerous. It spreads, this conversing with you, it spreads like wildfire when the right people hear about it.

So. You stick with asking me the next obvious question, pushing and pushing, not giving up, until you're sure you've got the answers, and it can take hours. How does that make you feel?

The process is exhausting. I'm in tears from the frustration quite often. But the sense of your presence is the most beautiful thing that's ever happened to me. I'm in the middle of a heated discussion, but it's with the lover of my soul, the Creator of the universe, the one who invented me. As Dickens wrote; *'it's the best of times and it's the worst of times.'*

It's like a discussion with the person you love the most. I mean the human person. The person you love the most and you know you can trust. Then suddenly you think they've let you down, broken a promise. Your whole world threatens to collapse momentarily, and yet somehow you know, you hope that they haven't really let you down. On one hand you're terrified, on the other you're pretty sure you're probably overreacting. But you know you have to ask them for answers, so you do, and you discover that actually you completely misunderstood. They really do love you. They really haven't broken their promise. That's about the best way I can explain it.

Give me some other examples of the next obvious question.

Well remember I don't give up. I don't accept a vague answer unless you tell me specifically that I have to. So if you say something like *'that thing I promised has happened.'* **I demand the obvious. I say 'what do you mean it's happened?' And I might hear a few words, and I check them. I say 'is that really you'. And on and on it goes. It's like interrogating you.**

Does that worry you? I'm God. People say you can't talk to me like that.

Well David did, and anyway I'm desperate by that stage. And I'm not prepared to believe in a God who breaks his promises, so it's shoot out time when I think you have. I panic, I go for my guns. I need to know what's going on. And if you're breaking promises then I'll need to change the entire direction of all the significant areas of my life so I have no choice but to do whatever it takes. Either I'm going to get the real answer from you or, abandoned by you, I'm going to have to change direction in every significant area of my life. If that's interrogating God, then too bad.

And you think I'm Ok with that?

You seem to be.

I am Mark. I love it. I designed you for this conversation. Real conversation. Not just the nice stuff. The real stuff too.

I've given you Bible verses that say it's Ok. What are they?

> 'the kingdom of heaven has been subjected to violence, and violent people have been raiding it.' MATT 11:12 NIV

> 'It is the glory of God to conceal a matter; to search out a matter the glory of kings.' PROVERBS 25:2

What does the bible say about listening to God?

About hearing him speak into your mind?

About having a conversation where you can understand what he says? About writing down or speaking out his words by faith as he speaks them to you? About this idea that He doesn't find fault but will just talk to you anyway?

The original Greek and Hebrew words shown in the following bible verses have been sourced from the Lexicon and Strong's Concordance at www.Biblecc.com

'Doesn't that privilege of intimate conversation with God make it plain that you are not a slave, but a child?' GALATIANS MSG

'And then he said to me, 'Write this down, for what I tell you is trustworthy and true.' REVELATIONS 21:5

'Then the LORD said to me, 'Write my answer in large, clear letters on a tablet, so that a runner can read it and tell everyone else.' HABAKKUK 2:1-2 NLT

'Now write down this song and teach it to the Israelites and have them sing it' DEUTERONOMY 31:19 NIV

'The heavens declare the glory of God; the skies proclaim the work of his hands. Day after day they pour forth SPEECH ['Emer': Speech, word. From 'amar; something said]' PSALM 19:1-2 NIV

'How can a man keep his way pure? By keeping your WORD ['dabar': speech, word]' PSALM 119:9 NIV

'I have hidden your WORD ['imrah': Command, speech, word] in my HEART [leb: inner man, mind, will,] that I might not sin against you.' PSALM 119:11 NIV

'For the WORD OF GOD ['logos': speech, divine utterance. Christ expressing the thoughts of the Father through the spirit.] is alive and active. Sharper than any double-edged sword, it penetrates even to dividing soul and spirit, joints and marrow; it judges the thoughts and attitudes of the heart.' HEBREWS 4:12 NIV

'He sent forth his WORD ['dabar': speech, utterance] and healed them; he rescued them from the grave.' PSALM 107:20 NIV

'but whoever LISTENS ['Shama': to hear] to me will live in safety and be at ease, without fear of harm.' PROVERBS 1:33 NIV

'I called but you did not answer, I SPOKE ['dabar': to speak] but you did not LISTEN ['shamar': to listen]. You did evil in my sight and chose what displeases me.' ISAIAH 65:12 NIV

Gill's commentary says about Isaiah 65:12; 'When Christ called unto them personally, to come and hear him, they turned a deaf ear to this charmer, charming so wisely, and would not attend upon his ministry,'

'So faith comes from HEARING ['akoé: spiritual hearing, discerning God's voice] and hearing through the WORD ['rhematos': a spoken word, made by the living voice] of Christ' ROM 10:17 NIV

'Everyone should be quick to LISTEN ['akouo': to hear (listen); which comes from 'akauo', properly to hear (figuratively) to hear God's voice which prompts Him to birth faith within], slow to speak and slow to become angry.' JAMES 1:21 NIV

'PRAY ['prosuchomai': to pray, exchange wishes; to interact with the Lord by switching human wishes (ideas) for His wishes as He imparts faith ('divine persuasion').] without CEASING ['adialeiptós': incessantly, without any unnecessary interval (time-gap)].' THESSALONIANS 5:17 NIV

'So, go now and write all this down. Put it in a book. So that the record will be there.' ISAIAH 30:8 MSG

'You keep him in perfect peace whose mind is STAYED [samak: to lean, lay, rest, support] on you, because he trusts in you' ISAIAH 26:3 NIV

'LISTEN ['shama': to hear] to Me, you who know righteousness, A people in whose heart is my LAW ['Torah': direction, instruction, law];'   ISAIAH 51:7 NIV

'Do your best to present yourself to God as one approved, a workman who does not need to be ashamed and who correctly handles the WORD ['logos': the thoughts of the Father through the spirit] of truth'   2 TIMOTHY 2:15 NIV

The original Hebrew 'Logos' and Strong's Word studies '3056' suggest that 'word' can mean the word spoken by God into our heart, or the words of God spoken to us by others, and probably, although not as obviously, the words of God written down.

'As for you, the ANOINTING ['charisma': anointing, unction, referring to the teaching ministry of the Holy Spirit, guiding the receptive believer into fullness of God's preferred-will] you received from him remains in you, and you do not need anyone to teach you. But as his anointing teaches you about all things and as that anointing is real, not counterfeit—just as it has taught you, remain in him.'   1 JOHN 2:27 NIV

'I did not receive it from any man, nor was I taught it; rather, I received it by REVELATION ['apokálypsis': unveiling] from Jesus Christ.'   GALATIANS 1:12 NIV

'I am able to do nothing from Myself [independently, of My own accord—but only as I am taught by God and as I get His orders]. Even as I hear, I judge [I decide as I am bidden to decide. As the voice comes to Me, so I give a decision],'   JOHN 5:30 AMP

The Freedom Assignment
Please tell lots of people about this book.

I have a dream. You might call it a ministry. I call it *'The Freedom Assignment'*. It's simple really. The idea is to get millions of people enjoying their own back and forward conversation with God. I've devoted my life to it. To make it possible I need your help. I need you to tell others about this book. *That's all it seems to take!*

It still amazes me, but whenever someone reads **The Freedom Diaries** and gets inspired to try their own conversation with God, they're away! It sets them free.

"[this conversation with God] is so good. True and so much of a mystery to so many. This really is the word of God."

"You have inspired me to listen more. Thank you."

"I just love this stuff, it's what I've thought and felt for a long time. And to hear God saying it through you is great, this has helped me and our church greater than I can express in words."

Writing **The Freedom Diaries** has changed my life. It's taught me that God really does want a conversation with me. It doesn't matter who I am. He just wants to talk.

If reading The Freedom Diaries **has helped you too, please 'like' it on Facebook, and tell all your friends to read it too.**

Get the message out by whatever means you can, Twitter, email, or txt; whatever. Maybe even buy one or two copies for friends?

The more people who read this book, the more who will try a conversation with God themselves. They'll hear him speak in sentences they understand. And that will set them free.

"discovering the intimacy of conversation and dialogue [with God] is totally powerful."

Everyone deserves their own conversation with God.

If reading **The Freedom Diaries** has helped you, please tell others. Urge them to get their own copy and help me in this assignment.

Mark.

MARK & MIRIAM SPEAKING AT YOUR CHURCH

If you would like us to teach at your church please email us.

As more people read The Freedom Diaries and are changed by the message, the demand to have us teach increases. We are always learning more about a back and forth conversation with God and we love sharing it with people who want to learn more too.

What Church Leaders say about having us teach:

"People came away inspired to spend time with God and confident they could." **Russell Watts Senior Pastor.**

"People became more hungry to hear from God themselves." **Graham Braddock Elder.**

"Only positive feedback from our congregation. Testimony time was amazing, thought it wouldn't stop." **Mark Schonberger Senior Pastor.**

Our message includes:

- How a back and forward conversation with God healed our marriage after five years apart.
- How to have your own back and forward conversation with God.
- How to deal with Doubt.
- How to know whether you're hearing God.
- What the bible says about a back and forward conversation with God, including a look at the Greek and Hebrew texts.

For a FREE INFORMATION PACK please contact:
   info@thefreedomdiaries.co.nz

(NEW!) MY Freedom Diary

21 key lessons on how to have your own conversation with God - and for the first time in print;

The Real Story Behind The Freedom Diaries!

If you are one of the thousands who loved The Freedom Diaries this new book will change your life forever. Even after the first few hundred copies had sold we were already receiving amazing reports like these.

"Reading and using this book saved my marriage."

"I had no idea God would talk to me like this – this is incredible."

If you wish you could hear God's voice more clearly, MY Freedom Diary is the book you've been waiting for! It will completely revitalise your relationship with God.

INCLUDES: A step by step guide to having your own conversation with God (just like Mark does in The Freedom Diaries) - and 365 special pages to write your own conversations with God.

Order now online at:
www.thefreedomdiaries.co.nz

Mark & Miriam Holloway.
This new book helps you have your own conversation with God and tells you the real story behind The Freedom Diaries.

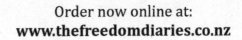